Praise for *Shan*

"*Shamanic Qabalah* by Daniel Moler provides an in-depth guide to the esoteric practices at the core of the magical revival in the Western Mystery Tradition."

—Peter J. Carroll, cofounder of Illuminates of Thanateros
and author of *Liber Null & Psychonaut:
An Introduction to Chaos Magic*

"Daniel Moler's *Shamanic Qabalah* is a strong contribution that will appeal to modern mystics in the emerging transformational community. This is a compelling book and Mr. Moler is to be acclaimed, as he has created very good medicine indeed."

—Hank Wesselman, PhD, anthropologist and author of nine books
on shamanism, including *The Re-Enchantment:
A Shamanic Path to a Life of Wonder*

"*Shamanic Qabalah* examines and then masterfully converges the mystic healing theories and practices of a variety of ancient and surviving faith traditions. ... Extremely well-researched, 'boots on the ground' researched, Moler's 'unified field' provides insight not just into ritualized practices common to peoples who have never encountered the others, but those yearnings common to all humankind from which these manifestations of hope spring. Scholarly, well organized, and enlightening."

—Gerry Stribling, author of *Buddhism for Dudes:
A Jarhead's Field Guide to Mindfulness*

"Met the Goddess last night. Glad I was reading Daniel's book at the time!"

—Eliott Edge, artist, philosopher, humorist,
and author of *3 Essays on Virtual Reality:
Overlords, Civilization, and Escape*

"Daniel Moler's *Shamanic Qabalah* is a testament to the oft-forgotten truth that the many paths eventually merge into the one Great Path, the recovery of the Undivided Self. His insightful and creative examination and interpretation of Qabalah—and its correspondences to a rich array of mystical traditions and mystery schools from the Andean *paqokuna* to tarot—is a richly detailed map to help guide us on this personal journey."

—Joan Parisi Wilcox, author of *Masters of the Living Energy:
The Mystical World of the Q'ero of Peru*

"It's exciting to see people re-engaging with the Qabalah in new and creative ways, and this is exactly what Daniel Moler has done in *Shamanic Qabalah*, drawing on eminent sources like Dion Fortune, Gareth Knight, and even, uniquely, Peruvian shamanism to explore the Qabalah not as somebody interested in dry book learning and rote memorization, but as a head-on psychonaut concerned with living, creative, psychedelic ritual."

—Jason Louv, author of *John Dee and the Empire of Angels:*
Enochian Magick and the Occult Roots of the Modern World

"Intricately woven, yet profoundly understandable, this brilliantly conceived treatise parts the veil to reveal the beauty of life, magic, and human purpose. Rooted, yet transcendent, like the Tree of Life itself, *Shamanic Qabalah* is a compendium of esoteric mysteries. Daniel Moler is a shaman and humanitarian of the highest order."

—Steve Guettermann, mythologist, ritualist, and author of
How to Get Even with the Universe by Getting Right with the World:
Working within Sacred Space and Time

SHAMANIC QABALAH

© Elaina Cochran

About the Author

Daniel Moler is a writer, artist, educator, and shamanic practitioner. Formerly an adjunct professor, he has extended his teaching, which includes professional training and independent academia, to other areas of life. Daniel is a sanctioned teacher of the Pachakuti Mesa Tradition, a form of Peruvian shamanism brought to the United States by respected *curandero* don Oscar Miro-Quesada. Trained in multiple spiritual disciplines, Daniel uses the art of shamanic healing to help others during times of transition and transformation. In order to provide the most holistic healing environment, he works within a wide variety of modalities, including energy healing, curanderismo, herbalism, Zen, and Hermetic alchemy via the Holy Qabalah. As a writer, he has published fiction and nonfiction works around the world in magazines, journals, gaming modules, and online, including *Positive Health Magazine, Cannabis Culture, The Tattooed Buddha, Sacred Hoop, Elephant Journal*, and *A Journal of Contemporary Shamanism*. He is the author of two books, *RED Mass* and *Machine Elves 101*, as well as a contribution on San Pedro healing ceremonies in Ross Heaven's book *Cactus of Mystery*. Visit Daniel online at www.danielmolerweb.com.

SHAMANIC QABALAH

A MYSTICAL PATH TO UNITING THE TREE OF LIFE & THE GREAT WORK

DANIEL MOLER

Llewellyn Publications
Woodbury, Minnesota

First Edition
First Printing, 2018

Cover design by Kevin R. Brown
Illustration on page 22 by the author
Figure 26 and figure 27 by Mary Ann Zapalac. All other art by the Llewellyn Art Department. Figure 29 by Mary Ann Zapalac and the Llewellyn Art Department

Llewellyn Publications is a registered trademark of Llewellyn Worldwide Ltd.

The Golden Dawn by Isreal Regardie © 1971 Llewellyn Worldwide, Ltd. 2143 Wooddale Drive, Woodbury, MN 55125. All rights reserved, used by permission.

A Garden of Pomegranates: Skrying the Tree of Life by Isreal Regardie, Chic Cicero, and Sandra Tabatha Cicero © 1999 Llewellyn Worldwide, Ltd. 2143 Wooddale Drive, Woodbury, MN 55125. All rights reserved, used by permission.

The Training & Work of an Initiate by Dion Fortune © 1967 Society of Inner Light used with permission from Red Wheel Weiser, LLC, Newburyport, MA.

A Practical Guide to Qabalistic Symbolism by Gareth Knight © 1965, 1993 Gareth Knight used with permission from Red Wheel Weiser, LLC, Newburyport, MA.

The Mystical Qabalah by Dion Fortune © 1935, 1998 Society of Inner Light used with permission from Red Wheel Weiser, LLC, Newburyport, MA.

The Book of Thoth: A Short Essay on the Tarot of the Egyptians by Aleister Crowley © 1999 Ordo Templi Orientis. All rights reserved, used by permission.

Dark Night of the Soul by John of the Cross © 1953 E. Allison Peers. Used with permission from Dover Publications, Mineola, NY.

Library of Congress Cataloging-in-Publication Data
Names: Moler, Daniel, author.
Title: Shamanic Qabalah : a mystical path to uniting the tree of life & the
  great work / by Daniel Moler.
Description: First edition. | Woodbury, Minnesota : Llewellyn Publications,
  [2018] | Includes bibliographical references and index.
Identifiers: LCCN 2018033819 (print) | LCCN 2018040114 (ebook) | ISBN
  9780738757698 (ebook) | ISBN 9780738757636 | ISBN 9780738757636 (alk. paper)
Subjects: LCSH: Cabala. | Shamanism—Peru.
Classification: LCC BF1623.C2 (ebook) | LCC BF1623.C2 M65 2018 (print) | DDC
  135/.47—dc23
LC record available at https://lccn.loc.gov/2018033819

Llewellyn Worldwide Ltd. does not participate in, endorse, or have any authority or responsibility concerning private business transactions between our authors and the public.

All mail addressed to the author is forwarded, but the publisher cannot, unless specifically instructed by the author, give out an address or phone number.

Any internet references contained in this work are current at publication time, but the publisher cannot guarantee that a specific location will continue to be maintained. Please refer to the publisher's website for links to authors' websites and other sources.

Llewellyn Publications
A Division of Llewellyn Worldwide Ltd.
2143 Wooddale Drive
Woodbury, MN 55125-2989
www.llewellyn.com

Printed in the United States of America

Other Books by Daniel Moler

RED Mass: A R.E.D. Agency Novel
Machine Elves 101

Featured In

Cactus of Mystery: The Shamanic Powers of the Peruvian San Pedro Cactus
Don't Walk in Winter Wood

Dedicated to the Ancient Ones,
for keeping these traditions alive through the ages.

Acknowledgments

This work could not have been accomplished without the undying support of my wife and muse, Autumn Paige-Moler. *Shamanic Qabalah* is just as much her work as it is mine, as she walked through this process every step of the way with me, editing my work, inspiring countless ideas, and never allowing me to give up. Thank you, *Sonqo Suwa,* for always believing in me, most especially when I couldn't believe in myself!

Also, a bow of gratitude goes to John Nichols. This concept never would have been possible if it wasn't for his work in the Mysteries. And another bow to my *maestro,* don Oscar Miro-Quesada, for your continual advice and support, as well as putting up with my monkey brain when it got out of hand (which it occasionally does). And to my editor, Lauryn Heineman, who transformed my inane ramblings into a coherent structure that finally made sense … your hard work has been invaluable!

And to others who contributed greatly to the development of this project: Gerry Stribling, Mary Gustafson, Dolores Ashcroft-Nowicki, Hank Wesselman, Eliott Edge, Elaina Cochran, Joan Parisi Wilcox, my fellow pathworkers from the Mystic Path, and all the amazing souls at Llewellyn Worldwide.

Disclaimer

Contents

Foreword … xv

Introduction … 1

PART I: THE GREAT WORK

Chapter 1: Preamble of the Stone … 11

Chapter 2: Initiation … 19

Chapter 3: Illumination … 29

PART II: SHAMANIC QABALAH

Chapter 4: The Tree of Life … 43

Chapter 5: Malkuth, the Elemental Pacha … 57

Chapter 6: Topography of the Inner Worlds … 69

Chapter 7: The Campos and the Pillars … 89

Chapter 8: Sacred Anarchy … 101

Chapter 9: Psychonautics in Practice … 115

PART III: SIMULACRA

Chapter 10: The Astral Foundation … 137

Chapter 11: The Ethical Machine … 175

Chapter 12: The Supernal Firmament … 217

Conclusion … 241

Bibliography … 243

Index … 249

When Man had observed in the Father the creation of the Creator, he himself wished to create; and he was given permission to do so by the Father, being begotten in the sphere of the Creator, he observed carefully the creations of his brother from which he obtained every power. The Father and the brother loved him, and each gave him of their own authority. Having acquired knowledge of their essence and partaking in their nature, he wished to break through the circumference of the spheres and to come to know the power of him who was set in authority over the fire.

—POIMANDRES TO HERMES TRISMEGISTUS, *THE CORPUS HERMETICUM* (BOOK I:13)

—

We will never know world peace until three people can simultaneously look each other straight in the eye.

—PUSCIFER, *SIMULTANEOUS*

FOREWORD

There is no such thing as an immortal work of art. There is one art—the greatest of all, the art of making a complete human being of oneself.

—A. R. ORAGE, *ON LOVE / PSYCHOLOGICAL EXERCISES:*
WITH SOME APHORISMS & OTHER ESSAYS

With the passion of an enraptured mystic, the erudition of a veteran scholar, and the eloquence of a virtuoso storyteller, Daniel Moler has accomplished something truly extraordinary in writing *Shamanic Qabalah: A Mystical Path to Uniting the Tree of Life & the Great Work*. Not only has he convincingly laid bare the shamanic foundations of our most enduring Western Mystery Tradition—the esoteric Jewish theosophical doctrine of Qabalah—he has simultaneously managed to demystify the raison d'être of our contemporary human estrangement from the sacred dimensions of life.

At heart, *Shamanic Qabalah* is a breathtaking tour de force about the anarchically aroused shamanic longings of the soul for rescue from the tyranny of an unexplored human mind, from the confining structures and strictures of literalism in all its forms. It is a consummately articulated visionary sermon on spiritual human freedom. Reading *Shamanic Qabalah* is itself a process of divine gnosis, a self-transformational plunge into the timeless waters of our Remembering as immortal souls. It offers both the novice and seasoned initiate of shamanic ritual arts or Western Hermetic traditions a necessarily ego-annihilating path of communion with the great primal Abyss and subsequent embodiment of the ten Sephiroth hierarchically nested within the sacred Tree of Life.

I thus encourage you to read this remarkably insightful book by allowing it to touch your heart and not only awaken your mind. For in order for us to live with more soul in a global culture increasingly entranced by consumerist values—which are falsely justified by a materialistic and mechanistic worldview—it is incumbent upon each of us to do everything from a deeper, more reflective, shamanic soul experience of divine interdependence with the living cosmos.

Shamanic Qabalah is a veritably life-transforming, soul-animating field guide to the Great Work. All aspiring psychonauts keen on exploring astral realms stand to greatly benefit from the hands-on practices elucidated within this fascinating book. The perennial wisdom foundation of *Shamanic Qabalah* is adroitly punctuated with in-depth esoteric and exoteric ritual guidance derived from theurgy, gematria, tarot, astrology, pathfinding, and Pachakuti Mesa Tradition cross-cultural shamanism, all woven together into a seamless ceremonial companion guide for skillfully navigating and befriending our wildly sentient multiverse.

Any finely written book about the Great Work and the Golden Chain of Initiation (*Aurea Catena*) that preserves it inescapably becomes a book in the Great Chain, a radiantly connective golden link of treasured wisdom and illumined guidance replete with shamanic power to elicit a Remembering of our divine immortality as human souls. *Shamanic Qabalah* is precisely one of these books. Exposure to the soul-educing gnosis divulged within the pages of this captivating book shall irreversibly transform your life for the better— please proceed to read *without* caution!

It is quite a challenge to adequately express the depth of esteem and gratitude I feel for Daniel Moler as the unapologetic, daemon-intoxicated hollow bone that gave expression to this unique opus; for his unassailable dedication to the Great Work as a sanctioned teacher of Pachakuti Mesa Tradition cross-cultural shamanism; for his assured honesty as my trusted friend and shamanic soul brother in faith. For these reasons and many more, I respectfully offer my humble support and service to his calling as an adept Shamanic Qabalist.

In sacred relationship,
Don Oscar Miro-Quesada

Oscar Miro-Quesada is a respected *Kamasqa* curandero and *Altomisayoq* adept from Peru, founder of the Heart of the Healer (THOTH), originator of Pachakuti Mesa Tradition cross-cultural shamanism, and coauthor *of Lessons in Courage: Peruvian Shamanic Wisdom for Everyday Life*.

INTRODUCTION

You must realise clearly that the aim of the work is to train for initiation, not to convert the world.

—LORD ERKSINE, CHANNELED BY DION FORTUNE, *DION FORTUNE & THE INNER LIGHT*

Instead of spaceships, we have our minds. In futility, we assumed it was outer space that we have been called to traverse into uncharted territory, but it is actually *inner* space that is our true destiny to explore.

It was on Day of the Dead 2013 that one particular psychonaut crossed the threshold of my front door and into my living room with strange eyes that were full of conspicuous mystery. Adorned in an overly large trench coat that reached down to his ankles, he waddled in with a stack of worn books tucked under one arm. His white-gray disheveled hair, a goatee braided into beads, and his prickly eyebrows all formed the same sort of otherworldly demonic look as Max von Sydow playing Ming the Merciless in the horrendously campy 1980 *Flash Gordon* film. Physically, his stature was tiny, but his ambience radiated huge throughout the room.

My wife, Autumn, and I had invited him over to speak to a group gathered for a *Día de los Muertos* event, as we have a great interest in South and Central American ceremonial practices and were excited to delve deeper into the ceremonial aspects of the culture. He was a noted local expert in all things esoterica and had agreed to "pull something together" for us.

But John Nichols had other ideas.

With a warlock grin—the kind that made you feel like you were caught up in some grand cosmic joke that only he knew you were a part of—he sat down cross-legged, avoiding the head of the room, and immediately informed us all that this would be less of a presentation and more of an informal discussion. At that time, I eyed the tattered spines of the tomes he placed on the floor in front him: the *Yoga Spandakarika*, *The Sea Priestess* by Dion Fortune, and *The Forgotten Mage* by C. R. F. Seymour. *What do any of these texts have to do with Day of the Dead?* I thought.

And then, he began: "The thing about Day of the Dead, or just this time of year in general, is that it seems to be a period of time in which the veil separating this world from the unseen world is thinnest…"

And that was the last mention of Día de los Muertos for the rest of the evening. The conversation breathed its own life from there, from discussing other dimensions of existence to the expansion of consciousness, from shamanic techniques of ecstasy to something called the Tree of Life.

I had known about the Qabalah Tree of Life for years. Because it is a vital component to a robust career in the magical arts, I understood its importance but somehow always likened it to the quantum physics of mysticism. At some level, I knew, I needed to acquire my so-called mystical "undergrad" and "graduate" degrees first before taking on "PhD"-level territory. I had mentioned this at some point during the conversation that night, feeling like I wasn't ready yet to take on the Tree of Life.

As a response, John pulled out his well-read copy of the *Yoga Spandakarika*, one of the most important Tantric texts in Kashmiri Shaivism, translated by Kalu Rinpoche–disciple Daniel Odier. John and his partner teach Tantra, a highly misunderstood discipline that is less about sex and more about the fulfillment of sensory experience, around the world. *Spandakarika* translates from Sanskrit to "Song of the Sacred Tremor," the "sacred tremor" being the infinite fluctuation of creation and death, which the tenets of Qabalah identify with.

"Check this out." John eyed me with a court-jester glance. "Odier is talking about meditation, and the fellas who stay quiet all day and deprive themselves of experience, to gain some sort of enlightenment… and how great that is, and everything, but that Tantra, resonating with the sacred tremor… well, let me just read it: 'In general, this is what happens: we have this presence to inner feeling, then we come to a situation where there is a great variety of stimulations, and we get lost in order to taste what is outside.'[1] Wow." He closed the book, a shiver of elation jolting through his body like he'd been overcome with some invisible ecstasy. He looked back up with wide, determined eyes. "You see, incarnating in

---

1. Daniel Odier, trans., *Yoga Spandakarika: The Sacred Texts at the Origins of Tantra* (Rochester, VT: Inner Traditions International, 2005), 67.

this life … I see it like a massive buffet splayed out before us—'a great variety of stimulations'—and it's our duty to try a little bit of this, a little bit of that, not to deprive ourselves, but to 'get lost in order to taste what is outside.' The inner world grows through the experience of the outer, and vice versa. They augment each other. There's nothing you need to prepare for, because life itself is the preparation, the experience to gain the knowledge you need."

Hours later, John and the crowd left. Autumn and I looked at each other with an earnest expectation. We knew there would be no going back from here.

We were going to execute an initiatory pathworking into the Qabalah Tree of Life.

After five months of intensive study and preparation, we gathered a cadre of like-minded folks to join in on the pathworking together. Historically, these rites were always done in groups, from the mystery schools of old to the secret societies of the modern age. The Lodge of People, run from our home temple, was a hodge-podge of bright individuals from a variety of spiritual disciplines but with one common goal in mind: exploring the Tree of Life together as a sacred community.

On the evening of March 20, the spring equinox of 2014, the Lodge candidates all gathered together to launch the Great Work, a collective pathworking into the Qabalah Tree of Life. From the outset, we dubbed our endeavor "the Mystic Path."

Initially, almost tongue-in-cheek, we likened our venture to that of the television show *Star Trek*: explorers going where no human has gone before. In some respects, we had no idea how true this sentiment would be as the weeks, months, and then years rolled by. However, the interesting thing about this Work is that others *have* gone to these places before. This is what makes the Tree of Life function as a vital spiritual architecture: it is powered by those who have previously worked it throughout history, but it is up to us to take that knowledge and move it forward, to explore further and deeper into the unknown based upon what has come before.

As with any voyage of discovery, there are times of both rapture and despair. Regardless of the difficulties, Autumn and I knew that this information would have to be communicated out to the world. Even though there have been countless texts written through the ages about Qabalah and the Tree of Life, it has been said that a good Qabalist takes what they have been taught and makes it simpler for the coming generations. After completing a full initiatory pathworking of the Tree of Life, we indeed now consider ourselves justifiable Qabalists.

Lineage

"We need to get away from this crap," John told me once. "Lineages and fraternities—we no longer need that shit to be legitimate." In a way, he is absolutely right. However, I am reminded of a quote from one of John's (as well as my and Autumn's) own inspirations in Qabalah, the great mystic Dion Fortune. She once wrote,

> One of the chief advantages of initiation into a fraternity having a long line of tradition behind it lies in the fact that many souls will have entered into their freedom through its discipline and be working on the Inner Planes, and into their comradeship the newly-initiated brother enters. He is therefore in a very different position from the psychic who ventures on to the astral by means of his own unaided psychism. The latter is like a person who comes to live in a great city without any letters of introduction; it will be a long time before he gets to know anyone, and those with whom he scrapes casual acquaintance will not be among the best of its citizens.[2]

I take this to include some sort of a shamanic or esoteric lineage as well, not just a fraternal order. Let's then consider living a sacred life in the modern world. The sacred life (in other words, spirituality) contains two epistemological ingredients that, ideally, should reinforce each other: mythology, which denotes our connection to something Other than the Self, to the unknown, the Unseen; and geosophy, which denotes our connection to the land around us, its history, and its agrarian impact.

The problem we have in Western culture, specifically America, is that we are displaced due to colonialization. The majority of Americans have no geosophical connection to the land, and what mythological connection we may (or, likely, may not) have with our ancestry has been watered down through the industrious expediency of the modern age.

The predicament of North Americans is that this land we are on has been co-opted from an ancestral lineage that is not our own. America is a melting pot of immigration: a member of every culture on the planet can be found within its borders. And as the generations evolve, very few can trace their ancestral lineage to the land they live on.

As Dion stated, an ancestral lineage has power and is vital to maintaining a strong connection to both the inner and outer landscapes, tapping into their mythological souls. The methodology outlined in this book is based upon much of the training my wife and I had

---

2. Dion Fortune, *The Training & Work of an Initiate* (San Francisco, CA: Weiser Books, 2000), 76.

received from the lineages that we have adopted (or have been adopted by) as our sacred path of living. We feel it is important to honor and recognize the teachers and their wisdom before us, not only to recognize the unique blend this particular breed of Qabalah has provided for us, but to trace a family tree of power for future initiates to be able to draw upon in their own individual pathworkings.

The Western Mystery Tradition (WMT) is a broad set of esoteric disciplines rooted in magical and mystical practices. Distinguishable from Eastern mysticism, many of the WMT branches claim to be derived from the Greek and Egyptian mystery schools, embodied in the enigmatic teachings of Thoth-Hermes, Hermes Trismegistus, the "Thrice-Great." Although there really is no definable origin or pedigree of doctrine, the nineteenth century saw a rising interest in spiritualism and theosophy, which gave birth to a renewed interest in the various tributaries of WMT knowledge. From alchemy to Gnosticism to Masonry, the WMT template encompasses a variety of mystical cultivations that can normally be found on the fringes of an institutionalized religion, rather than being the primary infrastructure or face of the religion itself.

Dion Fortune is the cardinal influence on the tenets of our process. Born Violet Mary Firth in 1890, she later changed her name to a variation of her family motto *Deo, non Fortuna* (God, not Fortune) as a commitment to her spiritual work. There can be no doubt that Dion Fortune, with the exception of S. L. MacGregor Mathers and Aleister Crowley, was perhaps the most influential occultist of the early twentieth century. She was a prolific author with an entire library of works, and *The Mystical Qabalah* could arguably be her greatest contribution to WMT scholarship, as well as her fiction novels, such as *The Sea Priestess*, *Moon Magic*, and *The Winged Bull*. Much of the material in this book is acquired from her vein of the WMT, as her independent break from the secrecy of the fraternal magical orders of her time brought clarity to the legacy of mystery school teachings.

Other primary influences which Dion's career propagated that inspired many of the teachings in this book are her peers and students C. R. F Seymour, W. E. Butler, Israel Regardie, and Gareth Knight, as well as Dolores Ashcroft-Nowicki, the director of studies at the Servants of Light mystery school. Dolores's pathworking meditations in her two books *The Shining Paths* and *Inner Landscapes* were the driving fuel of our pathworking initiation with the Tree of Life. I could not recommend these books any more highly as a guide to initiation. Along with Gareth Knight's *A Practical Guide to Qabalistic Symbolism*, there really is no need for anyone to ever be replicating this knowledge to the outer world. However futile the effort, I still make the attempt, based upon their exceptional leadership, to keep communicating the Great Work to future generations in the hopes that a new audience is reached.

The *Pachakuti Mesa Tradition* (PMT) is a shamanic lineage that is Peruvian in foundation, though cross-cultural in implementation. Autumn and I are both sanctioned teachers within this lineage, so it is undeniable that many of the teachings of our Qabalistic process would be in alignment with our shamanic roots. Brought to the Western world by *Kamasqa curandero* don Oscar Miro-Quesada and originally taught to us by don Daniel Baxley, the PMT was developed to enact a transformative medicine into the world as tasked by don Oscar's teachers, don Celso Rojas Palomino and don Benito Corihuaman Vargas. Over the years, the PMT has seeded multiple communities across the globe into a new type of lineage that has transcended borders, race, gender, religion, and all the other divisions in humanity. Historically, the PMT is an amalgamation between two Peruvian traditions of don Oscar's teachers.

The *Paqokuna* lineage comes from the *Quechua* peoples of the Andes Mountains. The Quechua claim to be the direct descendants of the Incas and lead peaceful lives at one with their environment as farmers, llama herders, and so on. *Paqokuna (paqos)* of this particular shamanic lineage are healer-priests who execute their craft by making *pagos* (offerings) to the *apus* (mountain lords), which they consider an integral influence of their everyday existence. Indeed, the practice of *ayni* (sacred reciprocity) is the lifeblood of the people, maintaining a relationship with the beings of nature required for their survival. The paqos are also skillful at healing sickness, just like the healers of the *curanderismo* lineage.

Curanderismo of the northern coastal region of Peru is a practice that mixes ancient folk healing with ceremonial practices based upon Catholic iconography. The practice—other than the utilization of an altar called a *mesa* (explained later)—revolves around the usage of a sacrament called San Pedro, a mescaline-infused tea which produces visions and healing capabilities. Many *curanderos* (curers) are expert herbalists and often spend their time combating sorcery and misfortune in others.

Lineage is important not so much as to justify a system of knowledge but to understand its framework. However, in truth, wisdom needs no lineage.

Going Forward

After my initiation into treading the paths of the Tree of Life, utilizing my foundations of shamanic training, I uncovered a strong connection between the two. After years of training, notes, journals, and blog posts, the information was compiled into the volume you now hold in your hands. The goal of this book is to provide an introduction into the initiatory mysteries of Hermetic Qabalah, correlated with the philosophy of shamanic practice. It is my assertion that shamanism and Qabalah go hand in hand, as they are both methods for facilitating direct relationship with the unseen powers of the universe.

I have organized this book into three parts. Part I, "The Great Work," lays out the philosophy, aim, and makeup of what exactly this thing called "initiation" is and why it matters. Part II, "Shamanic Qabalah," details the definitions and meanings of both Qabalah and shamanism and dives into the particular methods of interacting with each school of thought. Finally, part III, "Simulacrum," takes one through various paths of the Tree of Life as a practical initiatory tool for use by the modern reader. It has been my experience that coming across viable information on all +the paths of the Tree of Life all in one volume is difficult. I hope to provide all the information a practitioner needs to get started working with the Tree of Life in one volume, albeit in a shamanic way of creating sacred trust with the natural world.

Part I
THE GREAT WORK

1

PREAMBLE OF THE STONE

Enlightenment is about truth. It's not about becoming a better or happier person. It's not about personal growth or spiritual evolution. An accurate ad for enlightenment would make the toughest marine blanche. There is no higher stakes game in this world or any other, in this dimension or any other. The price of truth is everything, but no one knows what everything means until they're paying it. In the simplest of terms, enlightenment is impersonal, whereas what is commonly peddled as enlightenment is personal in the extreme.

—JED MCKENNA, *SPIRITUAL ENLIGHTENMENT: THE DAMNEDEST THING*

It is undeniable the state of the world is in chaos.

In the rapid technological prowess and innovation of the twenty-first century, leading a life in tune with the sacred can be an arduous task: our current day-to-day routine is a product of centuries of industrial expansion; our unchecked rate of growth has exploited the earth's resources and natural habitats; it is becoming increasingly more obvious to the scientific community that we have disrupted the balance our planet has previously maintained in order to sustain the conditions of life for millions of years; and through this exploitation and abuse at our hands, we have disintegrated our connection to the natural world and, in turn, ourselves.

Conversely, our technological progress has developed a global culture of unity and awareness the likes of which has never been seen in recorded history. If I wish, I can have a close friendship with a citizen of Pakistan, I can purchase wares from a market in Bolivia, and I can keep track of the on-ground tactics of a revolution in Egypt—all without ever leaving my home. The interconnectedness of our communications has exceeded the limits of science fiction. So, in the context of our continued abuse toward the planet and ourselves, we have to ask ourselves, why are we doing this? And what can we do to make it better?

Dagara medicine man Malidoma Patrice Somé writes, "I have come to suspect that in the absence of ritual, the soul runs out of its real nourishment, and all kinds of social problems then ensue.... I suggest that the road to correcting ills goes through the challenging path of ritual."[3] I also assert that transcendence, through some means of ritualized connection with the sacred, is the way our collective psyche can try to surpass these gluttonous addictions pervading our society. This is the aim of the shamanic Qabalah, a field guide to assist fellow psychonauts (astronauts of the psyche) through the process of initiation via the Great Work.

Gary Lachman is the former guitarist for the rock band Blondie, now turned mystic scholar. He is convinced we are indeed here to be stewards not only of the earth but of the entire universe itself. In his book *The Caretakers of the Cosmos*, he outlines the duality of human existence as shown in various mystical traditions throughout history (Gnosticism, Hermeticism, etc.) and asserts that, taken together, these traditions present a path forward in the human predicament:

> I believe that nature, the world, the cosmos, separated us off from itself in order for it to become *conscious of itself through us*. It is in this way, through our own increasing consciousness, that the work of creation is completed, or at least carried on. Drawing on the work of different "participatory" thinkers, it is my belief that our evolutionary task now is to regain an experience of participation and all that it entails, without losing our independence as conscious egos, capable of free will and creative action, something our ancestors, more at one with the cosmos, lacked. Our task, then, is to become *more* conscious, not less, which means facing the sense of separation from the world firmly, and *getting through it*.[4]

But what exactly does being "more conscious" mean? That answer, I believe, can be found in the process of initiation. It can only be explored to be known.

---

3. Malidoma Patrice Somé, *Ritual: Power, Healing and Community* (Portland, OR: Swan/Raven & Company, 1993), 121.

4. Gary Lachman, *The Caretakers of the Cosmos: Living Responsibly in an Unfinished Universe* (Edinburgh, UK: Floris Books, 2013), 27.

Getting Started

I was sitting in a circle of people. It was a spiritual gathering, a workshop centered on self-transformation and what have you. We were taking turns one by one to introduce ourselves and share the state or county where we were from.

The first woman stood, covered in beads and tattoos, bells jingling off her hemp dress as she rose.

"My name is Priestess Ishtar Blue Feather Woman, and I'm from Atlantis."

Actually, her name was Maggie Smith, and she was from downtown. But her creative opening remarks inspired everyone else in the group. Light bulbs sprung over their heads all throughout the circle, a Fourth of July spectacle of compulsive, lemming rapture. The next person stood, a guy in dreadlocks with a t-shirt that stated proudly in bubblegum letters, "Spiritual Gangster."

"My name is Bear Claw, and I'm from, um…." He thought about it for a little bit, a childish grin on his face. "Orion's Belt … hehe, yeah!"

Everyone laughed. The next person stood, and it continued.

"My name is White Buffalo Seeker, and I'm from Jupiter."

"My name is Star Child, and I'm from Dimension X."

"My name is Standing Tall Man, and I'm from the Pleiades."

And on and on it went, everyone getting more and more creative with their fictionalized names and origins, until the group came to me.

"My name is Daniel Moler, and I'm from Olathe, Kansas."

They all kept smiling, but there were no more giggles. They were the kinds of smiles painted on forcefully to keep a composure of calm, but underneath their flow had been interrupted. I'd been a killjoy. I wasn't trying to be. I was actually just being me. That was who I am; I was just introducing myself, rather than an invented or channeled persona from a previous, assumed lifetime. The point of an introduction was to get to know the people you were in circle with. This was a workshop on self-transformation; it was time to get real. I didn't have a sense of who anyone was from their super-identities. Plus, to be honest, I did want to make a point…

I've heard numerous times from seekers in alternative spirituality and transformational communities that they are dissatisfied with the world. That is indeed why they want to transform, because they are dissatisfied with their current state of being. But too often I interact with others who are so uncomfortable in their skin they even make comments like, "I wonder if there was some mistake when I was sent to this planet" or "Just waiting for my star relatives to pick me up." Coupled with the ornamental introductions from above, often I get to the place where I just want to ask them:

"Why do you keep disassociating yourselves from the earth?"

Why are we discarding the lineage of being children of the earth? It's the same situation in fundamentalist religious institutions. I grew up in a Christian church, and I was taught from an early age that God created the earth, and then we were created from God. The Christian creation myth (like other creation stories) denotes that we were basically plucked out of the sky and placed here on the planet as a sort of test of our mettle. Almost as if we *are* alien to the earth!

But I believe in science—in reality—even though I am a highly spiritual person. To harken to our *Terra* heritage, we literally *grew* out of the earth. Starting in the seas, we began as cellular organisms that evolved into multicellular organisms, which eventually ended in us walking out of the primordial waters to become sentient beings on the land. Again, *literally*, the earth is our mother. This is not an abstract or metaphorical concept. It is as real as the oxygen we breathe.

We should not want to be from anywhere else. We should be proud of our heritage. This is who we are: earth-beings having an earthly experience.

I understand the disenchantment with being human, though. Frankly, we live in a shitty world right now, a world we ourselves have created. At the moment, there are mass-shootings and mass-bombings happening all around the globe. There is unprecedented environmental devastation putting pressure on our lives, and nobody wants to do what it takes to change the course. Roughly 80 percent of the world is in poverty. The list goes on and on, and for some it goes on all too long until the point where all our fragile brains can do is shut down. But none of this is Earth Mother's fault. Don't disown her.

We must have our resolve. And we must do something about this. Part of the problem of wanting to effect change is that there is too much to do. We become overwhelmed and lose sight of what we *can* do, because we can't do everything. Wisdom teachers around the world agree, though, echoing the popular statement attributed to Mahatma Gandhi: "We must be the change we wish to see in the world."

But Gandhi didn't actually say that. What he said was simplified and turned into a meme that's easy to copy and paste onto a tweet for a motivational uplift. What Gandhi actually said was this: "We but mirror the world. All the tendencies present in the outer world are to be found in the world of our body. If we could change ourselves, the tendencies in the world would also change. As a man changes his own nature, so does the attitude of the world change towards him. This is the divine mystery supreme. A wonderful thing it is and the source of our happiness. We need not wait to see what others do." [5]

This statement—actually an esoteric commentary—has been co-opted into an exoteric pretext for a form of religious exploitation pervading our modern culture. It has been taken literally, instead of mystically, to promote a commercialized narrative that seeks to secularize true spiritual seeking into a success-oriented pyramid scheme.

Former Zen monk Mu Soeng is now an author and program director at the Barre Center for Buddhist Studies in Massachusetts. Soeng is a critic of what he calls the "happiness industry" pervading Buddhism, but also our entire culture of spiritual and social media. He states that the overlaps between the happiness industry and spirituality have forced religions—including Buddhism—into traffickers of bliss. Consequently, a spiritual path can no longer be legitimate unless it caters to the benefit of people's happiness.

Soeng continues his analysis of happiness-seeking belief systems as something separate from the liberation or illumination sought after in mysticism. America especially has adopted religion in general to be the basis of a manifest-destiny mindset inherent in all Western life, from the smallest of daily banalities to the gaining of favor from on high. It's almost as if religion has turned into a principle of self-gratification, that God itself is invested in the minutiae of every person's innate desires. Soeng explains, "Throughout history, all popular religions ... have sought to convey a prosperity gospel through faith in one deity or another. What's distinctive about the prosperity gospel in America is that it fits into a distinctly American narrative about happiness starting with what Max Weber has called 'the spirit of Protestant Ethic.' This is the Calvinistic idea that God rewards prosperity to those who work hard." [6]

So, in effect, we have developed a spiritual culture that is based on materialism. Our store shelves and TV commercials are filled to the brim with prosperity evangelists like Joel Osteen and advertisements selling us the next big thing on better health and better financial success ... all to reach the goal of *your* dreams! But what is most disconcerting about all of this—whether or not you are okay with the consumer merits of such an ethic pervading our society—is that our material success has nothing at all to do with having a spiritual life.

---

5. Mohandas Gandhi, *The Collected Works of Mahatma Gandhi,* vol. 3 (Ahmedabad, India: Navajivan Trust, 1960), 241.

6. Mu Soeng, "Worldly Happiness/Buddhist Happiness," *Parabola* 41, no. 2 (Summer 2016): 48.

The universe (God) only cares for one's material gain as much as the human body cares about the individual success of a single cell in the whole of the entire organism. We, as human beings, care little for the personal desires of every single cell inside of our bodies, as long as it serves its function for the whole of the body. Likewise, that is the function of the mystical path, a true spiritual life. It is the path of the cell, of a function, to serve the needs of the greater whole of the body of the earth, and thus the universe.

One of the greater twentieth-century philosophers of the mystery traditions, Manly P. Hall addresses this notion of service that makes up the life of a mystic in his book *The Mystical Christ*. In this treatise of mysticism, he writes, "To cultivate the attributes of spirituality in order to satisfy frustrated ambitions or to make an otherwise useless life appear useful is to invite disaster; yet religion [or any spiritual system] has always served as an outlet for the neurotic. The halt, the lame, and the blind have always demanded the consolation of their faith, but have contributed little of strength and integrity to the sects which they have joined. In mysticism it is what we give and not what we gain that determines spiritual progress."[7]

Inherent in the notion of mysticism is the quality of sacrifice: one's entire life is surrendered to the mysteries of the universe, rather than just Sundays. In any case, if indeed the religious life assumes God is a personality—with personality enough to be jealous of false gods (which are, by that logic, not even real)—then the spiritual life, and most especially the mystical one, is about having a relationship with that personality. If I were to have a relationship with my wife by making every decision in accordance with what I can acquire for my own gain from her, then what kind of relationship is that? If I ask for this and ask for that, she would be willing to give at first because of her love for me, but at what point does she begin to hold back because of lack of reciprocation? What about the giving? What about decisions that are actually of mutual benefit, not just mine or hers alone?

Our spiritual culture is a capitalist one. We need to stop cultivating spiritual practices that promote the acquisition of "stuff," of "things." We seek "liberation," we seek "success," and we seek "abundance," among other things. However, just as I am not in relationship with my wife to *get* things from her but am in relationship with her for the sake of relationship, why then can we not be in relationship with God for the sake of just being in relationship? Why must we have some deep, ulterior motive for having belief, for having faith? Must we always have some sort of gain?

---

7. Manly P. Hall, *The Mystical Christ: Religion as a Personal Spiritual Experience* (Los Angeles: The Philosophical Research Society, 1951), 86–87.

Recheck yourself, because you have just convinced yourself that you have no ulterior motive. But look deeper. You do.

When Gandhi said "this is the divine mystery supreme," he was not talking about some exclusive secret that is concealed from the common person. Every mystic versed in the symbology of the mysteries understands exactly what he means here. Gandhi is saying the only thing you do have control over is the temple that is you. Your body, and less so even the physical vehicle and more so the mental and emotional capacities. Our power resides within.

As was stated by one of the greatest mystics ever known, Yeshua, the Christ, in the Gospel of Thomas: "When you know yourselves, then you will be known, and you will understand that you are children of the living father. But if you do not know yourselves, then you dwell in poverty and you are poverty." [8] He is, of course, not speaking of literal poverty in terms of financial success.

There is a mystical substance known to the ancient alchemists, whispered in legends and written about in arcane tomes, called the philosopher's stone. This stone was said to have such great power that it could bestow eternal life and enlightenment and turn base metals into gold. One can imagine a king's reaction to such a feat! As faux chemists were tasked by their leaders to spend years and years toiling away in laboratories and traveling the globe in search of such a lucrative object, the authentic alchemists knew that the philosopher's stone was a symbol. It was never a physical thing to be found or formed, but a spiritual, mental, and emotional process to be developed and matured.

In alchemy, there is a Latin phrase—*Visita interiora terrae rectificando invenies occultum lapidem*—which reveals that one must visit the interior of the earth, purified, in order to find the stone. This means we must delve deep within ourselves, become redeemed, to achieve the attainment sought by philosophers and mystics through the ages.

We do not fly into the stars or take flights of fancy to find the stone, in order to live a life of spiritual virtue. No, we delve into the depths of the earth. We go inward, to the truth of who we are. We are children of the earth—let us not forget that, ever.

---

8. Willis Barnstone and Marvin Meyer, eds., *The Gnostic Bible: Gnostic Texts of Mystical Wisdom from the Ancient and Medieval Worlds* (Boston: Shambhala, 2009), 3:7–10.

2

INITIATION

Go in the narrow door; because the door is wide and the road is broad leading off to destruction, and many people are going that way. Whereas how narrow the door and how constricted the road leading off to Life, and how few people find it!

—YESHUA (JESUS) TO THE CROWD ON THE MOUNT, MATTHEW 7:13–14,

AS TRANSLATED FROM THE ORIGINAL GREEK

The path of the mystic is not a hobby or an amusement. It is a calling.

 As a child, I often found myself plagued by insomnia, my gut clenched with the anxiety brought on by the greatest of mysteries: *Who—or what—is God? And how can I get to know him, her, or it? What in the hell is this thing called reality?*

From the very beginning, I was trying so hard to just figure out life. I wanted to know what this thing was. What the hell is happening?

Since the beginning of human history—indeed, since the beginning of consciousness—we have been trying to figure this one out.

We are at least aware that we exist … philosophy has figured out this much.

Cogito ergo sum, as is often paraphrased from René Descartes's seminal work *Discourse on the Method*. "I think, therefore I am." Another version of the translation is "I am thinking, therefore I exist," and this has seemed to reign supreme throughout history as Descartes's own "first principle of philosophy," as well as the fundamental basics of consciousness studies.[9]

---

9. René Descartes, "A Discourse on Method," *Descartes: Philosophical Writings*, trans. and ed. Elizabeth Anmscombe and Peter Thomas Geach (New York: MacMillian Publishing, 1971), 31.

We each have a brain; therefore, we receive the reality perceived by the brain. For some, this is enough. However, those called to the Work of the Great Mystery need more. Indeed, it is the Mystery which lures us, like Ariadne's thread leading us out of the labyrinth of the mundane.

One highly regarded scholar of the Mysteries, Charles R. F. Seymour (known as "the Colonel"), speaks of this inner calling to those who cannot settle for simple answers, those who yearn for a deeper connection with the Source of All Creation: "There is a 'divine discontent' that urges one on to seek beyond the skyline where strange roads go down. As a rule it is only the restless soul, who, driven by this strange but divine feeling of discontent, seeks for the Ancient Mysteries…"[10]

It is those whose souls grapple with the Mystery of God that are often called to the path of initiation, otherwise known as the Great Work, the pursuit of the philosopher's stone. Throughout history there have been mystery schools of various fraternities, orders, and grades that have sought—outside of the confines of core religious institutions—an authentic path of transcendence. From the earliest pangs of Neolithic shamanism to the Rites of Mithras, from the pyramids of Egypt to the Temple of Apollo, from the Freemasons to the Theosophical Society, the Great Work has manifested in one way or another throughout history as an enigma. Most typically, the Great Work found itself in the tracks of so-called secret societies, the subject matter of most conspiracy theories.

However, there was always good reason for the rites of these organizations to remain in the dark (oftentimes literally). Partially, it was to avoid persecution. Even before persecution had become the customary reaction of the establishment, though, secrecy was vital to maintaining the integrity of the ritual processes. For an example, turn on the television and watch the news for five minutes. It takes no effort on the part of the populace to take a piece of information and distort it based either on ignorance or political gain. Like mathematics and other sciences, the Mysteries take a lot of training to fully understand. Certain pains were taken by the priests and priestesses of these ancient mystical orders to cover up their ceremonies and methods with symbols and abstractions in order to protect the sanctity of the knowledge they were tasked to carry.

Indeed, this is where the word *occult* comes from. Contrary to popular opinion, it does not in any way relate to anything "satanic" or "evil." The term was bastardized by religious fanatics intending to demonize any sort of mystical practice that did not match their own.

---

10. Charles R. F. Seymour, *The Forgotten Mage: The Magical Lectures of Colonel C.R.F. Seymour* (Loughborough, Leicestershire, UK: Thoth Publications, 1999), 19.

Occult is derived from the Latin *occultus*, which means "secret" or "hidden." All occultism really is or has been is the knowledge of the hidden, such as magic, mysticism, and religion, especially in regard to esotericism (which is often used interchangeably with occultism). Occultism became the common moniker used for ideas regarding the Great Work in the eighteenth century as a reaction to the rationalistic epistemology of the European Enlightenment. Gareth Knight elucidates:

> Much portentous nonsense has been written about "occult secrecy," the "Keys to Power" and the like in past years, mainly to cloak ignorance in the writer, or else for cheap self-aggrandisement. The reason why the Mysteries, which are really the Yoga of the West, are called hidden, and for the few, is because they *cannot* be explained to outsiders. The barrier is purely one of communication. To try to describe a mystical experience is like trying to describe the scent of a flower, one cannot do it. The best one can do is to tell the enquirer how best he can obtain the particular flower so that he can smell it for himself. If he cannot be bothered to follow your directions or flatly refuses to believe that the flower exists there is nothing one can do about it.[11]

It is the goal of the initiate, through the vistas of occult, esoteric methodologies, to interpenetrate the unseen in order to unveil the Mysteries of God. So, what exactly is happening when an initiate is "unveiling the Mysteries"?

In the year 1888 a very peculiar image made its appearance in French astronomer Camille Flammarion's *L'atmosphère: météorologie populaire*. Often referred to generically as the "Flammarion engraving," it is believed to have been the print of a wood engraving made by either Flammarion himself or an unknown artist. The image shows a man—sometimes noted as a traveler, for he carries a walking cane—kneeling down and stretching his upper body into a breach in the earth and sky horizon, revealing on the other side of this breach another world of cosmic symbols and machinery. In other words, he is moving into the world existing behind—or *beyond*—the one we currently see with our very eyes.

---

11. Gareth Knight, *A Practical Guide to Qabalistic Symbolism*, one-volume edition, vol. 1 (Boston, MA: Weiser Books, 2001), 5.

Figure 1: The Author's Reimagining of the Flammarion Engraving

Flammarion's caption for this engraving reads, "A missionary of the Middle Ages tells that he has found the point where the sky and the Earth touch…" [12]

"Where the sky and Earth touch" would of course be the horizon line. However, there truly is no horizon, is there? You can't reach it. There is no true point where the sky and earth touch; it is an illusion. But, it is through that illusion, breaching that smokescreen, that the true machinery of the universe reveals itself. This horizon is what is referred to, especially in mystery traditions, as the veil.

The Colonel has discussed at length the process of lifting the veil, or what he calls "the unveiling of the self," as the prime objective of initiation. The second objective is to raise the veil of the cosmos itself. Paraphrasing G. R. S. Mead, Seymour writes, "To raise it man has to transcend the limits of individuality, to break the bonds of death, and so become conscious of immortality. To raise the veil is to see Nature as she is, and not as she appears to be." [13] He makes a point to say no mortal human has yet achieved this state of being. However, we see its echoes in the legends and mythologies of our world history, in the Christ of Christianity, White Buffalo Calf Woman of the Lakota, Horus of Egypt, Muhammed of Islam, Elijah of Judaism, Siddhartha of Buddhism, Pachakuteq of the Inca, the avatars of Vishnu in Hinduism, and so on and so forth. There are certain figures in every

---

12. Camille Flammarion, *L'atmosphère: météorologie populaire* (Paris: Hachette, 1888), 163.

13. Seymour, *Forgotten Mage*, 126.

spiritual tradition across the planet that have some sort of story representing the human's reach for transcendence, for breaching the veil between earth and sky.

Somewhere engrained in our consciousness, as a collective, we obviously strive for a touchpoint with the unknown. We express this in a variety of ways but most generally through our search for knowledge (science) and our search for beauty (art). However, there are those who dare to push beyond even those limitations, to the fringes of consciousness, that horizon which separates the known from the unknown, the earth from the sky.

This is the mystic path, the strange road that leads beyond the horizon. Lifting the veil is the first task.

Out of the Cave

Plato, the father of Western philosophy, wrote a series of dialogues between himself and his teacher Socrates called *Republic*. Written sometime around 380 BCE, *Republic* was centered on defining an ideal society through character, justice, and the education of the soul. In book 7 of the text, Socrates points out that the aim of education is to change the desires of the soul, as outlined in one of the more famous parables in philosophy, popularly called the "Allegory of the Cave."

Socrates introduces the allegory to show how the lack of education can hinder civilization and then begins to metaphorically describe humanity as beings who live in a deep, underground cave. These beings have been in this underground dwelling since childhood, fixed in one place their whole lives, shackled by the neck and limbs so that they are unable to move and can only face one direction within the cave. They live their entire lives bound, only able to look upon this one wall. And upon this wall, shapes move about, images go to and fro, and they speak to and interact with those images, catalogue those images as they observe them, as those images are the only reality which they know.

But then for some reason, one of those bound beings is able to loosen their shackles and move their head. Imagine this liberated individual is then able to look around the cave—other than that one wall—and see a very disturbing thing: that the images on the wall that they thought were reality were actually just shadows cast by a great fire behind the shackled humans, one they could not see because of their bonds. This whole time what they thought was real was nothing but two-dimensional shadows cast by objects and instruments controlled by a company of puppeteers. Socrates then goes on to say, "Consider, then, what being released from their bonds and cured of their ignorance would naturally be like if something like this came to pass…. [H]e'd be pained and dazzled and unable to see the things whose shadows he'd seen before. What do you think he'd say, if we told him that what he'd seen before was inconsequential, but that now—because he is a bit closer to the things that are and is turned towards things that are more—he sees more correctly?" [14]

Imagine the trauma induced by suddenly seeing and knowing the truth! And if that human decided to investigate further, to explore the cave, they would eventually be led up a path which would take them to the surface, where they would be temporarily blinded by the great light of the sun for having lived their entire life in darkness. Imagine the shock of this whole new world about them, seemingly unlimited, strange, beautiful, and terrible.

But why do we start out living in darkness, shackled in the cave? Why are we born shrouded in the veil upon incarnation?

To the ancient Greeks, the river Lethe was the answer to this question. Upon death and journeying to their final resting place in the underworld, a soul was required to drink from one of five rivers, namely the waters of Lethe. *Lethe* literally means "forgetfulness" or "concealment." It was believed that a soul must forget their previous life before being reincarnated into a new one.

Whether or not you believe in reincarnation is irrelevant. The myths of old were the compass through which the ancient thinkers could navigate the perplexities of consciousness. It is doubtful they were ever taken literally, but the characters and places within the myths were symbols used to explore the mysteries of phenomena. According to mythologist Joseph Campbell, a myth is "the secret opening through which the inexhaustible energies of the cosmos pour into human cultural manifestation." [15] Myths are symbols that the psyche produces subconsciously, not through deliberate manufacturing. They keep us in touch with our origins, which are "secret," concealed.

We can see that the ancient Greeks had this notion of a concealed origin, a connection to the source of being that was disrupted or forgotten. The memory of our origin eludes us. Occasionally, it seems, there is an individual who claims to have refused libation from the River of Forgetfulness, but they are few and far between, and their story can prove quite nebulous at times. For the most part, we all share this commonality, even those who don't at least share the commonality of the underworld itself, as death waits for us all.

---

14. Plato, *Republic*, trans. by G. M. A. Grube (Indianapolis, IN: Hackett Publishing, 1992), 187–88.
15. Joseph Campbell, *The Hero with a Thousand Faces* (Princeton, NJ: Princeton University Press, 1973) 3–4.

So, we have the great concealer of the past—the river Lethe—and the great concealer of the future—death. What then of the present? Concealed in the past and future, some say the present is the clear point of immediate attention. However, it cannot be entirely that clear, can it? If it were, why would we be so confused? Why would we have so much hate, fear, and bewilderment, which have together cascaded into a societal landslide of near-inevitable extinction for our species?

The Toltec civilization from Mesoamerica proposes another scenario to give some context to our present plight. Don Miguel Ruiz, a Toltec *nagual* (shaman), discusses the concept called the *mitote* (mih-TOH-tay), a condition of consciousness that keeps us trapped in a perpetual state of concealment. He likens it to the Hindu concept of *maya*, an illusion, which is really what reality is.[16] The Aboriginal Australians have a similar concept, that life is really a dream. It is a state of being that we are somehow convinced is real, but it really is not. Ruiz writes,

> We live in a fog that is not even real. This fog is a dream, your personal dream of life—what you believe, all the concepts you have about what you are, all the agreements you made with others, with yourself, and even with God.
>
> … It is the personality's notion of "I am." Everything you believe about yourself and the world, all the concepts and programming you have in your mind, all are the *mitote*. We cannot see who we truly are; we cannot see that we are not free.
>
> That is why humans resist life. To be alive is the biggest fear humans have.[17]

We are all sleepwalkers: the vast majority of humanity is moving about, but we are asleep and unable to see each other, constantly bumping into one another, falling down, and walking into walls. How many times have you made the same mistake over and over again? How many times do you make that same New Year's resolution but are never able to relinquish your old, unhealthy habits? How many times do you keep ending up in the same shitty, destructive relationship?

It is often stated that we are in a collective state of amnesia. I am more apt to say we are in a collective state of anosognosia. *Anosognosia* is the brain's inability to be aware of a major deficit or illness with the body, typically due to physiological damage to certain parts

---

16. Miguel Ruiz, *The Four Agreements: A Practical Guide to Personal Freedom* (San Rafael, CA: Amber-Allen Publishing, 1997), 16–17.

17. Ruiz, *The Four Agreements,* 16–17.

of the brain. Maybe the damage we have done to ourselves through the trauma of history has created a physiological state in which we have become unaware of our own deficits. This might be a more updated model of the Christian concept of "original sin" or an explanation of mitote.

Symbols

We are rarely aware of our own collective sickness, our cultural malaise of anosognosia. The initiate on the path of mysticism awakens from this anosognosia, from the cave of our illusions.

After there has been time for acclimation from this awakening, wouldn't then that human want to return to the cave, to free their other sisters and brothers who are still imprisoned within their old reality? Also, wouldn't that liberated human also face difficulty in explaining to their shackled fellows the actual world which exists above them? The prisoners would lack the sufficient language and terminology to be able to comprehend these new things the liberator would be describing. They would be confused and confounded, rejecting the absurdities coming from the liberator's mouth. They would demonize, and maybe even attempt to kill, the liberator for challenging their preconceived notions. As Socrates explained, "In the knowable realm, the form of the good is the last thing to be seen, and it is reached only with difficulty." [18]

It is because of this difficulty to reach the masses—who are shackled to their shadow puppet show—that a liberator will most often resort to symbols and allegories to speak of the actuality of all things. This is the language of the Great Work used by the mystery schools.

A symbol, put simply, is a concept that represents something other than what it is. Examples of symbols are words, ideas, images, and especially numerals. They are abstractions that convey a whole other reality from how they are materially displayed. The word *symbol* comes from an ancient Greek custom that was used to bind a group of people together. A slate of burned clay was broken to pieces and each piece given to an individual within that group. When the group convened, the individuals would match (*symbollein*) together the broken pieces, confirming their legitimacy within that group.

Hence, symbols are like pieces of a vast puzzle that, when put together, give us a great understanding of the universal picture. Mathematics is the primary example of this process. However, in esoteric philosophy there is another set of symbols that convey this uni-

---

18. Plato, *Republic*, 189.

versal picture in a different way. Unfortunately, there have been dogmatists throughout the ages who have literalized these symbol sets in the spiritual literature and, from that, tyrannized the religious process into a structure of fundamentalism.

Symbols are not meant to be taken at face value. That defies the very nature of a symbol. Gareth Knight states, "The whole aim of symbolism is its own destruction so that one can get to the reality which it represents." [19] Like the liberator in the cave, symbolism can, with all hope, communicate to those of us shackled to the illusion a bigger reality that exists around us, which the *mitote* of the Toltecs blinds us to.

Symbols are the language of mysticism, and that language needs to be learned in order to tread these strange paths.

The biggest mistake one can ever make while undertaking the Great Work is to take the imagery of mysticism literally. As Knight stated, the aim of the symbol is its own demise. One has to get past what the symbol seems to represent (its façade) and understand what lies behind it. Symbols are a system of mathematics that initiates use to decipher the secrets of the Mysteries.

Initiation, the Great Work, engages with these symbols in a conscious way—via ritual—to reach the subconscious recesses of the mind. Each symbol (whether it be a Hebrew letter, the image of a tarot card, an astrological glyph, a mythological figure, an angelic being, etc.) represents a key that unlocks a certain dimension existing within the subconscious of the individual. The subconscious can be likened to encrypted data, and the symbols of the Mysteries have been designed over millennia to be the code that unlocks the information already inside us but that we otherwise do not have access to. We may or may not be consciously aware of this unlocking right away. Often, especially as one moves into higher and deeper levels of initiation, it becomes more difficult to consciously discern and put into words the experience.

Each symbol accounts for a factor within the cosmos, within one's self. When the mind concentrates upon the symbol, and when it is charged through consistent ceremonial processes, it is able to come into contact with the force behind the symbol. There then is the open portal to establish a channel between the aspirant and the World Soul, the realm behind the veil.

Naturally blinded, we are driven by discontent. That much is true. Using symbolic ceremony, the aim of initiation is to lift the Veil of Mystery surrounding us. It is not a singular operation that only happens once in a person's life; rather, it is a continuous approach to

---

19. Knight, *Qabalistic Symbolism*, vol. 1, 20–21.

exploring the reality of both the seen and unseen. As the Colonel relays, "… an initiation into the Mysteries by means of ritual is a long-drawn-out process of self-development, that does not take place in a world of time and space. [...] In a genuine initiation few can say where or when or at what moment 'realisation' came to them. [...] *Initio* means 'I begin', and even the most successful initiation merely means a mental and spiritual process in the soul of the candidate. To this process there is no finality." [20]

With no finality, to be a true Initiate then is to align one's life with the standard that is required for success in the Great Work.

---

20. Seymour, *Forgotten Mage*, 21.

3

ILLUMINATION

The wind turns a ship
From its course upon the waters:
The wandering winds of the senses
Cast man's mind adrift
And turn his better judgment from its course.
When a man can still the senses
I call him illumined.

—SRI KRISHNA TO ARJUNA, *BHAGAVAD-GITA*

Religion has a bad rap.

Nowadays it is quite popular to decree oneself "spiritual, but not religious." This is the rallying cry of many spiritual paths lately, perhaps the by-product of generations of guilt-laden religious institutionalism. Even some mainstream religions have adopted the motto in the hopes of appealing to younger generations.

Unfortunately, this has created a new religious paradigm in which the focus has steered away from spirituality entirely and turned into a new breed of corporatization. This new paradigm has mutated, focused more on individuation than rituals of reverence. Modernization is fine, but why can't one seek self-liberation and also be devoted to God (however that concept applies to you) at the same time? What we have now is a generation that is leaving God out of the equation of a spiritual life.

Modern spirituality has offered up a puffball abstraction of a God that is all-loving no matter what—exactly what we all hoped for as children—instead of the cruel despot that would condemn us to damnation if we were bad. This abstraction of God is a being who wants you to succeed in your worldly endeavors no matter what, who cares about your sense of self-worth, your sense of self-fulfillment; indeed, the universe is even "conspiring for your happiness."

The modern human has certainly created a god in their own image, a god always rooting for their cause, a god in which no darkness could ever enter. But it is a false god.

The late mystic Jiddu Krishnamurti once stated, "If we are seeking God merely because we are tired of this world and its miseries, then it is an escape. Then we create God, and therefore it is not God." [21] The spiritual life is, and always should be, the search for truth, whatever the cost. It should not be, ever, a vehicle for positive reinforcement.

The universe is a vast, empty, dangerous, scary—yet beautiful and awe-inspiring—concept. True awareness is a direct experience, through the senses of the body, of the world around us (which is the true goal of yoga, not aerobic exercise). Ultimately, though, the universe does not care about your bank account and most certainly is not invested in whether or not you feel good about yourself.

The universe—God—will kill you in the blink of an eye, and it will not care. Just as the body will kill off cells that no longer serve their function.

That right there is the ultimate spiritual experience. If you truly live within that experience *fully*, then you will actually have a great weight lifted off of your shoulders:

You are not the center of the universe!

It may be hard for the ego to swallow, but once one realizes that God does not lose sleep over anyone's personal struggles, you begin the path of initiation.

Perhaps this is due to the misunderstanding of the images—symbols—inherent in religious texts throughout the centuries. *Lux* (Latin for *light*) in most all spiritual paths is the end goal of the spiritual experience. For the mystery schools, the path of attaining lux is even more apparent, and it most especially came to fruition and accuracy during the blossoming of the Hermetic Order of the Golden Dawn at the end of the nineteenth century.

The Hermetic Order of the Golden Dawn initiated a renaissance of the Mysteries in Europe during the tail end of the industrial revolution, as a sort of Romantic response to the assembly-line modernization of society at that time. Coming into contact with some supposedly ancient Rosicrucian manuscripts, along with their Masonic and theosophical leanings, a collection of aspiring occultists created one of the more succinct and thorough magical systems of initiation, which has survived—in one shape or form—to this day.

---

21. J. Krishnamurti, *On God* (New York: HarperCollins Publishers, 1992), 43.

In the late twentieth century the author and adept Israel Regardie published a compendium of the teachings, rites, and ceremonies of the order, simply called *The Golden Dawn*. Regardie discusses the importance of understanding the role of lux in initiation. Certainly, to reach and attain direct contact and communion with the Light of God is the goal, if ever there was one, of spirituality. Light has been likened to the spiritual experience of God in almost every religious context imaginable throughout history.

Yet, according to Regardie and the Golden Dawn, when we speak of light in the Great Work, it is not the physical rays of luminescence we may typically conceive of. It is not literal. It is also not always benevolent. It is a metaphor for an experience … the experience of the fruition of the Great Work itself:

> As we know, the experience of the rising of the Light in both vision and waking state is common to mystics of every age and of every people. It must be an experience of the greatest significance of the treading of the Path because its appearance seems always and everywhere an unconditional psychic thing. It is an experience which defies definition, as well in its elementary flashes as in its most advanced transports. No code of thought, philosophy or religion, no logical process can bind it or limit it or express it. But, it always represents, spiritually, a marked attainment, a liberation from the turmoil of life and from psychic complications and, as Dr. C.G. Jung has expressed the matter, it "thereby frees the inner personality from emotional and imaginary entanglements, creating thus a unity of being which is universally felt as a release." It is the attainment of spiritual puberty, marking a significant stage in growth.[22]

This shows that the function of initiation, in seeking light, is shepherding oneself into a process of labor. It is an alchemical endeavor, just as the ancient alchemists were initiates themselves. Turning the lead within oneself into gold—*chrysopoeia*—is the prime goal. The whole aim of magic, alchemy, and mysticism is to purify one's soul through illumination of the divine light, which is in fact an inner light. This is initiation.

---

22. Israel Regardie, *The Golden Dawn* (St. Paul, MN: Llewellyn Publications, 1989), 24–25.

Character and Conduct

One cannot receive the light, cannot receive initiation, just by wanting it. Desire alone is not sufficient. One must condition oneself accordingly so that the light of spiritual illumination may be received, for the light will not fill a container that is impure.

This sounds dangerously close to puritanism, which admittedly scares most people away from a truly religious life. Run if you must, but truth remains adamant…

Initiation is a state of mind. It comes as a result of discipline, rather than circumstance. Spiritual illumination can only be exemplified though embodying its principles in a concrete, physical form.

In *The Mystical Christ*, Manly P. Hall expresses a great deal about the task of the initiate to live a religious life. Indeed, the knowledge acquired within the Great Work inspires one toward a standard behavior: "Where mysticism motivates conduct, it flows through ourselves into collective society. We live outwardly, but from within ourselves. It becomes our moral duty to bear witness through conduct to the majesty of conviction. To fail in this is to break faith with something we know to be beautiful and necessary." [23]

Enacting a proper code of conduct to groom one's character is absolutely essential to readying oneself for the illumination of initiation. This is where the lineage of Dion Fortune came into play for me, personally. One of Fortune's most notable works is a sort of instruction manual on how to prepare oneself for the path of initiation, called *The Training & Work of an Initiate*. In it, Fortune describes that in the Western Mystery Tradition, it is mandatory for an initiate to cultivate their character for contact with the light, the higher realms of being, of what she calls the "Masters." It should not be our base desires which drive our life, but Will. This Will is a will not of our own but of the Divine.

Fortune clarifies exactly what character type is needed in order to properly set out toward the role of initiation. In this, one can see that mysticism truly is a way of life. Some of the attributes that need to be developed by a candidate of the Great Work are as follows:

- *Simplicity of Life:* The world is complex enough; avoiding drama helps eliminate unnecessary dross, which will need to be wiped clean anyway if one desires initiation.
- *Serenity in Demeanor:* To be unperturbed amid catastrophe results in the desired control of emotion necessary to calm the waters of the soul. A disturbed pond cannot accurately reflect the stars of the heavens upon its surface.

---

23. Hall, *Mystical Christ*, 43.

- *Quiet:* Fortune has stated that "the Great Initiator comes in the silence to the higher consciousness." [24] It is rarely through excitable states that the true illumination of light shines.

- *Cleanliness:* Cleanliness is next to godliness. This is true in so many respects. The body is your one and only *true* temple. It is okay to have our vices, but regular self-care is paramount as an initiate. The light requires a physically strong and stable receptacle into which it can flow.

- *Avoid Attention:* If gratification from others is what one desires, initiation cannot be achieved. True initiation is about the deepest of relationships with the self. Again we see another reason why the mystery schools were kept secret … as more eyes and ears seek to pick apart a spiritual experience, the light dissolves under the pressure of surveillance.

- *Skilled with the Hands:* All the great alchemists, magicians, and mystics were masters over one or more crafts, whether it be painting, woodworking, composing, and so on. Part of initiation, we shall see, is making Manifest that which is Unmanifest, the process of creation. Replicating that process on a physical level is a requirement of the Great Work.

- *Intellectually Adept:* It is recommended that the first things one learns before committing to the path are algebra and geometry, and from there, a healthy study of all the sciences, history, psychology, philosophy, and so on. The mind must be sharp and full of knowledge. That way, when one encounters an image or a situation upon the Path, one will be equipped to deal with it accordingly.

Many people will have issues with these requirements, but the school of initiation is not a flight of fancy. It is hard work. The ancient mystery schools were not weekend workshops and afternoon drum circles. To be inducted into a mystery school was a way of life that took dedication and tenacity; candidates were normally well versed in all the sciences, multiple languages, and the arts and were most especially skilled in some form of craft, if not many. Truly, they were Renaissance men and women, true embodiments of the balanced perfection displayed in Leonardo da Vinci's Vitruvian Man.

There is a place for our own spiritual wackiness as well as the logic of reason within our lives. They can coexist. We can have our ideas and reality too. In our efforts to dream big in the cosmic woo-woo, we can allow empirical research to guide our vibes and intuitions

---

24. Fortune, *Training & Work of an Initiate*, 49.

to a more practical state of living within the world and thus enact a more realistic effect on changing it for the better.

In Threes

An initiate, according to Dion Fortune, is "one in whom the Higher Self, the Individuality, has coalesced with the personality and actually entered into incarnation in the physical body." [25] Accordingly, there are three psychological elements at work within the self that are at play during the process of initiation:

- *Shadow:* Known in Hebrew as *Nephesch* and also referred to as the "unredeemed," the shadow is the animal soul of man. This is an aspect of being human that is primal and resides in the subconscious. In alchemical imagery, any human with horns or animal parts is representing the shadow aspect of ourselves. Its motivation is survival.
- *Personality:* Known in Hebrew as *Ruach*, the personality is the base human behavior set, reduced to a set of habit complexes. The personality is normally represented by the Moon in alchemical imagery, as it waxes and wanes through innumerable incarnations. It is motivated by desire and fueled by emotion.
- *Individuality:* Known in Hebrew as *Neschamah*, the individuality is also called the higher self and is built through the hard work of initiation. Represented as the sun, the individuality shines perpetually in the heavens, whether or not it is actually seen. Its motivation is the Great Work, the Will of God.

Initiation is successful through the victory of uniting the psyche. This happens not through a war of conquering the personality or the shadow, but through a harmonization among all the parts within the human soul. This process is called by many names in the esoteric traditions: the Knowledge and Conversation of the Holy Guardian Angel, the Alchemical Marriage, Individuation, or the Great Work. Most often in our lives, the personality is ruled by the shadow, but the goal is to have the personality most influenced by the individuality. When this happens, the human condition is alleviated from suffering and the real work of creating a better world can begin. Otherwise, the humankind will continue on its dim path toward ignorance and self-destruction.

---

25. Fortune, *Training & Work of an Initiate*, 34.

Across the globe, most shamanic traditions describe a three-realm cosmology that not only portrays the framework of the universe but is also relatable to the three parts of the human psyche. These three realms are commonly ascribed to the distinct regions of the Lowerworld, the Middleworld, and the Upperworld.

The three worlds are where shamanic practitioners travel to do their work, as they are the realms of being that make up the entire soul of man. A concise description of these worlds can be easily related to the three parts of the psyche above. The Peruvian Quechua—the possible descendants of the Inca—have one of the more cogent systems of cosmology, therefore their terminology for the three realms will henceforth be used:

- *The Lowerworld*: Known in Quechua as the *Ukhupacha* (OOK-hoo-pah-chah), this is the world below ground, the inner caverns of soul where our most repressed aspects of the psyche are stored. This is the place where the shadow resides, where we go to face those parts of ourselves we rarely wish to see or are unaware of.
- *The Middleworld*: Known in Quechua as the *Kaypacha* (KAI-pah-chah), this is the here and now, the physical world, where the personality abides.
- *The Upperworld*: Known in Quechua as the *Hanaqpacha* (hah-NAHK-pah-chah). The Hanaqpacha is the transcendent, the world above, and the realm of the highest state of consciousness. This, of course, then is where the individuality shines. Often thought of as celestial or angelic, this place can be thought of on a practical level as aspiration toward one's better self.

Referencing the work of the famous mythologist Joseph Campbell, shamanic practitioner and author Matthew Magee has correlated the experience of these three realms with the hero's journey. The hero's journey is the universal story Campbell has recognized in virtually all the myths and spiritual traditions around the world and throughout history. Magee suggests a way of understanding these three worlds: "In the hero's journey, a person must leave the familiar in order to fulfill a destiny (usually divinely inspired), overcome difficult obstacles, and finally, return to his or her community to share the message learned and to restore or enhance the lives of the people he or she represents. Campbell depicts this universal myth as having three stages: 'separation—initiation—return.' Similarly, in the shamanic journey the *curandero* leaves the realm of the familiar and either ascends to the *Hanaq Pacha* or descends to the *Ukhu Pacha*, gains otherwise inaccessible knowledge or power, then returns to the *Kay Pacha*." [26]

There is a perspective of seeing these other realms as literal, external dimensions or realities. Although that could be taken into consideration, understanding them as the tenets of the psyche mentioned above begets an understanding of the alchemical mechanisms at play in initiation.

Andean mysticism suggests that at one time these realms were highly integrated, and are *meant* to be integrated, and it was humankind's fall from grace that separated these realms. In fact, it is because these realms are separated that our society remains in its collective malaise of self-destruction and global destruction. The Kaypacha (Middleworld) is just an interface for the Ukhupacha and Hanaqpacha, which both should be realms that exist to serve us for our highest good.

A depiction of this process can be seen in the following images. Even though they are not literally displayed like this, conceptualize a life before the hero's journey, before initiation into any shamanic or mystery tradition. The three *pachas* (worlds) exist separately, without interconnection.

Now, imagine if you will the timeline of a person's life running left to right on this graphic. If we exist in a state of being without integration with these realms, we walk throughout our lives unaware of the shadow, the repressed notions of the psyche hidden deep within the Lowerworld, the Ukhupacha. Poet and activist Robert Bly has written extensively on the shadow, the repressed psyche. He likens this shadow to a bag in which we store these repressed notions of ourselves that we drag around with us. The bag gets heavier and heavier as we get older, because the older we get the more we store away the parts of ourselves we do not want to see, that others don't want to see, and so on. According to Bly, "when we put a part of ourselves in the bag it regresses. It de-evolves toward barbarism.... Every part of our personality that we do not love will become hostile to us. We could add that it may move to a distant place and begin a revolt against us as well." [27]

26. Matthew Magee, *Peruvian Shamanism: The Pachakúti Mesa* (Kearney, NE: Morris Publishing, 2005), 13.

27. Robert Bly, *A Little Book on the Human Shadow* (San Francisco: Harper & Row, Publishers, 1988), 21–22.

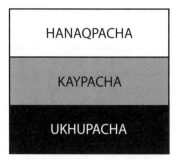

Figure 2: The Three Pachas

If the shadow is left unchecked and not tended to, it explodes unexpectedly into our lives, often leaving a fallout that bleeds over into the Middleworld, the Kaypacha. That manifests in outbursts that can involve hurting ones we love, undesired consequences, depression, and so on. As time goes on, the bag can get bigger, the outbursts more explosive.

Figure 3: The Three Pachas

This state of being creates a set of behaviors completely out of balance and affects the rest of the realms negatively. Unattended, the shadow can become worse, more out of control, and harder to manage as time continues. Additionally, the personality within the Kaypacha becomes confused and disoriented, and thus contact with the individuality in the Hanaqpacha becomes impossible.

When beginning the Great Work and in shamanic apprenticeship, the first realm one learns to interact with is the Ukhupacha. This is because the work of an initiate is to learn to manage the potencies of the Ukhupacha, to harness what is necessary from the shadow and return what is no longer needed back to the below, to be composted in the regenerative soils of the Ukhupacha so new things can grow. Assuredly, when one works within this realm correctly, life begins to look a little more like this:

Figure 4: The Three Pachas

So, even though the out-of-control qualities of shadow arising from the Ukhupacha into the Kaypacha have been mitigated, it can be clearly seen that they still interact. Shadow doesn't go away. However, it can be managed and integrated more harmoniously into the interface of the Kaypacha. But, the integration of the three realms is still out of balance … There needs to be interaction from the Hanaqpacha to achieve this balance.

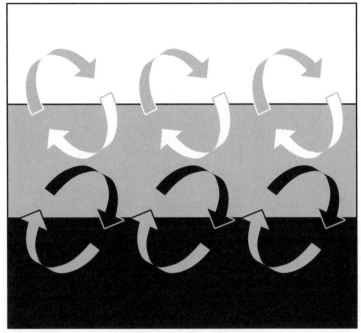

Figure 5: The Three Pachas

While working with the Ukhupacha and its many teachings, it often helps to receive guidance from on high. The Hanaqpacha acts as a sort of beacon here in the Kaypacha, a guiding post helping us aspire to be the absolute best we can be. Essentially, we sit here in the Kaypacha, looking to the Hanaqpacha for guidance while working with the Ukhupacha.

This is the formula of living religiously as an initiate, engaging with the Great Work. As we will see, integration of these three realms promotes the most effective practice of shamanic Qabalah.

Part II
SHAMANIC QABALAH

4

THE TREE OF LIFE

The human body, like that of the universe, is considered to be a material expression of ten globes or spheres of light. Therefore man is called the Microcosm—the little world, built in the image of the great world of which he is a part.

—MANLY P. HALL, *THE SECRET TEACHINGS OF ALL AGES*

Qabalah

Qabalah—also seen as *Kabbalah* or *Cabala*—is known most primarily as the esoteric doctrine of Judaism. The term's Hebrew root QBL (*Qibel*) means literally "to receive." So, in its simplest of definitions, Qabalah is a spiritual discipline of reception. Rabbi Gershon Winkler has described exactly what is being received in Qabalah: "'Receiving,' in turn, means being open to the ever flowing river of wisdom and insight, magic and enlightenment, that emanates unceasingly from what the *kabbalah* calls קודשא בריך הוא *kud'sha b'reekh hu*, meaning *Sacred Wellspring*." [28]

In essence, it is a system of initiation. And although it is associated primarily with Jewish mysticism, even Rabbi Philip Berg of the well-known Kabbalah Centre refers to it as "the spiritual heritage of all humankind." [29] Qabalah has a long and complicated history, not all of it based upon traditional Jewish orthodoxy. Evolution works never in a sequence but rather like the weaving of a spiderweb. Many spiritual and ethnic traditions have touched upon or contributed to the narrative of Qabalah over the centuries.

---

28. Gershon Winkler, *Magic of the Ordinary: Recovering the Shamanic in Judaism* (Berkeley, CA: North Atlantic Books, 2000), 71.

29. P. S. Berg, *The Essential Zohar: The Source of Kabbalistic Wisdom* (New York: Three Rivers Press, 2002), 3.

Many mystics attribute ancient beginnings to the system of Qabalah. Their attribution of its inception comes directly from the divine order itself: God handed the system of Qabalah directly to Adam, from Adam to Noah, from Noah to Abraham, who eventually brought the mystical tradition to Egypt, where Moses himself became an initiate. Egypt is often considered one of the origin points of the mystery schools, where the processes of initiation were not only refined, but institutionalized. From there, Qabalah branched out to the Eastern nations and beyond, infiltrating many religious and philosophical systems across the planet.

This is one of many accounts ascribing the origins of Qabalah to Egypt, rather than it being strictly of Jewish ancestry. The genesis mythologies can dive even further into the oceans of imagination, with influences said to have stemmed also from Atlantis and Lemuria (if you are in to that sort of thing). Regardless of the actual historical record, it is the mythology that is important, for it carries the essence of the tradition into the work of the initiate.

Though the essential historical texts of Qabalah—the *Zohar* and the *Sepher Yetzirah*—are archaic and allegorical, centuries of academic interpretation have provided us with an accessible and comprehensive system of initiation. Indeed, Qabalah has become one of—if not *the*—key elements of the Great Work. The *Zohar* and *Sepher Yetzirah*, through layers of numerological symbolism and poetry, illustrate and elucidate in essence the most profound emblem in all mystery traditions: the Tree of Life.

The Tree

The Tree of Life is a symbol, or symbol composite, that can be viewed as a graph of the unseen universe, both inner and outer. As a diagram, it exhibits every component and ingredient in the soul, tracing each of its disparate parts together so that a reintegration of its parts can be obtained. It integrates psychology, spirituality, and science into a holistic design whose sole purpose is to better understand our cosmic heritage. The Tree of Life seeks to define the ineffable: the nature and purpose of the universe and the individual (which are both one and the same, as well as autonomous).

I ascribe the Tree of Life to be a roadmap—*the* roadmap—of consciousness, used to explore the nature of God, the Divine, the self, the soul, and all the myriad dimensions of being that exist in the unseen realms. On this roadmap, there are pathways and there are destinations, like any map would have. It is the role of the initiate to traverse this roadmap as on a journey of discovery.

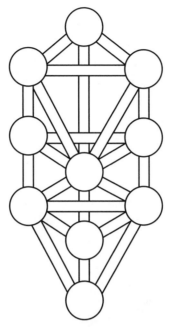

Figure 6: The Tree of Life

The importance of symbology was stressed in an earlier chapter. This is because the Tree of Life is not only a symbol itself, but a composite—a symbol composed of multiple symbols. Meditation upon the exoteric design of the Tree of Life without the proper study in meaning behind it is equivalent to neglecting to fill the gas tank: you may have a pretty map but no means of getting started on your journey. Traditionally, it takes years (likely decades) of study before a Qabalistic initiation can be undertaken by an individual. Part of the job for an initiate in the mystery traditions is to be schooled in all the sundry parts and layers of the Tree of Life, to learn its esoteric abstractions before the exoteric can be realized.

As a composite symbol, the Tree of Life can be broken up into numerous assortments of patterns, motifs, and classifications. The first of these, which are an absolute requirement for understanding the Tree, is its basic infrastructure: the Sephiroth and Paths.

Sephiroth

The primary construction of the Tree of Life consists of ten circles or spheres, called *Sephiroth* (SEH-fear-oht). Referred to in the singular, one is called a *Sephirah* (SEH-fear-ah). The Sephiroth are stages, traditionally called emanations, of manifestation from which the

Source of Creation (God) advances from its noumenal reality to a physical one. Conversely, the Sephiroth also represent the stages of the soul's journey from material incarnation to union with the Divine.

The primal undergirding of any magical or mystical process is the act of creation itself. Imagine the Tree of Life as a flow process chart that represents the processing activity performed in the creation of the universe (and consciousness). In essence, the Tree of Life replicates the process of creation.

So, in following the flow of creation, the Sephiroth represent certain stages of the creative activity in the universe. To follow that flow within a sequence, one would trace that process of creation from top to bottom, each sphere, or Sephirah, being a phase in that process which establishes itself as its own emanation but then precedes the force of movement toward the next phase. The Sephiroth—as spheres, emanations, stages—indicate phases in the evolution of nonphysical existence (the Unmanifest) to physical existence (Manifest). Here then we see the metamorphosis of spirit into matter, the materialization of the physical world as indicated by the bottom Sephirah on the tree.

How then was the universe created?

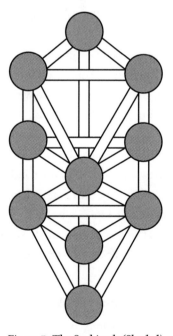

Figure 7: The Sephiroth (Shaded)

In the Western world, it is perhaps common to recall the seven days of creation as portrayed in the account of Genesis in the Christian creation story. Of course, the Qabalists understand this is not to be taken literally, but as a metaphor for the creative process. In fact, certain Sephiroth on the Tree of Life even represent the creation story in the Torah, as described by Rabbi Berg: "The biblical account of the Seven Days of Creation describes the Lower Seven *Sefirot*.... The word 'day' is the cosmic code for *Sefira*, or a life-form intelligence, as deciphered in the *Zohar*."[30]

Qabalah is a natural creation story, even beyond the orthodox Judaic framework.

In Qabalah, everything is numbers. As many have stated both in and outside the world of science, mathematics is the language of the universe. It is no different in Qabalah. We cannot ever truly understand God, the Great Mystery; however, mathematics provides for us an abstraction with which we can at least get an *impression* of that mystery. To understand the Tree of Life as creation, we must gain some understanding of the Sephiroth and their numerical sequence. It would be helpful to understand the following as a creation story.

0: Ain Soph Aur

Before any number, of course, there is zero. So before creation, there was nothing, what is generally called the Unmanifest.

According to Qabalah, the Unmanifest is actually the *true* substance of reality. Anything other than the Unmanifest—the Sephiroth, the Manifest, the universe as we know it—is only a result of the Unmanifest, a shadow.

We can never truly know the Unmanifest. We can only attempt to ponder it through abstractions. Therefore, any language used to describe the Unmanifest can only be metaphor. This gives us insight already into working with the Tree of Life, for the further up the tree we go from matter into spirit, the more abstract the concepts. In fact, Dion Fortune was certain that the only possible way to have knowledge of the Unmanifest was through the auspices of geometry.

Her most complex work, *The Cosmic Doctrine,* is a channeled masterpiece that requires some advanced foundation in algebra before undertaking its reading. In it, she attempts to describe the Unmanifest. She describes, through analogy, how the Unmanifest became Manifest. It all started with the desire for movement. When that happened, two distinct factors were at work. Fortune writes,

---

30. P. S. Berg, *The Energy of Hebrew Letters* (New York: The Kabbalah Centre, 2013), 53–54.

When space moves two forces are at work:
   (a) The force which causes it to move, being the desire of space for momentum.
   (b) The force which had hitherto caused it not to move, being the desire of space for inertia.[31]

Fortune talks of a tug-of-war pull between these two forces that causes a series of rings of movement that geometrically begin to build the foundational building blocks of the Manifest. She calls them the Ring Cosmos, the Ring Chaos, and the Ring-Pass-Not (which holds the balance between the two extremes of Cosmos and Chaos).

In traditional Qabalah, these are known in order as the Hebrew terms *Ain*, *Ain Soph*, and *Ain Soph Aur*. Put simply, their meaning implies the veiling of reality, of the Unmanifest from the Manifest, the three Veils of Negative Existence:

• *Ain*: Meaning "no-thing"; the only true speculation we can ever have of the nature of God.

• *Ain Soph*: Meaning "without limit"; God is beyond the nature of duality, male or female, good or evil.

• *Ain Soph Aur*: Meaning "limitless light"; the first known indication we can ever have of God is light brighter than any other, beyond our own conceptions.

If we can imagine these three aspects as the rings of Fortune's mythology, we can conceive of a series of three concentric circles intertwined together in a gyroscope of movement.

This gyroscope-type movement, propelled by the immense force of gravity, concretizes and then forms a center. Thus, the first emanation materializes into the potential of the Manifest universe. *Kether* is the first Sephirah on the Tree of Life, represented of course by the number 1. Consequently, we can now conceptualize the manifestation of the Sephiroth in sequence, as depicted by their numerical values seen here:

---

31. Dion Fortune, *The Cosmic Doctrine* (Boston, MA: Weiser Books, 2000), 20.

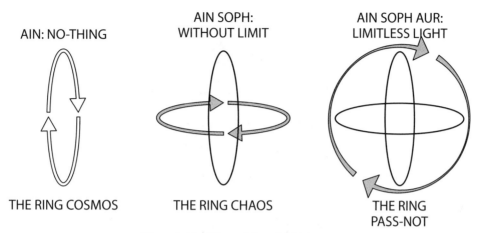

AIN: NO-THING

THE RING COSMOS

AIN SOPH:
WITHOUT LIMIT

THE RING CHAOS

AIN SOPH AUR:
LIMITLESS LIGHT

THE RING
PASS-NOT

Figure 8: The Rings of Negative Existence

Before studying each individual Sephirah, it is important to understand how they are formed from each other. All the Sephiroth come from the first, from Kether, which itself comes from the Unmanifest. Dion Fortune explains this cascading effect of the tree: "Let us conceive of Kether, then, as a fountain which fills its basin, and the overflow therefrom feeds another fountain, which in its turn fills its basin and overflows. The Unmanifest for ever flows under pressure into Kether, and there comes a time when evolution has gone as far as it can in the extreme simplicity of the form of existence of the First Manifest."[32]

All possibility, all the following Sephiroth, are formed then in the first Sephirah, in Kether. However, all that possibility is in its simplest, most pure, form; the following Sephiroth then lay out the process of breaking down that simplicity into more complex forms. This is the overall machination of the tree.

Our creation story continues. Let us now consider the individual Sephiroth, which will be explained in more detail later in this book.

---

32. Dion Fortune, *The Mystical Qabalah* (Boston: Weiser Books, 2000), 37.

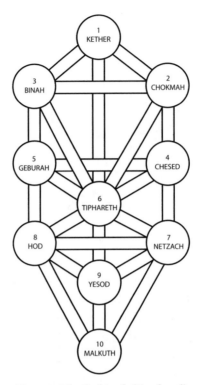

Figure 9: The Sephiroth (Numbered)

1: Kether

Kether translates to "crown" in English, as it is the reigning Sephirah of all creation. It is the basic life force of all root forms in existence. It is the most androgynous of all the Sephiroth, as before Kether there was no duality. What is formed in Kether will be reflected throughout the rest of creation. In Kether, though, it is all one, all unity. There is no division in Kether. In essence, Kether is the highest essence of God that can be conceived.

2: Chokmah

Chokmah is Hebrew for "wisdom." To begin the process of manifestation, Kether (God) could not create anything separate from itself, for all that is in existence is in Kether. However, it could *reflect* itself. Chokmah represents the first reflection of God; therefore, it represents the ultimate thrust or drive of spiritual *Force* into existence. Because of this, it is the prime masculine identity of the universe. It is the vision of God face-to-face with itself, now exemplified as Him. This denotes the holographic nature of reality ... that the resulting manifestation of which we are aware is nothing but a reflection of a reflection of a reflection (ten-fold) of the only true reality: the Unmanifest, of which Kether is the only *true* reflection. Chokmah is the first attempt of Kether, of God, to disembark from its unity and understand itself through separateness, through disparity.

3: Binah

Binah means "understanding." Chokmah could not really have been considered a masculine identity until it reflected itself as Binah, the prime feminine identity of the universe. If Chokmah represents the ultimate drive of spiritual force, then Binah encapsulates that Force and contains it into Form. *Form* in the esoteric arts is defined as an interlocking of free-moving Force into patterns that can then operate as a unity. All Forms inherent in the universe first beget their construction from Binah. With Binah, we get the first trinity found in almost all spiritual traditions; we get the intrinsic duality of manifestation. Without the concepts of both masculine and feminine, and the androgyny from which they spring, the material universe of the Manifest would not be.

4: Chesed

Chesed is Hebrew for "mercy." In Chesed we begin to see prime imagery of godhood begin to formulate into being. Truly, we cannot as humans contemplate or experience in physical form the likes of Binah, Chokmah, and especially Kether. However, in Chesed are the prime images that we associate with God, most especially the benevolent All-father of numerous mythologies. Chesed is where the Will of God begins to move into manifestation, that Will being equated with the spiritual experience of universal love (which is far beyond our limited understanding of "love").

5: Geburah

Geburah translates to "severity" in English. Here we see in the creation process the breaking down of the Will of God into the actual Forms which will be experienced in the Manifest. As was stated before, form makes its first appearance in Binah, but it is only experienced as the *idea* of Form. In Geburah we find the engine that actually produces the Forms of Manifested reality. Contrary to popular opinion, this is a harsh and severe process equated with the travails of birth; therefore, the image types of the Goddess are highly represented in this Sephirah.

6: Tiphareth

Tiphareth means "beauty." Understanding Chesed as the center of masculine Force (Joseph) and Geburah as the center of feminine Form (Mary) the resulting birth would be the mediating balance of integration and regeneration (Christ). Tiphareth not only represents the mediation (and result of) Chesed and Geburah, but also of the whole of the entire Tree of Life. It is the central harmony of all things, the Golden Dawn of the Great Work. As the mediating intelligence for the tree, all sacrificial gods and mythologies hold their place in this sphere: to give of oneself and be of service is the root of the Great Work. Without that sacrifice, one cannot climb the tree. Tiphareth ensures that. This is the beauty of initiation. Tiphareth is the individuality of creation before it is then broken down into the more fractured aspects of existence, into personalities.

7: Netzach

Netzach is Hebrew for "victory." As Forms are broken down in Geburah and receive their individual components in Tiphareth, in Netzach is the victory of achievement. Netzach is the celebration of diversity, but before ideas can come into full Form, they must be inspired. This is where creative imagination of the universe resides. Here is where poets and painters receive their muses, sparking the inspiration needed to begin the process of creation into Manifest.

8: Hod

Hod translates to "glory" in English. As the Force of imagination moves through the spheres, in Hod that inspiration is designed and fashioned so that it can be forged into a physicalized reality. Here is where the formulations of language, numbers, and philosophy find their root, so that ideas can be taken from the muses of Netzach to be brought forth into the Manifest. If Netzach is the place of heart, then Hod is the place of the mind. Within Hod, ideas are made concrete.

9: Yesod

Yesod means "foundation." Just as Tiphareth is the equilateral result of Chesed and Ge-burah, so is Yesod to Netzach and Hod. Yesod is truly the foundation of all manifestation. It is the architectural undergirding of all physical reality. Together, Netzach and Hod make up the structural framework of what indeed becomes *actual*. Known as the "Storehouse of Images," Yesod is the astral realm itself. Whatever exists has its skeleton in Yesod. As the primary Sephirah of magicians and alchemists throughout the ages, manipulation of Yesod results in the manipulation of matter itself. Yesod is the final fount of the creation process into the Manifest.

10: Malkuth

Finally, we come to Malkuth, the Manifest world. *Malkuth* means "kingdom." Malkuth is here, this existence that we understand as "reality," but is actually "actuality." It is earth, the physical realm of matter and life. Though those who consider themselves "spiritual" seek to attain the higher realms of existence, it is really mastery over Malkuth that allows one to travel the higher realms unimpeded. In essence, the physical world holds the key to true spiritual development. Malkuth is the kingdom, the fully realized creation of God. Libera-tion from physical existence is not the goal of the Great Work; rather, a full immersion into the fabric of creation is necessary.

Perhaps the most vital mantra of Qabalah, if one were to remember nothing else, is that *Kether is the Malkuth of the Unmanifest*. Meditation upon this statement could take life-times. It is a realization that Malkuth and Kether are one and the same, just reflections of each other. When one seeks heaven—truly, heaven does exist here on earth—there are po-tentialities even beyond our own universe, as the crown of all creation is just a Malkuth for another entire different universe of which we have no understanding.

This axiom is highly reminiscent of the Hermetic phrase from the Emerald Tablet, as translated by the great Persian alchemist Jabir ibn Hayyan: "That which is above is from that which is below, and that which is below is from that which is above, working the miracles of one. As all things were from one." [33]

It is important to understand the flow of the Sephiroth is only sequential to our limited understanding of past, present, and future. The process of creation is not something that happened long ago but is an ongoing phenomenon that always exists within us, throughout

---

33. *The Emerald Tablet of Hermes & The Kybalion,* ed. Jane Ma'ati Smith (Lexington, KY: Enhanced Ebooks, 2008), 8.

us, and beyond us. However, because we operate within a consciousness that seems linear, it is helpful to look at creation via the Sephiroth in a series of stages. Each Sephirah contains within it the potentiality of the following Sephiroth that issue forth from it; it is as if each Sephirah represents a specific manifestation of creation. At the same time, each Sephirah is a reflection of those Sephiroth preceding it. That which is above is also below, and vice versa. Gurus and shamans from around the world have spoken widely of this concept and have said that time is not the sequential series of past, present, and future stages it appears to be. The key to understanding the Sephiroth is that they are currently in manifestation right now, even as you read this, and will continue to do so until the universe ceases to exist.

The Paths

As can be seen, the Sephiroth are connected by a series of lines that act as roadways of association among the emanations of creation. They allow travel throughout the tree, as well as a configuration of relationship that assists the individual in communing with the unseen. The paths between the spheres allow one to traverse the various stages on the Tree of Life, acting as subjective correspondences to the objective Sephiroth.

The paths help us understand that there is no stagnation within the tree. No Sephirah can be understood in and of itself, by itself; it can only be understood in relation to the other Sephiroth around it. Life itself is a multifaceted synthesis of relationships, as is the tree. Life *is* relationship; therefore, the paths represent our experience upon the tree, our experience within the dynamic landscape of the cosmos. Therefore, no one Sephirah on the Tree of Life can be understood in isolation; a Sephirah can only be understood in its relationship to the other Sephiroth around it, and the dynamic of relationships among them (the paths).

Atop the vestibule of one of the greatest mystery schools in ancient Greece, the Temple of Apollo in Delphi, was inscribed the maxim *Gnōthi seauton*, translated as "Know thyself." Exploring the consciousness of one's own being is the closest—and truly *only*—way of having a relationship with God. As Dr. Carl Jung had proposed time and time again, in more ways than one, over the course of his career, "The goal of psychic development is the self. There is no linear evolution; there is only a circumambulation of the self." [34]

This is even pointed out by the Christ, a Qabalist in his own right, in the Gnostic Gospel of Thomas. In now understanding the basics of the Tree of Life, including the mean-

---

34. C. G. Jung, *Memories, Dreams, Reflections*, ed. Aniela Jaffé, trans. Richard Winston and Clara Winston (New York: Vintage Books, 1989), 196.

ing of Malkuth as the kingdom, a vital understanding can be gained from these verses: "Yeshua said, If your leaders tell you, 'Look, the kingdom is in heaven,' then the birds of heaven will precede you. If they say to you, 'It's in the sea,' then the fish will precede you. But the kingdom is inside you and it is outside you." [35]

The paths provide the thoroughfare of consciousness for us to be able to tread the three realms of the Ukhupacha, Kaypacha, and Hanaqpacha throughout the emanations of creation. They supply to us a wealth of information to ensure a fruitful initiation.

---

35. Barnstone and Meyer, *The Gnostic Bible*, 3:1–10.

5

MALKUTH, THE ELEMENTAL PACHA

The student who is not grounded in the elements cannot understand the advanced teaching.

—DION FORTUNE, *THE TRAINING & WORK OF AN INITIATE*

In order to begin work upon the Tree of Life we must first know the world around us, the world of the elements. This means we must first begin an intimate relationship with the tenth Sephirah, in which we consciously reside: Malkuth.

One evening, Autumn and I were getting ready for bed. Like she does sometimes, she pulled a statement out of thin air as if we were already in the midst of a conversation.

"That's why I love shamanism," she said pointedly.

"Why's that?" I asked, immediately trying to find the answer to my own question.

"Because it grounds you. No matter what, it always pulls you back here, in this world, to what's happening right in front of you."

She could not have been more correct (as always). Autumn was referencing higher states of being—like the Sephiroth—altered states of consciousness, meditation, and so on. Being teachers in a shamanic tradition (and Autumn is a yoga instructor as well), we have more than our fair share of touchpoints with a wide variety of spiritual seekers and practitioners. More often than not, unfortunately, we see a lot of escapism: seekers addicted to seeking, participants whose heads are so far up in the clouds that they have lost touch with the real world. Some even lose all ability to function in reality.

One of our favorite definitions of shamanism comes from anthropologist and psychiatrist Dr. Roger Walsh from the University of California. Dr. Walsh characterizes shamanism as "a family of traditions whose practitioners focus on voluntarily entering altered states of consciousness in which they experience themselves or their spirit(s) interacting with other entities, often by traveling to other realms, in order to serve their community." [36]

This description is comprehensive, and it acknowledges shamanism as a method of practice—or interaction—rather than a specific religion or spiritual path. In fact, almost any religion on the planet stems from, and comprises a branch of, shamanic practice. These are some examples:

- Shaktism, a shamanic subset of Hinduism
- The Bon of Tibetan Buddhism
- A rebbe, often considered a shamanic rabbi in Judaism
- The Muttaqin of Islam
- Curanderismo of Latin America, a synthesis of indigenous shamanism and Catholicism, part of the lineage to which Autumn and I ascribe

The list goes on and on. Essentially, when going back to the origins of any religious or spiritual path around the world, one will find shamanic roots tied to it. It is humankind's first spiritual tradition, spanning back to the Paleolithic age, and is often considered the first known profession in the world by anthropologists.

Shamanism has evolved over the centuries, becoming an all-inclusive, cross-cultural paradigm for interacting with the unseen realms. However, the shamanic method is not as "otherworldly" as this definition, and common perception, implies.

We cannot be relieved of the burden of everyday life. Seekers are always looking for something "other," something beyond the pain of living they currently are unable to liberate themselves from. Rabbi Gershon Winkler, who has taken it upon himself to reconnect with the shamanic roots of Judaism, points out, "The shaman in the Judaic tradition does not rush into a spiritual experience like a famished desert traveler arriving at an oasis. Moses [considered the first Qabalist and shaman of Judaism] is not desperate for a vision because he knows that *looking* for one often gets in the way of *seeing* one. When we put all of our energies into seeking we risk not finding, we risk rushing past it." [37]

The problem is, the audacious thirst for spiritual experience is a mode of self-deception, and shamanism (or any legitimate mystery school) does not condone this sort of delusion.

36. Roger Walsh, *The World of Shamanism: New Vision of an Ancient Tradition* (Woodbury, MN: Llewellyn Publications, 2007), 16–17.
37. Winkler, *Magic of the Ordinary*, 22–23.

Thus, explains Joan Parisi Wilcox, an initiate of the *Paqokuna* lineage, "By taking the pulse of the metaphysical, the paqo learns to reveal the condition of the physical." [38] *Paqo* is the term for the shamanic priests/healers of the Quechua peoples of Peru. The goal of shamanic practice is to have touchpoints with the otherworld but to bring back the information for healing and renewal in *this* world, the here and now, the kingdom. Any information gained in the metaphysical that is inapplicable to this world is moot and therefore counterproductive.

Shamanic ceremonies are designed to heal conditions of this world, to bring the soul in contact with the earth and physical senses. From soul retrieval to *pagos* (offerings or payment to spirits), from animal allies to trance drumming, the elements of shamanic ritual are designed to cement the person in their body and in the acceptance of the material life in which they are now living.

This earthly experience, induced by shamanic ritual practices, reminds the body of its place in space and time. We spend so much of our waking day distracting ourselves from life (via television, internet, jobs, phones, traffic, alcohol, etc.) that when it comes to having a spiritual experience, we often cling to spiritual habits that end up doing the exact same thing these other distractions do: take us away from the present moment.

As an initiate, one should recognize this is actually an affront to God. Malkuth is the full realization of Kether. Why would one want anything other than this experience?

This is why shamanism is so important to a Qabalistic practice: a true shamanic experience thrives on the present moment. It supports the fact that right now—with your aching back, your hungry stomach, your kids banging on the walls, your glasses cracked in the left lens, your neighbor's barking dog, your dirt-covered floor—*that* is your spiritual experience, *that* is your experience of God, of spiritual union with the Source of All Being. Gareth Knight reiterates: "The physical world is the world which should be thoroughly grasped by the soul…. The physical world, in that one has to return to it time and time again, must hold the key for spiritual development. And this development is surely not to be gained in regarding all physical nature as a trap and temptation which must be strenuously denied and put away from one." [39]

In this way, a shamanic practice is much like Zen. Both are based upon the philosophy that the pursuit of the good without the recognition and acceptance of the bad is an illusion.

---

38. Joan Parisi Wilcox, *Masters of the Living Energy: The Mystical World of the Q'ero in Peru* (Rochester, VT: Inner Traditions, 2004), 100.

39. Knight, *Qabalistic Symbolism*, vol. 1, 190.

To become more than what you are now is folly, for you are already whole just as you are. Even when you are sick, even when you are depressed, even when you are poor, you are already exactly what you need to be in order to have a vital spiritual experience of union with life and death, for they are two sides of the same coin.

It seems oxymoronic that the goal of these rituals, practices, and philosophies of the Mysteries would be to realize that we do not need all these rituals, practices, and philosophies … but that is exactly how it is. Reality is a paradox. We have a bad habit of not realizing we are already out of Plato's cave; we need to be constantly reminded. Shamanic ritual pulls you out of the distraction, out of the sleepwalking fog, and opens your eyes to what is truly around you.

Engaging in shamanic ritual, as stated by *maestro* curandero don Oscar Miro-Quesada, assists us out of the mitote and into a balanced state of consciousness: "Through participation in earth-honoring ceremonies we are able to shift from fear to love, from desire to grateful acceptance of 'what is,' and from separation to wholeness." [40]

When we seek answers from someone or something else, we separate ourselves from our own inherent wisdom. Initiation is about empowerment. Shamanic Qabalah should connect us to our own intrinsic wholeness, which allows us to see the beauty in everything, to see God in everything, so that one does not have to stick to flights of fancy in order to feel what most mistake to be "unity."

Shamans do not travel to other worlds for kicks. They do it, as Dr. Walsh wrote, "to serve their community." So the practice of trance and altered states of consciousness should not become a staple of the everyday experience, but a rarity to remind the everyman that true divinity and harmony reside in the material world, Malkuth. This is the world we must all participate in. We have a lot of problems in Malkuth: racism, sexism, terrorism, mass-consumerism, environmental destruction, war. We can't solve them in the clouds. We can only solve them here.

The Pachakuti Mesa

Initiation demands a physical experience; we can only go so far meditating upon images. The key to this lies in tapping into the elemental factors governing Malkuth. Israel Regardie states, "The personality must be harmonised. Every element therein demands equilibration in order that illumination ensuing from the magical work may not produce

---

40. Bonnie Glass-Coffin and don Oscar Miro-Quesada, *Lessons in Courage: Peruvian Shamanic Wisdom for Everyday Life* (Faber, VA: Rainbow Ridge Books, 2013), 62.

fanaticism and pathology instead of Adeptship and integrity. Balance is required for the accomplishment of the Great Work.... Therefore, the four grades of Earth, Air, Water and Fire plant the seeds of the microcosmic pentagram, and above them is placed ... the Crown of the Spirit, the quintessence, added so that the elemental vehemence may be tempered, to the end that all may work together in balanced disposition." [41]

It is the staple template of most indigenous traditions that the elemental powers of Malkuth are recognized, honored, and culled from as a vital component of spiritual practice. From the medicine wheel of the First Nations people of the Americas to the pentagram of the pagan Celts, the Platonic elemental powers of earth, air, fire, and water are represented as an altar set to be used in some way, shape, or form.

The Western Mystery Tradition has an established practice that has been refined over the centuries to include an altar set that replicates the elemental essences to be channeled and utilized in the Great Work. Known as the primary tools of the magician, the implements are symbols, abstract representations of the elemental powers:

- The *pentacle* or *coin* represents earth. Essentially, it is a disc made of wood, copper, or tin inscribed with a five-pointed star—or some other representation of the initiate's spiritual attainment—and acts as the link between the initiate's godhead and their life on earth.

- The *cup* or *chalice*, of course, represents water. Its function is to contain, to form, being the prime feminine implement in a magical toolset. It is in polarity—and used in conjunction—with the wand, the prime masculine tool. Together, they represent the creative act of reproduction as the womb (cup) and phallus (wand).

- The *sword* represents air. Its purpose is to defend and banish anything corrupt and defiled in the initiate's path (magically and metaphorically, of course). The sword also acts a reservoir of strength and inspiration, bringing with it a long-standing tradition of chivalry.

- The *wand*, finally, is fire. The wand is a physical manifestation of the initiate's Will. When conjuring an image of a wizard from a story, a magical wand or staff will likely be in the picture. It is the magician's primary implement.

However accurate these are to portraying the elemental faculties of consciousness, I have always found the shamanic implementation closer to source. The WMT methodology works

---

41. Regardie, *The Golden Dawn*, 29.

for many, but for some it generates a layer of abstraction. These tools are symbols, not the elements themselves. For instance, a sword is a symbol for air, but there is a layer of abstraction between sword and air, for there is no direct conceptual relationship between them.

Shamanic symbols, on the other hand, get right to the elemental root, tapping into the elemental matrix of Malkuth itself. In the shamanic context, if one were to represent air, a bird or feather would be sufficient, as these are concepts that have a direct relationship with the element of air. There is little to no layer of abstraction. A most pristine example of this is the mesa framework from the Peruvian-based Pachakuti Mesa Tradition, as developed for the Western world by don Oscar Miro-Quesada.

Put simply, a mesa is an altar that is used ritually for healing and connection with the natural (seen and unseen) world. One way to understand the mesa, per author Matthew Magee, is as "a living control panel, co-created by Spirit and the curandero, to become a vehicle for experiencing the ineffable."[42] The mesa can be understood as a console in order to drive the operations of one's spiritual work.

The word *mesa* is a Spanish term meaning "table." It denotes the typically flat surface area in which a mesa is generally used, sometimes even on top of a table or shelf, but most of the time laid directly upon the ground. The mesa geographically comes from Latin America, most specifically Peru, but can exist in surrounding regions. There are many styles and variations depending on both the region and the individual user. This makes pinpointing a distinct and categorical definition of the mesa challenging to anthropologists. In essence, there is no one way or tradition of the mesa that is *the* way.

The mesa altar is a created space where religious rites are performed to gain access and connection to whatever source of spiritual awareness one may have (God, Goddess, the Tree of Life, etc.). Anyone can use a mesa; there is no special priest or priestess hierarchy to go through in order to work with it. It is a very personal, individualized tool one uses in their spiritual work.

After many years of being trained under two distinct Peruvian lineages—the Northern Coastal curanderismo and Andean Paqokuna traditions—Miro-Quesada was faced with the task of assimilating these two particular utilizations of the mesa and pondered how to best transcribe its ancient wisdom to the modern world. Through his academic work in psychology, a fascination for the archetypal work of Carl Jung, and his own inner guidance, Miro-Quesada developed the Pachakuti Mesa Tradition as a lucid, well-defined system of shamanic correspondence with the unseen realms. It was designed to articulate a clear

---

42. Magee, *Peruvian Shamanism*, xvi.

transmission of indigenous practice inside a cross-cultural context that could be understood and used in the fast-paced business of the West.

Pachakuti is a Quechua word meaning "world-reversal," or "turning over the earth." The ritual schema and practices are specifically fashioned to facilitate an alchemical transformation within the self, and thus the world at large. It draws upon the elemental powers of the universe through ritual objects (called *artes*) that represent that particular element in its most primal form. So when you are working with the elemental powers, you are working with them kinesthetically, through the primary vehicles of their manifestation in our world.

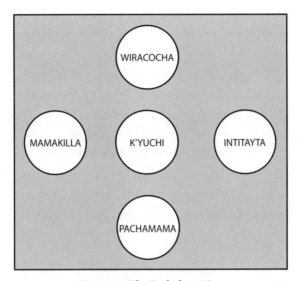

Figure 10: The Pachakuti Mesa

Consider the basic makeup of a Pachakuti mesa and the meaning of its components:

- *Pachamama* (PAH-cha-MAH-mah): Meaning Mother Earth, Pachamama is the section that resides in the south of the mesa. It represents, of course, the element Earth and material existence. It is where physical healing is called forth and is often connected with the tutelary animal spirit of the boa or anaconda, whose body is always intimate with the earth.
- *Mamakilla* (MAH-mah-KEE-yah): Meaning "Mother Moon," Mamakilla resides in the west and epitomizes the emotional realm of being. It evokes the element of water. The tutelary allies are considered the dolphin or whale, as their adept navigation of

the ocean personifies what is needed to navigate the deep waters of the emotional psyche.

- *Wiracocha* (WIHR-ah-KOH-chah): Also known as Great Spirit, Creator, and so on, Wiracocha resides in the north of the mesa and represents the Great Originating Mystery. Embodied by the element of air, it is often exemplified by the tutelary guidance of the eagle or condor, whose flight on the sacred winds personifies the heights we strive for in all spiritual work.
- *Inti or Intitayta* (IN-tee-TAI-tah): Meaning "Father Sun," Intitayta resides in the east and characterizes the element of fire. It is the more intellectual realm of being, where the higher mind outmaneuvers our normal brain processes of the day-to-day. The puma and jaguar express these attributes with their clarity of sight and leanness of equilibrium.
- *K'yuchi* (kooy-EE-chee): K'yuchi is the full spectrum of light we know as the rainbow. It embodies the center of the mesa, the unifying essence of the elemental matrix of Malkuth. Its element is ether, the quintessence material that all things in the material world come from and return to. The llama and alpaca, as animals of service, hold the space of the center as the primary attribute of the self-awakened soul.

The ritual objects, artes, placed upon the mesa to represent each direction, are archetypal models that manifest the most evocative power that exists within these elemental distinctions:

- *Pachamama*: Any object that exemplifies the elemental power of *allpa* (earth element) will do, but most often a stone or crystal is used.
- *Mamakilla*: Any object that exemplifies the elemental power of *unu* (water element) will do, but most often a shell or bowl (sometimes filled with water) is used.
- *Wiracocha*: Any object that exemplifies the elemental power of *wayra* (air element) will do, but most often a feather is used.
- *Intitayta*: Any object that exemplifies the elemental power of *nina* (fire element) will do, but most often a single white candle is used.
- *K'yuchi*: A person's most sacred object that exemplifies the harmonious power of *t'eqsikallpa* (aether element) is used.

The Pachakuti mesa is "awakened" before ritual use by following the logarithmic spiral—found in nature through spiral galaxies, nautilus shells, and so on—throughout the altar space in a clockwise direction, starting from Pachamama in the south and ending at center with K'yuchi.

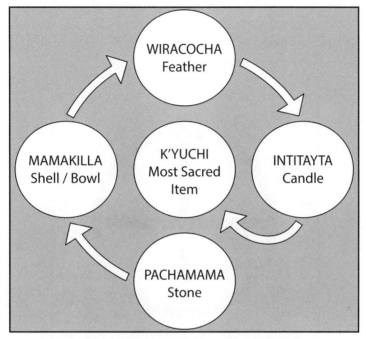

Figure 11: Mesa Opening Spiral and Artes

In activating the altar space by way of this design, the initiate is automatically replicating the act of creation found naturally in Malkuth. The reader is encouraged to initiate this activation through their own intention. However, this is not the only way to understand the elemental matrix as experienced through mesa.

The Cross

In 1970 Princeton University Press published famous psychoanalyst Dr. Carl G. Jung's final, and most influential, work on alchemy, *Mysterium Coniunctionis: An Inquiry into the Separation and Synthesis of Psychic Opposites in Alchemy*. In this lengthy tome, Jung unveils that the key to solving the problems plaguing modern man is found in the alchemical process.

Jung expresses that the primary template of the Great Work can be found in the *coniunctio*, the unification of opposing elements within Malkuth: "The idea of the cross points beyond the simple antithesis to a double antithesis, i.e., to a quaternio. To the mind of the alchemist this meant primarily the intercrossing elements.... We know that this fastening to a cross denotes a painful state of suspension, or a tearing asunder in the four directions. The alchemists therefore set themselves the task of reconciling the warring elements and reducing them to unity." [43] So, if we are to experience Jung's cross of unity on the mesa—the coniunctio—it may look something like this:

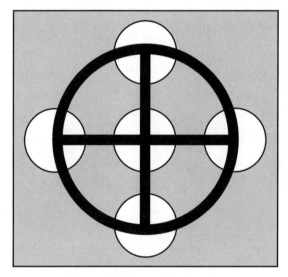

Figure 12: Mesa and Coniunctio

Coincidentally, or serendipitously, the elemental placements upon the mesa correspond to the elemental placements on the symbol of the equal-armed cross. This symbol, known sometimes as the "wheel cross" or "Odin's cross," is one of the oldest images represented in human history, dating back to the early Bronze Age. According to symbologist Carl Liungman: "In ancient China this sign was associated with *thunder, power, energy, head,* and *respect....* It appears in the earliest systems of writing used by the Egyptians, Hittites, Cretians, Greeks, Etrusians, and Romans. In ancient Greece ◯ signified a *sphere* or *globe*. It was

43. Carl G. Jung, *Mysterium Coniunctionis: An Inquiry into the Separation and Synthesis of Psychic Opposites in Alchemy* (Princeton, NJ: Princeton University Press, 1989) 421–22.

also used as a natal chart pattern in ancient astrology. In modern astrology it is the sign for the *planet Earth.*" [44]

This design is also found in Native American medicine wheels, circular stone monuments oriented to the sacred directions. The directions naturally convened in the center as well, creating a sort of equal-armed cross enclosed in a circle similar to the image above.

A spiral represents the circular, more organic or noumenal, way of the natural world; the cross, on the other hand, is indicative of our limited, microcosmic understanding of the world of phenomena. Jung interprets the cross in his alchemical work *Mysterium Coniunctionis* as a symbol of integration for the human soul:

> Man, therefore, who is an image of the great world, and is called the microcosm or little world (as the little world, made after the similitude of its archetype, and compounded of the four elements, is called the great man), has also his heaven and his earth. For the soul and the understanding are his heaven; his body and senses his earth. Therefore, to know the heaven and earth of man, is the same as to have a full and complete knowledge of the whole world and of the things of nature.
>
> The circular arrangement of the elements in the world and in man is symbolized by the mandala and its quaternary [cross] structure.[45]

Thus, the mesa—or any other sort of similar altar set—is a ritualized reminder that the universe must be experienced through the body. This may seem obvious. But, again, we so often sleepwalk in the mitote fog. To awaken from the slumber and begin the path of initiation into the "higher" realms in the Tree of Life, a full realization and awareness of the senses via the elemental matrix is essential.

It seems we are too often stuck in mystical endeavors; the tendency is to dilute the senses, to move beyond the physical, emotional, and mental states of being to attain the spiritual. But that is not the true mystic approach. Our anosognosia has conditioned us to doubt our own wholeness. Too many of us feel fragmented, incomplete.

By accepting and working with the material aspects of existence in Malkuth, a sort of synthesis is achieved that can allow one to then open a space, or gateway, for which the initiate can begin the Great Work. As the opposites are harmonized, and thus then subsided

---

44. Carl G. Liungman, *Dictionary of Symbols* (New York: W.W. Norton & Company, 1991), 328.

45. Jung, *Mysterium Coniunctionis*, 388.

into union (coniunctio), the pathways of mysticism open into wider vistas and horizons that begin to defy the capacity for language to communicate.

Figure 13: Mesa Coniunctio as Gateway to the Tree of Life

Malkuth depicted in the esoteric traditions is, according to Dion Fortune, "the only Sephirah that is represented as part-coloured instead of a unit, for it is divided into four quarters, which are assigned to the four Elements of Earth, Air, Fire, and Water." [46] In this differentiation of elements we see the unification of opposites, harmony in duality. These parts, or phases, can also replicate the cycles of our own experience, as also depicted in the calendar year.

Thus, no magical or mystical endeavor bears any fruit if it does not begin and end in Malkuth. If reality is not tangibly affected in some way or another, then spiritual work is useless. This sentiment has been stressed many times by don Oscar Miro-Quesada: "As we begin to engage in this Great Work, living in harmony with the natural order, ceremonially aligning to the pulses, rhythms, and cycles of our sacred earth, our purpose as earth-bound souls is revealed." [47] Therefore, working within the elemental pacha of Malkuth as the foundation of any ritual endeavor ensures a successful process ahead.

---

46. Fortune, *Mystical Qabalah*, 248.
47. Glass-Coffin and Miro-Quesada, *Lessons in Courage*, 95.

6

TOPOGRAPHY OF THE INNER WORLDS

Esoteric tradition declares that as soon as a mind is sufficiently advanced to be able to grasp its significance, it is made aware of the esoteric theory of evolution, so that, knowing the plan, it may be able to co-operate with the work. But long before the individual is ripe for the conscious realisation of this great task, his mind is being schooled and prepared in readiness.

—DION FORTUNE, *THE TRAINING & WORK OF AN INITIATE*

Just as an astronaut must study the physics of outer space in order to survive, so too must a psychonaut be well versed on the landscape of inner space. A deeper analysis is absolutely required before embarking upon an initiatory pathworking on the Tree of Life.

The absolute goal of the Great Work is referred to in a variety of different ways: the philosopher's stone, the *elixir vitae*, the Chemical Marriage, as well as the Knowledge and Conversation of the Holy Guardian Angel. In the mystical Judaic tradition of Qabalah, it is known as "Adam Kadmon."

Adam Kadmon is the Heavenly Man, the essence of the ten Sephiroth as an undivided unity. The objective of the Great Work is the realization and experience of this state of being, the mind and body in union. This is the meaning of *yoga* in Eastern terms. In the Western Mystery Tradition, however, it is designated by the God-name formula *tetragrammaton*, comprised of the Hebrew letters *Yod*, *Heh*, *Vav*, and *Heh* (YHVH):

יהוה

Over time this traditionally unutterable name came to be known as *Yahweh*. This formula can be laid out upon the Tree of Life to gain insight on how the Adam Kadmon concept is achieved via the marriage of the conscious and subconscious self as described in alchemy. In Judaism each letter in the Hebrew language holds a wealth of meaning, as well as a mathematical equivalent (known as *gematria*). In fact, some speculate the Torah is basically one giant formula whose meaning is lost if the Bible is to be taken literally. If we are to break out the letters of the tetragrammaton (*Yod-Heh-Vav-Heh*) onto the Tree of Life, they would look like this:

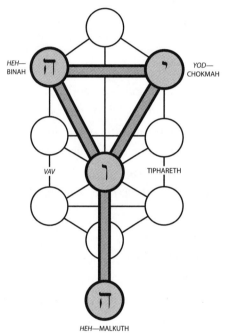

Figure 14: Tetragrammaton

The letters displayed onto the Sephiroth in this way convey the alchemical process in its most pristine form. The final *Heh* in the formula (residing in Malkuth) is referred to as the Unredeemed Virgin or Daughter, symbolizing the subconscious mind of the human being. Earlier, this was referred to as Nephesch, the shadow. As we discussed, this is usually in dire conflict with the conscious mind designated by *Vav* in Tiphareth, otherwise known as the Son, dubbed earlier the Neschamah, the individuality. Confusion and disruption of one's total consciousness is the result of this conflict, causing a fog of bewilderment for the personality (Ruach) in Yesod. The task of the Great Work is reconciliation of the individuality (*Vav*) with the shadow (the final *Heh*), thus establishing equilibrium within the personality.

Alchemically, this marriage between the Son and Unredeemed Virgin results in the impregnation of the Mother (the first *Heh*), which resides in Binah, resulting in the meaning of that Sephirah: understanding. Only through understanding can the true wisdom of the Father in Chokmah arise within the human (*Yod*).

Understanding + Wisdom = Purpose of Life Divined

Taking this one step further is the formula for the pentagrammaton. According to gematria, the Hebrew letter *Shin* is equal to the number 300, which is the embodiment of the Hebrew phrase *Ruach Elohim*, meaning "Spirit of the Gods":

Therefore, *Shin* is ascribed to the essence of Holy Spirit as described in the New Testament (in Hebrew, *Shechinah*). Engaged in this process of the Chemical Marriage, a reception (Qabalah) is happening in which the descent of the Holy Spirit fills the cup that is the initiate; it the descent of *Shin* into the midst of the tetragrammaton on an elemental level. That being said, it should be noted that there is an elemental designation to YHVH:

- *Yod*: Fire
- *First Heh*: Water
- *Vav*: Air
- *Final Heh*: Earth

As *Shin* descends, *Yod Heh Vav Heh* then becomes *Yod Heh Shin Vav Heh*, the pentagrammaton; in Hebrew this is designated as *Yeheshua* (from the Aramaic *Yeshua*), related to the personification of Christ. This is where the glyph of the pentagram actually comes into play in the Western Mystery Tradition; it is a symbol for the emulation, invocation, and evocation of the Christ Consciousness on an elemental level.

This is the truest manifestation of Adam Kadmon come into physical form, a newly created being, the adept, or *Tzaddik*: a righteous one, a saint, or one in whom the birth of

Spirit has established equilibrium with the base and unredeemed elements of matter. This depicts the whole of the constitution of man.

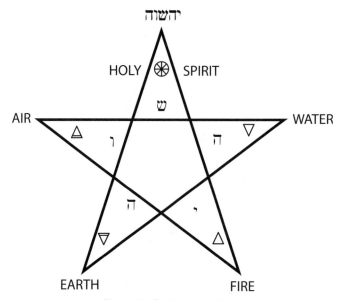

Figure 15: Pentagrammaton

But, a more granular understanding of the body of the tree will help provide a framework for this Marriage, this *yoga*.

Hebrew *Aleph Beth*

You will notice that an understanding of some Hebrew is necessary for an exploration of the Qabalah. Not only is Hebrew the original language of the Old Testament of the Christian Bible (i.e., the Torah), but in fact the letters of the Hebrew alphabet have a direct correlation to not only the Sephiroth but also the paths on the Tree of Life. Rabbi Rav Berg writes, "The first line of Genesis is interesting though its translation is not entirely accurate. Something indeed was created in the beginning, but it was not Heaven and Earth. We read in the *Zohar* that two thousand years prior to the Creation spoken of in Genesis, the all-embracing Creation reflected upon and brought into being the twenty-two energy-intelligences that constitute the master communications system through which all subsystems of energy evolve, and which today are expressed as the letters of the Hebrew *Alef Bet* [alphabet]." [48]

As each one of these letters has its own numeric value, and intrinsic meaning, so too does each have an exact correlation with each of the paths on the tree. The correlations are as follows:

Value	Letter	Letter Name	Name Meaning	Path
1	א	Aleph	Ox	Path 11, Kether to Chokmah
2	ב	Beth	House	Path 12, Kether to Binah
3	ג	Gimel	Camel	Path 13, Kether to Tiphareth
4	ד	Daleth	Door	Path 14, Chokmah to Binah
5	ה	Heh	Window	Path 15, Chokmah to Tiphareth
6	ו	Vav	Nail or Hook	Path 16, Chokmah to Chesed
7	ז	Zain	Sword	Path 17, Binah to Tiphareth
8	ח	Cheth	Fence	Path 18, Binah to Geburah
9	ט	Teth	Serpent	Path 19, Chesed to Geburah
10	י	Yod	Hand	Path 20, Chesed to Tiphareth
20	כ	Kaph	Fist	Path 21, Chesed to Netzach
30	ל	Lamed	Ox-goad	Path 22, Geburah to Tiphareth
40	מ	Mem	Water	Path 23, Geburah to Hod
50	נ	Nun	Fish	Path 24, Tiphareth to Netzach
60	ס	Samech	Prop	Path 25, Tiphareth to Yesod
70	ע	Ayin	Eye	Path 26, Tiphareth to Hod
80	פ	Peh	Mouth	Path 27, Netzach to Hod
90	צ	Tzaddi	Fishhook	Path 28, Netzach to Yesod

48. Berg, *Energy of Hebrew Letters*, 47.

Value	Letter	Letter Name	Name Meaning	Path
100	ק	Qoph	Back of Head	Path 29, Netzach to Malkuth
200	ר	Resh	Head	Path 30, Hod to Yesod
300	ש	Shin	Tooth	Path 31, Hod to Malkuth
400	ת	Tau	Cross	Path 32, Yesod to Malkuth

Table 1: Hebrew Letters

Note that the numbering of the paths begins at 11 and ends at 32, equaling twenty-two in total. It is generally considered that the first ten "paths" are the Sephiroth themselves. Therefore, we have a complete numbering as denoted in the first passages of the *Sepher Yetzirah* as translated by William Westcott: "In thirty-two wonderful Paths of Wisdom did Jah … engrave his name…. Ten are the ineffable Sephiroth. Twenty-two are the Letters, the Foundation of all things." [49]

Each of these paths, each of these letters, holds a wealth of meaning. It is not just the emanations of the Sephiroth that carry value in the Great Work of the Qabalah, but the paths as well. Rabbi Berg says the twenty-two Hebrew letters are the primary symbols that God enacted manifestation through: "Twenty-two sublime tonalities emanated, and it pleased the Lord to use them to fashion His universe…. The Lord created all of the souls through these twenty-two emanations, each of whom was a trading partner with Him, as stones hewed from mountain are of the mountain but are not the mountain itself. Thus, He could derive pleasure from imparting, just as they would derive pleasure from receiving." [50]

---

49. William Wynn Westcott, trans., *Sepher Yetzirah: The Book of Formation and the Thirty Two Paths of Wisdom*, 2nd ed. (London: Theosophical Publishing Society, 1893), 15.

50. Berg, *Energy of Hebrew Letters*, 42–43.

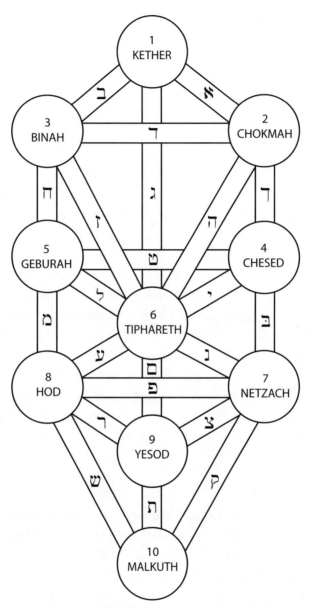

Figure 16: The Hebrew Letters on the Tree of Life

Tarot

The tarot is perhaps one of the most misunderstood divinatory tools. Its actual significance has been reduced to Hollywoodesque gypsy fortune-telling. Alphonse Louis Constant, whom many call the grandfather of the Western Mystery Tradition, was a nineteenth-century French socialist and Christian mystic, otherwise known as Éliphas Lévi. Lévi created one of the foundational syncretic tomes of the movement of Western Mystery initiatory practices, called *Transcendental Magic: Its Doctrine and Ritual*. In it, he unveils the legendary origin of tarot as the heart of all spiritual—indeed all *human*—traditions.

Éliphas Lévi's *Transcendental Magic* is one of the first instances in the history of the Western Mystery Tradition in which a direct correlation between the tarot and the actual paths on the Tree of Life is made. In fact, Lévi has referred to the tarot as the foundation of all esotericism:

> All religions have preserved the remembrance of a primitive book, written in hieroglyphs by the sages of the earliest epoch of the world. Simplified and vulgarized in later days, its symbols furnished letters to the art of writing, characters to the Word, and to occult philosophy its mysterious signs and pantacles. This book, attributed by the Hebrews to Enoch, seventh master of the world after Adam; by the Egyptians to Hermes Trismegistus; by the Greeks to Cadmus, the mysterious builder of the Holy City: this book was the symbolical summary of primitive tradition, called subsequently Kabalah or Cabala, meaning reception. The tradition in question rests altogether on the one dogma of Magic: the visible is for us the proportional measure of the invisible.[51]

This "primitive book, written in hieroglyphs" is indeed Lévi's reference to the tarot, and describes it not just as a "symbolical summary" of ancient wisdom traditions (i.e., shamanism) but also equates Qabalah (or "Kabalah") with those ancient practices.

To the Golden Dawn's credit, they formulized the usage of the tarot within the Tree of Life in concrete, tangible ways that Lévi only seemed to allude to. The self-acclaimed Beast 666, Aleister Crowley—an initiate of the Golden Dawn who later created his own magical fraternity, Ordo Templi Orientis—had even gone on to say that Lévi made mistakes in his attributions between the tarot trumps and the Hebrew letters in order to still keep the

---

51. Éliphas Lévi, *Transcendental Magic: Its Doctrine and Ritual,* trans. Arthur Edward Waite (Mansfield Centre, CT: Martino Publishing, 2011), 95.

occult secrets hidden and in code. However the case may be, whatever manuscripts the Golden Dawn stumbled upon served to solidify and ritualize the attributions in a way that made sense. The tarot has a habit of being the subject of uncertainty throughout its history, and even in its beginnings.

Tarot has a mysterious history; as such, it is difficult to pinpoint its origin and evolution throughout time. Many authorities (like Lévi) trace its inception to the Egyptian Mysteries. Some say it originally existed as the Book of Thoth but was burned in the Library of Alexandria, thus taking on a new form in a series of pictures and symbols to shroud their true meaning from persecution. However, the incarnation of the tarot we are most familiar with today came from sixteenth-century Europe—most notably Italy, France, and Spain. The tarot has evolved into various styles and paradigms, and regardless of the historical evidence—or lack thereof—pertaining to it, the true power of the cards and their symbols comes from their practical application.

This is true of both the tarot and the Tree of Life. The power of any tool comes from its usage rather than when or where it was formulated. But, again, what *exactly* is the tarot? And what is its purpose?

"The tarot will teach you how to create the soul," says Alejandro Jodorowsky in his alchemical cinematic masterpiece *The Holy Mountain*.[52] The tarot is, in a nutshell, a pictorial key to the entire universe, both inner and outer space. If the Tree of Life is the design, and Hebrew its language, the tarot comprises the images that unlock the many vistas of experience existing in initiation.

The tarot is a deck of cards on which the traditional deck of playing cards is based. Within a single deck of the tarot are four suits—comprised of fourteen cards each—and twenty-two trump cards, equaling a total of seventy-eight cards altogether. The suits are divided into wands, cups, swords, and pentacles (or coins). Each of these suits of course holds a specific meaning, along with an elemental and Qabalistic correlation. Previously, we discussed three worlds or levels of existence. In Qabalah, the Sephiroth of the Tree of Life have a four-fold nature, traditionally called the four worlds. Each Sephirah is expressed not as a unit but as a composite of these four expressions. These worlds correspond to the four elements, and thus the four suits of the tarot, and are best understood as different levels of experience of the tree.

The four suits of the tarot are as follows:

---

52. Alejandro Jodorowsky, dir., *The Holy Mountain* (Mexico City, Mexico: Producciones Zohar, 1975), DVD, 115 min.

- *Wands:* The suit of intuition that gives birth to the creative process; fire is what propelled the evolution of our species. Its gender association is male.

    Element: Fire, the Pachakuti mesa association being Intitayta (Father Sun)

    Qabalistic World: Atziluth, the Archetypal World, which can only be expressed through the Ten Holy Names of God, the Divine Emanations; the most abstract of the four worlds

    Hebrew Letter: Yod

- *Cups:* The suit of intuition that represents feeling and emotion; cups are the receptacles of ever-shifting expression. Its gender association is female.

    Element: Water, the Pachakuti mesa association being Mamakilla (Grandmother Moon)

    Qabalistic World: Briah, the World of Creation, where the Divine Emanations can begin to manifest through the Ten Mighty Archangels; also called the World of Thrones

    Hebrew Letter: Heh

- *Swords:* The suit of intellect, logic, the seeking of truth; swords cut through deception and illusion. Its gender association is male.

    Element: Air, the Pachakuti mesa association being Wiracocha (Father Sky / Great Spirit)

    Qabalistic World: Yetzirah, the World of Formation, where the Divine Emanations become fully manifest through a variety of beings, the Angelic Host

    Hebrew Letter: Vav

- *Pentacles (Coins):* The suit of sensation and physicality; pentacles represent the completion of existence made manifest. Its gender association is female.

    Element: Earth, the Pachakuti mesa association being Pachamama (Mother Earth)

    Qabalistic World: Assiah, the World of Action, where the Divine Emanations manifest as the base elements of earthly matter

    Hebrew Letter: Heh

Notice that the Hebrew letter associations in order of the four worlds, from archetype to action, form *Yod-Heh-Vav-Heh,* the tetragrammaton. Within each suit, the numerical values from aces to tens represent the ten Sephiroth; therefore, each suit is the totality of the expressions of the Tree of Life via the four worlds of the Qabalists, as well as the elements and the totality of the most Holy Name of God.

The other cards of the suits are the court cards: kings, queens, knights (princes), and pages (princesses). These sixteen cards find their inherent value through both their suit association and rank. The kings are obviously male gender cards, representing a mastery, command, or dominion over that particular suit. Queens are obviously female and are less forceful than the kings, though they still represent a mastery of the suit, just via more internal processes. Knights are primarily male and represent the most extreme expressions of that suit, however positive or negative those expressions may be. Pages have a strong female association and are a more passive or playful expression of the suit. These four court cards correlate as well to the Sephiroth and four worlds: king (*Yod*, Chokmah), queen (*Heh*, Binah), knight (*Vav*, Tiphareth), and page (*Heh*, Malkuth).

The trumps, twenty-two in total, are the remaining cards. Numbered zero through twenty-one, they essentially tell the story of the human soul, of human evolution, of the entire process of life, death, and everything in between as well as beyond. They are the topography of the universe in man. Their significance cannot be overstated. Acting as the primary hieroglyphs of the tarot story, the trumps do not adhere to any suit. Although each trump card constitutes a single image (or symbol), the trumps are also all connected in sequence to communicate a larger composite. In the least, each trump image is an archetype for a different expression of human consciousness; at most, they are keys to unlock the Mysteries of the unknown.

Although there is much debate on how the tarot trumps correspond to the Tree of Life, they are most normally understood to align with the paths. Seeing as how there are twenty-two trumps and twenty-two paths, they are usually mapped to each other accordingly:

Path	Trump Number	Trump Name	Hebrew Letter	Path
11	0	The Fool	א	Path 11, Kether to Chokmah
12	1	The Magician	ב	Path 12, Kether to Binah
13	2	The High Priestess	ג	Path 13, Kether to Tiphareth
14	3	The Empress	ד	Path 14, Chokmah to Binah

Path	Trump Number	Trump Name	Hebrew Letter	Path
15	4	The Emperor	ה	Path 15, Chokmah to Tiphareth
16	5	The Hierophant	ו	Path 16, Chokmah to Chesed
17	6	The Lovers	ז	Path 17, Binah to Tiphareth
18	7	The Chariot	ח	Path 18, Binah to Geburah
19	8	Strength	ט	Path 19, Chesed to Geburah
20	9	The Hermit	י	Path 20, Chesed to Tiphareth
21	10	Wheel of Fortune	כ	Path 21, Chesed to Netzach
22	11	Justice	ל	Path 22, Geburah to Tiphareth
23	12	The Hanged Man	מ	Path 23, Geburah to Hod
24	13	Death	נ	Path 24, Tiphareth to Netzach
25	14	Temperance	ס	Path 25, Tiphareth to Yesod
26	15	The Devil	ע	Path 26, Tiphareth to Hod
27	16	The Tower	פ	Path 27, Netzach to Hod
28	17	The Star	צ	Path 28, Netzach to Yesod
29	18	The Moon	ק	Path 29, Netzach to Malkuth
30	19	The Sun	ר	Path 30, Hod to Yesod
31	20	Judgement	ש	Path 31, Hod to Malkuth
32	21	The World	ת	Path 32, Yesod to Malkuth

Table 2: The Paths

Of the entire tarot, the trumps are studied the most, as traversing the paths on the Tree of Life is a vital component to the process of the Great Work within the Western Mystery

Tradition. Each trump will be covered in more detail with each path in part III, "Simulacra." Regardless, for now, they just need to be understood as a crucial ingredient in the apparatus of the tree's topography.

Triads

While traversing the Tree of Life, it is important to be aware of the various relationships among certain sets of Sephiroth and paths. Within the tree are three distinct groupings of Sephiroth called the Triads.

Including all the Sephiroth, except for Malkuth, the triads are groupings of three Sephiroth each that represent distinct levels of the universe. In essence, they reveal the primary levels, or stages, of creation. The triads break down like this:

- *The Supernal Triad:* Composed of Kether, Chokmah, and Binah, the Supernal Triad represents, really, the only True Reality. All else in the universe is but a reflection of this one triad. It is the Supreme Godhead and can never truly be known. We can only conjecture its existence through symbols, abstractions, and metaphors.
- *The Ethical Triad:* Composed of Chesed, Geburah, and Tiphareth, this is the first, inverted reflection of the True Reality. The Ethical Triad is the realm of the universe in which the principles of manifestation are first generated; in essence, where the blueprints of matter are drawn up.
- *The Astral Triad:* Composed of Netzach, Hod, and Yesod, the Astral Triad is yet another, though denser, simulacrum of the inverted reflection that is the Ethical Triad. If the Ethical Triad is the blueprint of manifestation, the Astral Triad is the machinery that builds the material world.

A study of the triads can give us a sense of how the parts of the tree operate both in the formation of the outer and inner universes. They illustrate how the central Sephiroth—Kether for the Supernal, Tiphareth for the Ethical, and Yesod for the Astral—are actually the primary backbone. The other Sephiroth can be seen as extensions, the polarities that make up the central Sephiroth: Chokmah and Binah for Kether, Chesed and Geburah for Tiphareth, and finally Netzach and Hod for Yesod.

However, there is another aspect of the tree that the triads allow us to see with clarity. Israel Regardie explains this gap very clearly: "The Supernals are separated by a great gulf, the Abyss, from that which lies below them. The Supernals are ideal; the other Sephiroth are actual; the Abyss is the metaphysical gap between. In one sense, they have no connection or relation with the Inferiors, the lower seven Sephiroth, reflected by them—just as space itself is independent of, and unaffected by, whether there is or is not anything manifested within its emptiness." [53]

This gulf of separation is the eternal separator between God and matter. Whatever passes through the Abyss is completely dead to what it once was before, for nothing of the Supernal Triad can be truly understood in the lower two triads, just as nothing in the lower two triads can withstand the purity of the Supernals. Regardie is actually referring to a space upon the tree where there resides an eleventh, invisible Sephirah.

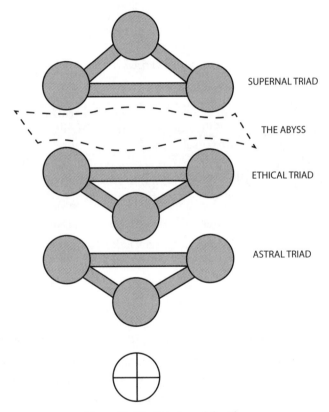

Figure 17: The Triads and the Abyss

53. Israel Regardie, *A Garden of Pomegranates: Skrying on the Tree of Life,* ed. Chic Cicero and Sandra Tabatha Cicero (St. Paul, MN: Llewellyn, 1999), 44.

Daath

Some Qabalists refuse to even acknowledge *Daath* (or *Daat*)—which means "knowledge" in Hebrew—the non-Sephirah prevalent in the space of the Abyss on the Tree of Life. Between the Supernal and Ethical realms is the void of the Abyss, where Daath resides.

Daath is the realm where the elements of existence that lie beyond our understanding become assimilated into the faculties of the human mind. Its name means "Knowledge," and as such it is the destination for all those who wish to "Know Thyself." Israel Regardie extrapolates on Daath's role and why knowledge is the tenet most ascribed to this area, this void within the Tree, in *The Golden Dawn*: "Fundamentally it is the ascent of the Dragon or, if you wish, an upwelling of the Unconscious archetypes—a highly dangerous and unbalancing ascent, until they are assimilated to consciousness—which first renders *Daath* a possibility. It is the Fall which is responsible for the acquisition of self-knowledge." [54]

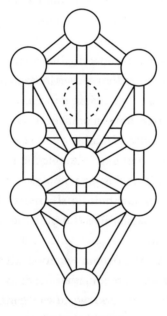

Figure 18: Daath

The symbol of the dragon is a useful image here in all esoteric and alchemical traditions. The dragon is emblematic of the struggles of humankind with their own inner selves, as a knight battles the winged fiend in tales of old. Carl Jung often postulated that

---

54. Regardie, *Golden Dawn*, 34.

the dragon reveals itself in many forms through dreams: a demon, animal, old man, cave, or even a walled garden. The dragon is a common theme in the work of psychotherapist and shamanic practitioner Dr. José Stevens, specifically as a means of turning one's own internal fears and personality patterns into objects of personal power. This is, in actuality, the goal of Daath, of the entire process of the Great Work itself. Stevens suggests the task of initiation is to submit the dragon (the baser elements of the shadow) to the Will of the individuality (higher self). Stevens writes,

> A dragon is merely an icon, a powerful image that represents danger and fear, and of course lies in wait on our path to roar out a terrible challenge to our progress. The dragon when first encountered represents fear itself. It is only later, with familiarity, that the dragon may actually give us clues to redemption—the necessary information to transform defeat at its claws to victory and passage. With victory, fear and separation are overcome. Fear flies, and the path leads to a greater reality encompassing unity, knowledge, wisdom, truth, and beauty.[55]

Daath can be the most uneasy and even dreadful Sephirah to encounter. For as one ascends the Tree of Life in earnest connection with the Supernal realms of being, Daath, the Abyss, is the where the last remnants of oneself—one's image of oneself especially—is shredded. We see this play out in the biblical story of the Garden of Eden. For as Eve encounters the serpent (dragon), she takes fruit from the Tree of Knowledge (Daath). As she and Adam partake of the fruit (Eve being a personification of Binah and Adam of Chokmah), their nakedness is revealed, and they are ashamed. They see their true selves. As a result, they are cast out of the Garden of Eden, of paradise. This is not a literal account but the mythology of our consciousness.

What comes as a result of this banishment of paradise is a separation between man and woman, and here we are in a world where neither the feminine or masculine are honored together, in balance. However, to return to paradise (the culmination of the Great Work), the serpent must again be reencountered and the Tree of Knowledge passed through. Knowing oneself completely, without shame, is true knowledge, which Colonel Seymour states is the prime maxim of the mystery schools: "Over the doorway of many of the ancient temples was written *Gnothi Se Auton* or, *Nosce Te Ipsum*, Know Thyself. This psycho-

---

55. José Stevens, *Transforming Your Dragons: How to Turn Fear Patterns into Personal Power* (Rochester, VT: Inner Traditions, 1994), 3.

logical process is sometimes called 'the unveiling of the self,' sometimes 'the knowledge and conversation of one's holy guardian angel,' or higher self. This is the first great goal. Its essential symbols are to be found on the Qabalistic Tree of Life…important symbols for the trained mind." [56]

To know oneself, dragons and all, is the motto of the Great Work. Entraining our mind to various symbols in the Mystery Traditions will incorporate all elements of the self into a whole. This is the essence of Daath, the non-Sephiroth of the Tree of Life.

The Chakana

It is important to understand that the Sephiroth and these levels of creation are not hierarchal levels of heaven that are separated from the "real world" and which we must attain through various stages of afterlife to get to God. This is an illusion beset on us from our modern way of life and mainstream institutions, in which one must climb the ladder of success (i.e., cleansed of sin) in order access the upper management of the heavens. This line of thinking can lead a soul's evolution into a trap, even beyond death, that contributes to our modern predicament of disharmony with the natural world.

All the Sephiroth—both individually and as a collective—encompass both positive and negative aspects of existence. In the Western Mystery Tradition, this is known as each Sephirah containing both a virtue and a vice. In the indigenous traditions of Peru, this concept is best represented by what is known as the Andean cross: the *chakana*.

Embedded within the ancient architecture of Peru, the chakana is a multileveled symbol that encompasses the astronomical means of reflecting the Southern Cross, the most significant constellation in the night sky to the Incas and other Andean people. The Quechua *chakana* means "stair" and comes from the word *chakay*, which means "to cross." The multitiered formation of the chakana not only emulates the crossing of the cardinal points of the four directions but was also revered as a pattern of creation. For instance, the tiers (or stairs) of the chakana form twelve points, each representing a month of the calendar year in mapping the sun's solstices and equinoxes.

---

56. Seymour, *Forgotten Mage*, 125.

Figure 19: The Chakana

Further, the chakana represents a bridging (or crossing) of the three worlds in the Andean cosmology (as discussed in chapter 3), converging into one universal whole. In the shamanic traditions of Peru, the Ukhupacha (Lowerworld), Kaypacha (Middleworld), and Hanaqpacha (Upperworld) are not three disparate realities that are supposed to exist separate from one another. These pachas are only separate because of our inability to be in harmony with ourselves. Indeed, in the Pachakuti Mesa Tradition, when these three pachas are united within and without—as emulated in the chakana—the *Qoripacha* (Golden Age) will arise on earth, an era of peace and tranquility.

Dante and Orlando Salas Delgado, brothers and archeological researchers from the National University of Saint Anthony the Abbot of Cusco, refer to the chakana as "la Flor de la Vida," which means the flower of life.[57] Modern mystic Drunvalo Melchizedek has taught and written extensively about the flower of life as a universal symbol of magic and creation. Manifesting in various forms throughout many cultures, including the mandalas of the East and the medicine wheel of the northern Native Americans, there is indeed a global symbolic pattern representing the totality of the universe. No one symbol is more

---

57. Dante Salas Delgado and Orlando Salas Delgado, *Arquitecura cósmica inka: Arqueoastronomía* (Cusco, Peru: Biblioteca Nacional del Peru, 2016), 188.

accurate than another, for they all communicate the same thing: that the entire cosmos is contained within one matrix of being.

In terms of the Tree of Life, let's revisit the idea of virtue and vice. It is known that for each Sephirah, a virtue and vice is contained. For example, the virtue—the prime attribute of manifestation—for the Sephirah of Hod is truthfulness. Therefore, when one is in alignment with positive attributes of the intelligence of Hod, then one is being truthful with oneself and others. However, it is in this same Sephirah that one's downfall in truthfulness can be achieved; it is normally the inverse of the virtue that creates the vice, and vice versa. If out of alignment, the vice of Hod manifests as the attribute of falsehood, or dishonesty. Thus, both the virtue (a characteristic of the Hanaqpacha, the individuality, or Neshamah) and the vice (a characteristic of the Ukhupacha, the shadow, or Nephesch) exist within the same sphere of potential (or Sephirah). The playing field where this potentiality takes place is the Kaypacha, where the personality, or Ruach, interacts in the scrimmage of life, choosing between the polarities of virtue or vice.

So, in this sense, the Tree of Life is not a map of heaven. It is both heaven and hell, as well as earth (Malkuth). In chapter 4, I describe the Tree of Life as a roadmap to explore the nature of God. God is the totality of all things: heaven, hell, and everything in between. In Quechua, this is referred to as the *Teqsemuyu*, the entirety of the universe that is God. God is not something separate from who we are, but we are a part of it. The chakana represents both the entire spectrum of the Tree of Life and its inversion, what the Qabalists call the *Qlippoth*. The Hebrew word *Qlippoth* means "shells" or "husks," and here we can trace the original term for what is known as a demon in occult lore. Demons are merely shells, husks empty and devoid of the Divine, which is what we become if we continually live in vice, rather than virtue. This means we are our own demons and angels at the same time; we are the source for our damnation or salvation. It all hinges on our ability, as initiates, to recognize that we are the microcosmic totality of the macrocosmic universe, the Teqsemuyu. We are and contain both the Sephiroth and the Qlippoth. We are the chakana. As we understand this truth, we pave the path for our own soul's evolution in consciousness.

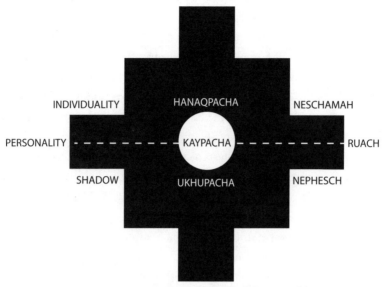

Figure 20: Chakana and the Three Worlds

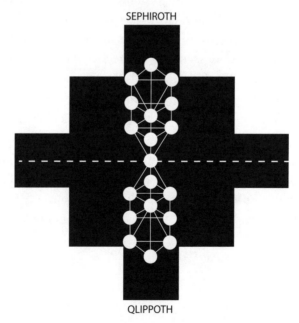

Figure 21: The Chakana as Teqsemuyu

7

THE CAMPOS AND THE PILLARS

Even within duality, the tantrika goes straight to the nondual source, because pure subjectivity always resides immersed within his own nature.

—VASUGUPTA, *YOGA SPANDAKARIKA*

The first time I ever drank the mescaline-containing psychedelic cactus called San Pedro—or *huachuma*—my maestro (coincidentally also named Daniel) called me up to his mesa. We were in an all-night healing ceremony called a *mesada,* in which participants imbibe the San Pedro medicine and receive healings (*limpias* and *levantadas*) from the curandero. It is usually held within a lodge space or patio and is most often performed (depending on the region in Peru) in complete darkness.

The medicine of the San Pedro was pulsing in full force through my body, so I struggled a little getting up off the floor. It didn't help me much that the darkness was pitch, but I managed to shuffle my way to the front of maestro's mesa. He told me then that the medicine was working strong and flowing through my system. Now, it was time to peak the medicine, for the full result of my healing. With the facilitation of his *auxillios* (assistants) I would be handed a shell, containing a tobacco infusion, that I would then need to imbibe through each nostril. The infusion was called *singado.*

As the prospect of this filled me with a heart-pounding terror, he began to pray to and call upon the assistance of San Cipriano.

San Cipriano (Saint Cyprian) was once a bishop of Carthage and is now a symbol of balance in curanderismo, the shamanic art of utilizing San Pedro as a healing sacrament.

As I was taught in my curandero lineage, San Cipriano began his path as a magician of Antioch, working the dark arts, and had become one of the more powerful sorcerers in his time. He had in his intention to bring down a pious nun from her servitude of Christ. Her name was Santa Justina. However, his magical attacks were futile against her faith. Through this, Cipriano fell in love with Justina but, seeing as she was a bride of the Church, was inspired to know Christ as well as she. He was received into the priesthood and soon became bishop, and she the head of her convent. Cipriano was even more powerful than most servants of the light because he had experienced the darkness and was able to reconcile the balance of two.

Although curanderismo from Peru is rooted in indigenous folk-healing practices, it is also a fusion of Catholic symbolism and iconography. When the Spanish invaded, the local populations were smart to adopt the Catholic cosmology and incorporate it into their own indigenous spiritual framework. After all, many of the saints, as well as the Holy Trinity, fit almost like perfect puzzle pieces into the Incan pantheon of deities. Anthropologists Donald Joralemon and Douglas Sharon have spent the bulk of their lifetimes studying Northern Coastal Peruvian curanderismo. They express that the amalgamation of native and colonial religions has proven to be a benefit to the healing practice: "Integrating two distinct historical and ethnic traditions—Spanish Catholicism and indigenous animism— the mesa dialectic provides a code for the problem-solving activities entailed in curing." [58]

Even though Peruvian, and especially Andean, archaeological evidence has always supported such a dialectic, it is perhaps due to this historical integration of traditions that curanderismo iconography is rife with a strong sense of duality. To the Peruvian curanderos, San Cipriano represents the arbiter between Christian and pagan beliefs, light and dark, exemplifying two sides of the same coin that is the curing process in ritual shamanism. Dr. Bonnie Glass-Coffin, professor of anthropology at Utah State University, expresses the important nature of opposites, of duality, in shamanic ceremony: "The binary oppositions of celestial/chthonic, straight/tangled, orderly/chaotic, and culture/nature that permeate cosmological beliefs … [are expressed] in *mesa* symbolism. Additionally, this emphasis on dualism and opposition seems to influence and reflect the healer's conceptualization of the harm that threatens his patients." [59]

---

58. Donald Joraleman and Douglas Sharon, *Sorcery and Shamanism: Curanderos and Clients in Northern Peru* (Salt Lake City: University of Utah Press: 1993), 187.

59. Bonnie Glass-Coffin, *The Gift of Life: Female Spirituality and Healing in Northern Peru* (Albuquerque: University of New Mexico Press: 1998), 150.

Maestro had me take in the singado, the tobacco infusion, from the left and then right nostrils. It went down hard, like daggers slicing through my nasal cavity and down my throat. My head swelled, my gut wrenched. He told me the infusion on the left side was taken in order to let go of what was no longer needed in my life. The one on the right side was to call in good fortune for myself. The left for dispatching, the right for raising.

Each side of a person, as well as the mesa (which are reflections of one another), represents certain powers and forces of the universe and psyche that are in opposition and need to come into some sort of harmony. Joraleman and Sharon state, "Curing rituals (including … nasal imbibing of tobacco juice …) activate a dialectical process by which the forces of good and evil in both man and nature are brought into meaningful interaction through the mediation of the middle field. The balance of forces or 'complementarity of opposites' achieved through ritual is then symbolically transmitted to the patient." [60]

Life is composed of dualities. It is the resistance and opposition of the dualities that cause suffering and disease, in the curandero paradigm. Additionally, the curandero understands that where there is duality, there is always triality. This is why the curandero's healing practice is always threefold: first to work one side of these polarities, then the other, and then to integrate a balance between the two. The curandero stands at the crescendo of these two forces, bringing them together to clash, to harmonize. This tug-of-war between dualities is reflected in every ritual process in a curandero's healing ceremony, as well as in the arrangement of the mesa altar space.

The Campos

There are many different types of mesa out in the world. What has been offered in this book, the Pachakuti Mesa Tradition, is just one of dozens (perhaps hundreds) of mesa traditions across the South American landscape. The mesa—as in all shamanic lineages—is not a dogmatic practice, like the Liturgies of the Catholic Church or the Pillars of Islam. Shamanic traditions are more like family lineages passed on from generation to generation, modified over time as the culture evolves.

I often liken shamanic lineages to that of a family Christmas tradition: grandmother carries her traditions to mother, mother carries it to daughter … A tree is still involved, maybe a Christmas meal, the reading of "The Night Before Christmas," but it gets changed as each generation modifies it to their own needs. Maybe the tree looks different, the meal switches from turkey to ham, or the reading of "The Night Before Christmas" turns into

---

60. Joraleman and Sharon, *Sorcery and Shamanism*, 6.

the viewing of the film *The Nightmare Before Christmas*. The traditions are still there, just adapted to the needs and desires of the current family unit.

Therefore, there are many different mesa traditions in Peru and in all of Latin America. However, despite the differing iterations, the mesa still accomplishes the same mystical goal: reflecting the practitioner's cosmology. As such, it is an arena of mediation between the opposing forces of the cosmos. Where the practitioner sits is the unification of these forces; the curandero is the cosmic axis.

It is because of this that most mesas in Peru and abroad include a cross or crucifix gracing the central field. The cross is the ultimate symbol of Christ's sacrifice, as the curandero must sacrifice of himself in order to serve others. As was discussed earlier, it is also a holistic symbol used the world over in almost every culture. The cross represents the *axis mundi*, the connection between heaven and earth where the four directions meet.

In the Pachakuti mesa altar, we saw earlier what the cross was conjoining in the mysterium coniunctionis: the elemental powers of Malkuth. But this isn't the only rendition of this harmonization of opposites in mesa shamanism.

The mesas from the northern coastal Peruvian tradition of huachuma curanderismo work with the elemental powers not from five directional quadrants—as in the Pachakuti mesa—but in three distinct, vertical fields called *campos*. The campos are divided into the left, middle, and right regions of the mesa. Traditionally, they are set up thus:

- *Campo Ganadero (Left)*: Known also as the Field of the Sly Dealer or the Field of the Magician, the Campo Ganadero contains artifacts regularly associated with black magic, the underworld, or evil. It is also associated with the past, as well as the feminine. Because this field is associated with darker forces, it is also capable of revealing and thus dispelling them.
- *Campo Medio (Middle)*: Known also as the Middle Field or the Field of Equilibrium, the Campo Medio contains artifacts that stimulate a mediating balance between good and evil, white and dark magic, or masculine and feminine.
- *Campo Justicerio (Right)*: Known also as the Field of the Divine Justice or the Field of the Mystic, the Campo Justicerio contains artifacts normally aligned with white magic and good. This field is also associated with the masculine and bringing forth positive attributes of the future.

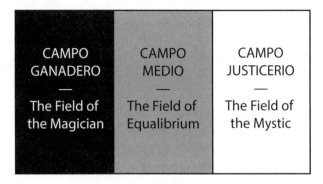

Figure 22: The Campos

The Campo Medio poses an interesting intersection of the dualistic nature of curanderismo, as well as a cosmology paradigm of universal structure. For a curandero, the Campo Medio represents the Middle Road or Middle Way as depicted in North American Indian spirituality. It is ultimate balance, the ability to live and operate the positive and negative faculties of consciousness, to be in two worlds at once. According to curandero don Eduardo Calderón,

> The *Campo Medio* is like a judge in this case, or like the needle in a balance, the controlling needle between those two powers, between good and evil. The Campo Medio is where the chiefs, the guardians, those who command, those who govern present themselves, since it is the neutral field—that is, the dividing field between two frontiers where a war can occur over a dispute. That is the place where one has to put all, all, all one's perseverance so that everything remains well controlled.[61]

This concept is inherent in the idea that duality is in fact a tripartite operation. There is always the positive, the negative, and then the dialectic between the two. In this case, the Campo Medio is less a field in its own merit than a field of interaction and discourse between the Campo Ganadero and the Campo Justicerio. This interplay actually aligns with the physical processes of curandero healing, which can fit within a three-phase operation of curing:

---

61. Douglas Sharon, *Wizard of the Four Winds: A Shaman's Story,* 2nd ed. (CreateSpace Independent Publishing Platform, 2015), 79.

1. *Limpia de Cuy:* A ritual cleansing of the body, normally done with artifacts from the Campo Ganadero (left). The goal of the limpia is to extract illness from the individual.

2. *Florecimiento:* A ritual flowering of the body, normally done with artifacts from the Campo Medio (middle). The goal of the florecimiento is to integrate the holism of the entire curing experience, sending the individual out into the world with good health and well-being.

3. *Levantada:* A ritual raising of the body, normally done with artifacts from the Campo Justicerio (right). The goal of the levantada is to bring good fortune to the individual in place of the previously extracted illness.

Again, Calderón further expresses the need for the integration of these three campos, three fields, within a ritualistic dialectic or discourse to maintain true harmony:

Equilibrium is necessary. If there is no equilibrium between these two forces, between good and evil, the thing changes aspect. It is necessary that equilibrium persist, and be influential.... If evil exists in a fashion that is much more eloquent, stronger, more expressive, more charged with force, good recedes; just as, when there is too much good, evil is separated.... By all means, there has to be this equilibrium, the duality of things so that all is in accord with this road, with the orientation of this equilibrium in the life of man.[62]

Pillars of Manifestation

The Mysteries have their own architecture. As we see in the cathedrals of Europe, mosques of Arabia, and stupas of Asia, the architecture of a sacred space emulates that which it is trying to invoke and evoke.

Probably the most profound building devoted to worship in the Western esoteric tradition is King Solomon's Temple from the Old Testament. Many iterations of this temple exist throughout all branches of the Western Mysteries, including (of course) Judaism, Hermeticism, Freemasonry, and even the Egyptian mystery schools. One of the most common depictions mimicked in these variations is the prevailing architectural feature of the two pillars.

---

62. Sharon, *Wizard of the Four Winds*, 175–76.

The first verifiable account of these pillars, as they are then recounted in all the Mysteries, comes from 1 Kings in the Nevi'im/Old Testament of the Holy Bible. In the passages dedicated to the descriptions of Hiram's bronze work within the temple, it is depicted: "He set up the columns at the portico of the Great Hall; he set up one column on the right and named it Jachin, and he set up the other column on the left and named it Boaz. Upon the top of the columns there was a lily design. Thus the work of the columns was completed." [63]

The relevance and meaning of the names Jachin and Boaz have created division among Biblical scholars for centuries. Some believe the names are variations of Babylonian or Phoenician deities that were adopted by the Hebrews, while others claim they translate clearly into "To establish in the Lord" and "Strength," respectively. [64] Either way, they communicate to those entering the temple that herein resides the presence of the Almighty.

Western esoteric scholar Manly P. Hall conveys a more naturalistic depiction of the pillars as a representation of polarity within one of the temples of Isis: "The World Virgin is sometimes shown standing between two great pillars—the Jachin and Boaz of Freemasonry—symbolizing the fact that Nature attains productivity by means of polarity. As wisdom personified, Isis stands between the pillars of opposites, demonstrating that understanding is always found at the point of equilibrium and that truth is often crucified between the two thieves of apparent contradiction." [65]

Another way to understand the conscious flow of the Tree of Life, and thus ourselves, is to engage the Sephiroth in terms of what Qabalists call the Pillars of Manifestation. Emulated as a simulation of the pillars in the temples of the Mysteries, the pillars upon the tree provide yet another template for understanding the way the universe works. As Kether came into manifestation, it split into a male aspect (Chokmah) and a female aspect (Binah). Each of these are distributed atop the heads of two columns, generating a vertical alignment of the Sephirah on the Tree of Life. The column on the left is called the Pillar of Severity, and on the right the Pillar of Mercy. In the middle, extending from Kether in the center, is the Pillar of Mildness or Equilibrium. The pillars on the left and right are noted in the Western Mystery Traditions as being representative of the entrance to King Solomon's

63. *Tanakh: The Holy Scriptures* (Philadelphia: The Jewish Publication Society, 1985), 1 Kings 1:31–32.

64. William M. Larson, "Those Mysterious Pillars: Boaz and Jachin," Pietre-Stones: Review of Freemasonry, accessed April 6, 2018, http://www.freemasons-freemasonry.com/larsonwilliam .html.

65. Manly P. Hall, *The Secret Teachings of All Ages: An Encyclopedic Outline of Masonic, Qabbalistic and Rosicrucian Symbolical Philosophy*, reader's ed. (New York: Penguin, 2003), 130.

Temple, the Pillar of Mildness being the candidate of initiation standing between the two, ready to enter the Mystery.

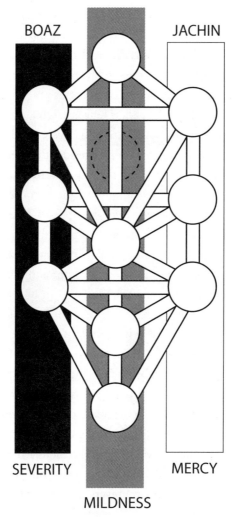

BOAZ   JACHIN

SEVERITY   MERCY

MILDNESS

Figure 23: The Three Pillars

The pillars within the context of the tree represent the paradigm of all creation, that the corporeal world is only manifest through the interaction of opposites. Just as it is shown in the yin-yang symbol from Eastern traditions, the Tree of Life also displays an interaction of the dualistic aspects of the universe in motion. Earlier the Sephiroth were described in their order (1 through 10) upon the tree, which when diagrammed in succession, forms a zig-zag motion across the entirety of the symbol.

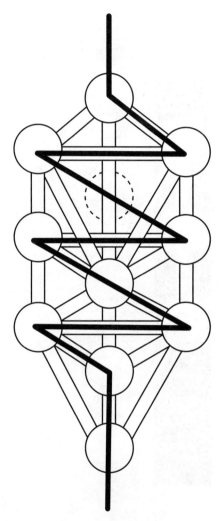

Figure 24: Lightning Flash

This is known as the Lightning Flash, the Descent of Power, or the Flaming Sword in esoteric orders. Following the path of creation, from Kether to Malkuth, from the Unmanifest to the Manifest, we can see that constant interplay between the two poles of duality on the tree. In fact, it is this interplay which creates the mediating presence of the Middle Pillar, which then results in the establishment of corporeality. A further study on the role of these pillars is necessary in order to understand the dialectic of the Pillars of Manifestation.

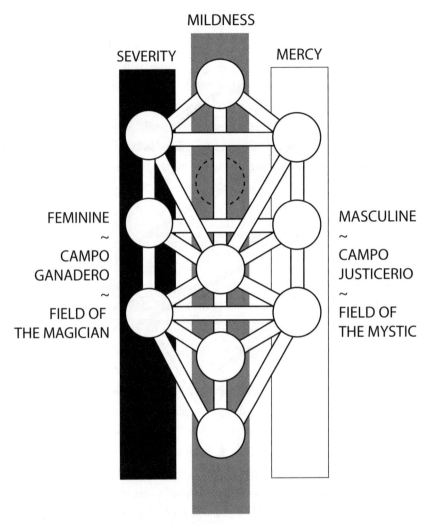

CAMPO MEDIO—The Balance of Power

Figure 25: The Pillars and Campos

• *Pillar of Severity:* Representing the Sephiroth on the left side of the Tree of Life, this pillar signifies the negative pole of universal interaction. It is the feminine side, passive, where the expression of Form is conceptualized into being.

- *Pillar of Mercy:* Representing the Sephiroth on the right side of the Tree of Life, this pillar signifies the positive pole of universal interaction. It is the masculine side, active, where the expression of Force is conceptualized into being.

- *Pillar of Mildness:* Representing the Sephiroth in the middle of the Tree of Life, this pillar signifies the equilibrium of the two poles. It is both feminine and masculine and neither at the same time. It is where the expression of consciousness is conceptualized into being.

Force and Form can correlate with the positive and negative poles, respectively. This presents to us a reflection on how interaction with spirit takes place. When descending the tree, all action is first derived in Force before manifesting into Form; therefore, spirit always begins with the idea of something before it becomes something. Conversely, when ascending the tree, all action begins with Form before moving into the thing behind the Form: Force. The universe constantly operates under this paradigm, like a water on seashore ebbing back and forth with the tide, waxing and waning, dancing. This is the cadence of the Sephiroth.

Viewed in this light, it is easy to see the correlations of the curandero mesa in accordance with the three campos. In fact, one could make an exact mapping of the three Pillars of Manifestation with the three campos and would be able to almost flawlessly replicate the operative processes among each triptych.

That these pillars or campos are divided into masculine and feminine attributes should not be taken literally. As clarified before, these are merely symbols to rationalize the positive and negative characteristics of the cosmos. This concept is among one of the toughest for aspiring esotercists to accept, but it also one of the most important to incorporate. Esoteric training is, in theory and practice, the act of making this dual consciousness a single reality. Dion Fortune elucidates that the positive and negative polarities of the Tree exist to create equilibrium:

> It is obvious that nothing can be evolved, unfolded, which was not previously involved, infolded. The actual course of evolution follows the track of the Lightning Flash or Flaming Sword, from Kether to Malkuth in the order of development of the Sephiroth previously described; but consciousness descends plane by plane, and only begins to manifest when the polarising Sephiroth are in equilibrium; therefore the modes of consciousness are assigned to the Equilibrating Sephiroth upon the

Middle Pillar, but the magical powers are assigned to the opposing Sephiroth, each at the end of the beam of the balance of the pairs of opposites.[66]

This Middle Way is indeed the modus operandi of shamanic Qabalah and distinguishes the prime differentiation between magic and mysticism. The Great Work can only be completed when the polarizing aspects of consciousness are in equilibrium, harmonized like San Cipriano to highlight the beneficial factors of both the left- and right-hand path.

---

66. Fortune, *Mystical Qabalah*, 52.

8

SACRED ANARCHY

It is of the nature of idea to be communicated: written, spoken, done. The idea is like grass. It craves light, likes crowds, thrives on crossbreeding, grows better for being stepped on.

—URSULA K. LE GUIN, *THE DISPOSESSED*

Anarchy.

The word itself conjures a multitude of feelings and imagery. Masked looters ravaging the streets, battling the police with Molotov cocktails. Vigilantes who have taken the rule of law into their own hands. Crumbling infrastructure. It invokes the most terrifying *Mad Max* future, a landscape of lifeless chaos, debauchery, and lawlessness. Our culture is obsessed with the idea of dystopia (a perversion of the perfect society) as evidenced through major hits that audiences can't get enough of, such as *The Hunger Games*, the Divergent series, or even *The Walking Dead*. We are afraid of it yet relish its excitement at the same time. Anarchy, in this day and age, has become synonymous with disorder.

But we have been led astray. This is not, nor has it ever been, the true essence of sociopolitical anarchism.

I believe that in order for a religious practice to be effective, it must adhere to the principles of a sacred anarchism.

At its base, etymologically, anarchy comes from the word ἄναρχος (*anarkhos*), which simply means to be without a chief or ruler. *An-* means "without"; *-arkhos* is derivative of *archon* and implies a single source, a hierarchy of importance from which the rule of law flows. At its root, anarchy, *anarkhos*, doesn't mean without law; it means without a single authority of law.

In seventeenth-century Europe, the word was used by royalty to demonize those who fomented disorder against the state. Their slander made the term derogatory in order to undermine criticisms toward the monarchies at the time, which were beginning to crumble in their political attempts to hold fast to an absolutist sovereignty over the people.

Having been the inspiration for revolutionary thought for centuries, *anarchism* as a term was never popularized until Pierre-Joseph Proudhon—a nineteenth-century French politician and philosopher—spearheaded its use in his 1840 treatise *What Is Property?* Proudhon's assertion was that man has no right to be owner of—and therefore to abuse—land, because that land is a gift provided by the natural world. Property owners were hoarding the surplus, creating monopolies on the fruits of what the earth had to offer to all people. "How can the supplies of Nature, the wealth created by Providence, become private property?" Proudhon asks. "We want to know by what right man has appropriated wealth *which he did not create, and which nature gave to him gratuitously.*" [67]

This sentiment fed wholeheartedly into Proudhon's proclamation as an anarchist. In fact, he considered the ultimate form of an effective government, as many did at that time, to be a republic, though a republic being representative as an anarchist organization. He writes in *Solution of the Social Problem* that "the Republic is a positive anarchy. It is neither liberty subject to order, as in the constitutional monarchy, nor liberty imprisoned *in* order, as the provisional government understands it, but liberty delivered from all its obstacles, superstition, prejudice, sophistry, speculation, and authority; it is reciprocal, not limited, liberty; it is the liberty that is the MOTHER, not the daughter of order." [68]

Liberty delivered from all its obstacles. Anarchism is about a true equality among people and their relationship to the world, where no prejudice, no hierarchy resides. Where order arises out of freedom rather than the other way around.

And so anarchism evolved into being one of the primary proponents of revolution across the world, most specifically rooted in the labor movement. Errico Malatesta, Emma Goldman, Peter Kropotkin, and others are just a small few of many activists and philosophers who sought a social revolution against the capitalist grip on the workforce, where the laborer rarely, if ever, enjoys the fruits of the product of their labor. The German Rudolf Rocker was one of these revolutionaries who helped define anarchism as an economic model for workers to gain control within a capitalist paradigm.

---

67. Pierre-Joseph Prodhoun, *Property Is Theft!: A Pierre-Joseph Proudhon Anthology*, ed. Iain McKay (Oakland, CA: AK Press, 2011), 103.

68. Prodhoun, *Property Is Theft!*, 280.

In his seminal work *Anarcho-Syndicalism*, a treatise on anarchistic industrial unionism, Rocker defines a society of anarchism through the desire of the anarchist: "Anarchists would have a free association of all productive forces based upon co-operative labour, which would have as its sole purpose the satisfying of the necessary requirements of every member of society, and would no longer have in view the special interest of privileged minorities within the social union."[69]

Anarchism would see the fulfillment of each individual's needs as a requisite to their common contribution to the community at large. Again, equality of economy and property is a key element in Rocker's philosophy, much like Proudhon's.

A prime contemporary advocate of anarchism as a sociopolitical movement is the linguist, historian, philosopher, and activist Noam Chomsky, who is one of the most respected intellectuals of our day. Chomsky is quick to note in conversations about anarchism that it is definitely not about chaos at all, but "a highly organized society, just one that's organized democratically from below."[70] Anarchism is not about an absence of order. It implies that the horse must lead the cart, rather than the cart before the horse. A government, the state, cannot govern the people as if it were some lone entity with powers from on high. The people *are* the government; therefore, they govern themselves. Rather than top-down leadership, anarchism promotes bottom-up collaboration.

The anarchist ideal has not always been just a political doctrine. In fact, its ideals have roots in the Greek's philosophy of self-governance, Loa Tsu's Tao Te Ching, and Jesus's Beatitudes, all the way to Rousseau's contributions about natural freedom to the Enlightenment.

In fact, anarchism's sensibility has even inspired modern-day business models of management. Major companies like IBM and the *New York Times* are proponents of bottom-up management styles because of the increase in employee morale and productivity. Research has shown how an anarchistic style of self-initiation in the workplace utilizes the full potential of workers. "In fact," writes Josh Bersin, contributor to *Forbes,* one of the leading business publications in the world, "our research shows that the best companies develop leaders from the bottom up."[71]

---

69. Rudolf Rocker, *Anarcho-Syndicalism: Theory and Practice* (Edinburgh, Scotland: AK Press, 2004), 1.

70. Noam Chomsky, *On Anarchism* (New York: The New Press, 2013), 20.

71. Josh Bersin, "It's Not the CEO, It's the Leadership Strategy That Matters," *Forbes,* July 30, 2012, http://www.forbes.com/sites/joshbersin/2012/07/30/its-not-the-ceo-its-the-leadership-strategy-that-matters/#7e91d7235a3e.

Perhaps the greatest example in literature that portrays a purist vision of anarchism can be found in Ursula K. Le Guin's *The Dispossessed*. The crux of the story inside this science-fiction classic revolves around two planets: Urras and Anarres. Urras is a wholly capitalist planet divided into numerous states that are constantly at war. Anarres, on the other hand, houses a smaller society that ascribes to an anarcho-syndicalist philosophy called "Odonianism," developed by Anarres's anarchist founder Laia Odo. The plot centers on Shevek, a scientist of Anarres who is invited to Urras as part of a research exchange between the two planets (who are usually mutually in opposition) regarding the development of a new theory in physics.

Lacking in action but not intrigue, the book itself is a discussion on the merits of a society based upon communal exchange or enterprise. The reader is threaded through numerous conversations on sociology, economics, science, and even relationships. The overall premise leans toward anarchism as a productive, but not necessarily utopian, means to a stable society. An example of Odo's philosophy shows some of Le Guin's attempts to answer some of the common criticisms of an egalitarian labor society: "A child free from the guilt of ownership and the burden of economic competition will grow up with the will to do what needs doing and the capacity for joy in doing it. It is useless work that darkens the heart. The delight of the nursing mother, of the scholar, of the successful hunter, of the good cook, of the skillful maker, of anyone doing needed work and doing it well—this durable joy is perhaps the deepest source of human affection, and of sociality as a whole." [72]

As you can see, like Rocker's anarcho-syndicalist philosophy, the ability for individuals to expresss themselves through their labor is in accordance with the needs of the community at large.

Reciprocity

Erudite and lucid, Le Guin goes to great lengths in her novel to describe the function of an individual in an Odonian (anarchist) society. Considering her depiction, I have often considered the Quechua shamanic peoples of Andean Peru to have a similar cultural framework. The Quechua are hardy people, living in the cold, harsh highlands of the second-highest mountain range in the world. An agricultural society, the Quechua are noted for likely being the descendants of the Inca from precolonial times.

---

72. Ursula K. Le Guin, *The Dispossessed* (New York: HarperCollins Publishers, 2015), 247.

It would be unfair to depict the Quechua in a strictly anarcho-syndicalist point of view; however, there are elements within their way of life that bear strong correlations to an anarchist approach to living.

The Quechua are known most for their farming and llama herding. While their bulk crop is potatoes (three thousand varieties of potato can be found across Peru, Bolivia, Ecuador, and Chile), they are also adept at growing coca, quinoa, and corn, among others. The conditions of the Andean environment are harsh; over the centuries, the Quechua have learned to adapt and build a community of interaction that benefits the whole rather than the individual. Catherine J. Allen, professor emeritus of anthropology and international affairs at George Washington University, has devoted much of her research to studying the Quechua people. Her book *The Hold Life Has* presents a comprehensive identity of the Quechua culture. She writes, "The essence of social relations [for the Quechua]...is to be found in the give-and-take of reciprocal relationships of mutual aid. Andean people are strongly conscious of reciprocity in its various manifestations, and the Quechua language contains a fairly elaborate vocabulary referring to modes of exchanging labor and goods. By far the most important modes are *ayni* and *mink'a*.... Life revolves around *ayni*. Nothing is done for free; in *ayni*, every action calls forth an equivalent response."[73]

Ayni is a reciprocal exchange of shared work among the Quechua in order to ensure an equality among their labor system. It provides a framework, a sort of hub, of social understanding. In a way, it could be considered their collective constitution, albeit in a non-written context. As with most concepts in the Quechua culture and language, everything is dual, everything has its opposite.

Symmetrical relationship implies a function of fulfillment among the people. Like Le Guin's Odonian, the Quechua citizen is happy to fulfill their role within the organism of their *ayllu*, or family unit. There is a difference, of course, between the fictional Odonian of Anarres and the Quechua of the Andes: for the Quechua there is integration with the modern world around them. The Andean language is an amalgamation of Quechua and Spanish, and often Quechua citizens will mill throughout the cities to buy or sell goods. Again, it is not a completely anarchist system, but there are connections nonetheless.

There is also a spiritual approach, not just a cultural one, to the principle of ayni. Author Joan Parisi Wilcox has written many accounts of her interactions and training with

---

73. Catherine J. Allen, *The Hold Life Has: Coca and Cultural Identity in an Andean Community,* 2nd ed. (Washington, DC: Smithsonian Books, 2002), 72.

the Quechua *paqos* (priest healers). She pinpoints ayni as one of the seminal components of Andean spirituality, essential to connecting with the unseen forces of the world:

> Ayni is the seminal operative principle of behavior and of being in the Andes. In the social structure, ayni expresses itself as a system of communal, shared labor, where, for example, farmers help work each other's fields. Ayni also is a guiding moral principle, similar to the Christian concept "do unto others as you would have them do unto you." In this light, ayni operates within a moral and personal code of conduct. Within the indigenous spiritual cosmology, however, ayni takes on an even greater significance, for it is an implicate, creative principle of the natural world.[74]

Ayni is a way of life. It is something to be lived as one's core philosophy and practice. While I was in Peru, my interactions with the local Quechua populace revealed to me that sacred reciprocity is—above all else—an agreement, a contract between the practitioner and the unseen. Before ever engaging in a ceremonial process—indeed before even treading into certain areas of the wild—the Andean peoples would be sure to honor the spirits of that land first and foremost. Wilcox says, "Andeans owe the very conditions of their lives [to the spirits and the earth]. Therefore, every action they undertake is necessarily an act of ayni, or reciprocity, with Pachamama. Before any food is eaten or liquid is drunk, a portion is offered to the Earth Mother."[75] As such, sacred reciprocity is the building of a relationship between oneself and the unseen. It is actually *the* language that allows one to interact with forces and energies that are otherwise unavailable to the normal human faculties of communication.

My own teacher don Oscar Miro-Quesada was taught by the esteemed paqo don Benito Corihuaman of Wasao. In his own autobiographical account, don Oscar relays a message he received from the unseen realms that was a direct proclamation regarding the style of shamanic sacred relationship. At one of the lowest points in his life, during his own dark night of the soul, don Oscar received this dictum: "This isn't about being delivered by some enlightened being. This is about promising to do something. Get on your knees and pray."[76]

Compare this to Le Guin's Odonian ideology on relationship, most specifically dissecting the practice of monogamous relationships. To an Odonian, marriage was a joint feder-

---

74. Wilcox, *Masters of the Living Energy*, 26–27.

75. Wilcox, *Masters of the Living Energy*, 27

76. Glass-Coffin and Miro-Quesada, *Lessons in Courage*, 50.

ation between two individuals. If it worked, it worked; if it didn't, each individual had the freedom to leave the partnership. The idea was based on the premise that one's freedom to be able to choose whether or not to leave the partnership actually made the partnership meaningful. Law in marriage did not a marriage make, as that would defy the validity of the vows made and the complexities inherent in relationship. Freedom is essential in any form of commitment in order to bring meaning to the commitment.

A spiritual walk, whether it be mystical or magical, must always be questioned as to the effectiveness of what it is trying to achieve. Why have a spiritual walk at all? Is it in trying to find a connection with God, the universe? It is in finding peace? Is it in trying to change something about yourself, or your environment?

Odo's promise, as outlined by Ursula K. Le Guin and referenced by Oscar Miro-Quesada, regards establishing a purpose, a function for one's work, whether it be spiritual, physical, etc. And through that pledge can be found the freedom within the individual soul that we all seem to seek in one form or another. It is through that promise that our human purpose is formed.

It is especially true of the mystic path, in which the primary focus is interacting with various intelligences within the unseen, that sacred relationship is so important. A relationship of mutual cooperation, of ayni, often populates the analogues of the soul realm.

Thus, Miro-Quesada elucidates the shamanic commitment that a connection with the sacred is indeed a relationship fostered by mutual benefit: "To harness the spiritual power of creation, as did our ancestral peoples, we need to return to a deep understanding of how sacred relationship works.... By doing earth-healing rites and ceremonies, we reestablish a conscious, awakened, sacred relationship with the Earth. This encourages all the conscious beings who inhabit our beloved *Pachamama* to feel more comfortable revealing themselves to nurture and support us. This is the nature of *ayni*." [77]

So it is understood why the shamanic system works so well within the Western esoteric context. As mentioned before, all the ideas explored during pathworking are symbols, *simulacra*. These simulacra—whether they be pictures, magical glyphs, Hebrew letters, Quechua words, or mantras—each have a force behind them, a living energy field (in Quechua, *kawsaypacha*), if you will. These images, in a sense, are alive, not static mechanical forces. When a magical image is built in the mind's eye—within our own consciousness—connected to an archetype in the collective consciousness in humanity, a catalyst of power

---

77. Glass-Coffin and Miro-Quesada, *Lessons in Courage*, 61.

ignites within the human soul. This power becomes a living thing to harness and utilize for the betterment of one's own life and the lives of others.

As these magical images become living things within the consciousness of the individual, they are then dependent on a rapport. A relationship must be fostered and nurtured, just like any other thing one might be in relationship with: a friend, a partner, a spouse. This rapport builds up skill. Just as with any skill, if one does not practice, if one does not dedicate oneself to the mastering of that skill, the inspiration or drive is lost. The magical images will then lose their power and effectiveness.

Managing the relationship of these magical energies is the prime modus operandi of the adept magician or mystic, who in effect should also be a proficient psychonaut.

Psychonautica

To be a psychonaut means to be a navigator of the soul.

According to Jan Blom's *A Dictionary of Hallucinations*, "The term psychonaut comes from the Greek words *psuchè* (life breath, spirit, soul, mind) and *nautès* (sailor, navigator). It translates as 'sailor of the mind' or 'navigator of the psyche.'" The term *psychonautics* "is used to denote the exploration of the psyche by means of techniques such as meditation, prayer, lucid dreaming, brainwave entrainment, sensory deprivation, and the use of hallucinogens or entheogens."[78]

This is exactly what the Great Work is, actually: sailing and navigating the mysteries of the mind and of the soul itself. The soul is both inner and outer, residing both within and without the universe and man. It is neither and both at the same time. It is paradox.

That all sounds rather nebulous, doesn't it? For centuries philosophers have sought to answer what *exactly* is the soul? This is a question, I think, that can never be truly answered; nor should it ever be, perhaps. Soul is the Great Mystery itself, with which we are always at play.

Much growth has been made in pinpointing a definition for *soul* throughout the centuries, specifically by the Rosicrucian movement. Known as the predecessor to the Golden Dawn and other modern mystical orders, Rosicrucianism dates back to 1378 with the birth of Christian Rosenkreuz ("Rose Cross"), who is cited as being the author of the first published Rosicrucian documents. Built upon a library of alchemical symbolism from Hermeticism, Christianity, and Qabalah, the Rosicrucian paradigm brought a scientific

---

78. Jan Dirk Blom, *A Dictionary of Hallucinations* (New York: Springer Science+Business Media, 2010), 434.

methodology to spiritual practice. Rosicrucian orders have evolved over time, much like and with many ties to the Masonic fraternities.

In 1930 the Supreme Grand Lodge of the Ancient and Mystical Order Rosæ Crucis (AMORC) published a manuscript by the Imperator of the Rosicrucian Order of North and South America, Dr. H. Spencer Lewis, called *Mansions of the Soul: The Cosmic Conception*. Although the book has more specifically to do with the Rosicrucian theory of reincarnation, it provides a very concise definition of the soul for our use:

> It is to the effect that the real part of man is the infinite, Divine, or intangible consciousness and essence which constitutes the inner self. For this inner self many names have been invented and universally adopted at various times. The most general of these names is that of *soul*, and we find it associated with another word, which means the *breath*; and for many ages the inner self of man was associated with the idea of breathing an invisible essence which constituted the spiritual nature of man. A second general principle most universally and consistently adopted was the idea that this soul of man is a distinct entity, or a spiritual something, that is immortal, and at times separates from the physical body. [79]

We see here that a description of soul is not so easy to pin down. Dr. Lewis gives us two distinct ideas to work with; maybe soul is both and neither at the same time. Probably one of the most underrated occult scholars of our current era, Patrick Harpur, wrote a comprehensive treatise of supernatural phenomena in his work *Daimonic Reality: A Field Guide to the Otherworld*. In the tradition of Jacques Vallee and Carl Jung, Harpur draws upon and alludes to the dual nature of soul. He suggests there is indeed a personal soul, but that it is incomplete to talk about soul without referring to the World Soul, *Anima Mundi*. Soul is both individual and collective. Harpur explains, "Soul is not a 'thing' in itself, not a substance (this is why I do not call it *the* soul); rather, it is the imaginative possibility in our natures, a set of *perspectives*. Soul, that is, imagines; and the images it imagines are daimons that not only manifest as personifications, but also—invisibly—as perspectives. They are the many eyes that see through our eyes. We call the particular perspective of our daimon

---

79. H. Spencer Lewis, *Mansions of the Soul: The Cosmic Conception* (San Jose, CA: Supreme Grand Lodge of AMORC, 1954), 39–40.

'the world'; but there are as many 'worlds' as there are daimons. Reality is primarily meta-phorical, imaginative, daimonic." [80]

Because we live in a world whose quality of knowledge has suffered in the analogues of quantity, it must be reiterated that a daimon is not a "demon" or "evil spirit." *Daimonic* means the Gnostic-Neoplatonic notion of an entity that is not entirely physical or spirit, not one or the other, but both *and* neither at the same time. As Harpur stated, they are images of soul.

Harpur references Jung's own terminology of individuation, which is essentially initiation, the process of transformation via making the unconscious conscious: "The daimons are archetypal images which, in the process of individuation, conduct us toward the archetypes (gods) themselves. They did not have to convey messages; they were themselves the message." [81] They are intermediaries between the worlds of gods and men.

Kamasqa

Nonetheless, navigating the soul can be an abstract task for some. It's a lot like looking at a painting from Mondrian, Rothko, Kandinsky, or even Matisse without any knowledge of an artist's philosophy or intentions … The surface level appears nebulous and even simplistic; the brain doesn't know what to do with the information.

This is one reason why learning the symbology of the unseen, the markers that point the way along the road, is important. Also, understanding the emanations of creation assists, at an unconscious level, the initiate with sailing the deep waters of soul. In Peruvian shamanism there is a concept—or an essence, if you will—called *Kamasqa*. Through her years in training with the Quechua paqos, Joan Parisi Wilcox portrays Kamasqa as a derivative of the word *Kamaq*, which is "the supreme creative principle in Andean cosmology. *Pachakamaq* is the creator of the world." [82]

She describes Kamasqa as also one who has been called to the sacred path without formal training, one who is the experience of the outpouring of creation, of soul, into the world. Even though he has had formal training, don Oscar Miro-Quesada is one of those whom I have met who is the embodiment of that outpouring. As a Kamasqa curandero and my own teacher, I went to him to uncover the mystery of Kamasqa, to pinpoint an

80. Patrick Harpur, *Daimonic Reality: A Field Guide to the Otherworld* (London: Viking Arkana, 1994), 126.

81. Harpur, *Daimonic Reality*, 38.

82. Wilcox, *Masters of the Living Energy*, 320.

accurate translation of this nebulous Quechua term and its relationship to the goal of the Great Work.

In a personal conversation with me, this was Miro-Quesada's explanation:

> As all power, Kamasqa is both an effluence, an etheric light fluid, as well as a dreaming. It is an active imaginative space. It has a temporal component, and it has a spatial component. It is always creative, just as any river that is born of the melting of the glaciers, which starts as a trickle and then becomes the roaring rivers that feed the ocean. Along its way it creates habitat through life, it creates opportunities, lands to be cultivated and the people to be fed from it. I, personally, as with everything that is good medicine, take the stance of the poet when it comes to my relationship with Kamasqa. I try not to define it too much. I try just to understand that it visits me in different expressions, and every one of the expressions allows me to be more creative as a soul because I am anointed and touched by its flowing through me. It never composes me, it never defines me, but it does inspire me. And it does help dream me into being. And that's how I understand Kamasqa to be. Creative power is a good definition, but there is much more to it.[83]

As the river forms the landscape, so too it seems that Kamasqa, the creative effluence, forms our soul growth along the sacred path. The key to this, as Miro-Quesada points out, is that Kamasqa is "an active imaginative space." Imagination, it seems, is the vital component to tapping into the divine outpouring from the higher realms, the Hanaqpacha, onto the physical plane.

The English poet William Blake once wrote that "Man has no Body distinct from his Soul."[84] Known perhaps as one of the greatest Western poets who ever lived, William Blake was a Romantic. Romanticism was a reaction to the modern destruction of nature and humanity brought on by the Industrial Revolution in the nineteenth century. The Romantic movement emphasized the expression and inspiration of the artist and the individual as not only a rebuke of modernization, but also as a re-engagement with the mysteries of the universe.

---

83. Oscar Miro-Quesada, personal communication with the author, February 2017.

84. William Blake, "The Marriage of Heaven and Hell," in *The Poetical Works of William Blake,* ed. John Sampson (London, New York: Oxford University Press, 1908; electronic reproduction by Bartleby.com, 2011), line 10, http://www.bartleby.com/235/253.html.

Blake was fascinated with the imagination; he saw it as a tool for connection with the Divine. As expressed by one of the phrases upon his engraving *Laocoön*,

The Eternal Body of Man is The Imagination, that is God himself } ‏עשי‎ Jesus we are his
The Divine Body } Members.[85]

Roger Whitson, professor of English at Washington State University and author of *William Blake and the Digital Humanities*, has presented Blake's relationship with the imagination as a means of liberation from his concept of the veil constructed by a celestial being that controls the material world: *Urizen*. Urizen was Blake's own take on the Gnostic concept of the demiurge, an antagonistic deity subordinate to the Supreme God yet who masks itself as God. Whitson expressed to me, "In some ways, Blake did believe that the imagination could help us move past the illusion of Urizen (note the play on words: U-rizen, your reason, horizon, etc.)."[86]

Whitson notes Blake's use of printmaking as a medium for expressing imagination as a means of liberation from Urizen. Blake is well known as a pioneer of the use of image and text working together in a singular context to convey an idea. Whitson then went on to explain Blake's imagery as a developed system that itself induces a form of interactive alchemy: "What's interesting here is that Blake is interested in a complete system, in a complete material practice, in a mode of communication that places all these contraries in a dialectic or dialogue. It doesn't mean that they agree, or that they synthesize, but they are interacting. Soul and body, image and text, materials and ideas, etc. Printing is, for him, a form of transmutation."[87]

Blake was a psychonaut if ever there was one. In his works, he regularly used his imagination as the vehicle for tapping into the fluidic depot of soul, the Kamasqa storehouse that both inspires and requires action upon the material plane. That Blake exposes this "dialectic or dialogue" as the schema of this interaction with soul is significant. Ayni, sacred reciprocity, is a relationship, a dialogue.

---

85. Irene Tayler, "Blake's *Laocoön,*" *Blake/An Illustrated Quarterly* 10, no. 3 (Winter 1976–77): 72–81, http://bq.blakearchive.org/10.3.tayler.

86. Roger Whitson, email correspondence with the author, February 10–February 23, 2017.

87. Roger Whitson, email correspondence with the author, February 10–February 23, 2017.

Anthropologist Catherine Allen writes that "reciprocity is like a pump at the heart of the Andean life," [88] and, likewise, it is most definitely the pump at the heart of shamanic Qabalah. For a mystic, an efficient psychonautic practice must be able to build a rapport with the unseen, create a dialogue. Otherwise, the system breaks down, and instead of an anarchistic aggregation of relationship … you get chaos.

88. Allen, *The Hold Life Has*, 73.

9
PSYCHONAUTICS IN PRACTICE

What we need now are the diaries of explorers. We need many diaries of many explorers so we can begin to get a feeling for the territory.

—TERENCE MCKENNA, *THE ARCHAIC REVIVAL*

In any endeavor, the question must always be asked: What are we doing? Why are we doing it? And are we getting results? If so, what kind? The mystic arts (whether shamanic, Qabalistic, or occult) are indeed an art form, but even the arts require, within the artist, the critical eye of scrutiny and testing that befits the methodology of science.

These inquiries must be considered on an individual level. Notwithstanding, we can collectively rest assured of esotericism's roots in classical philosophy—specifically Plato's legacy—providing an empirical framework for the mystic process. Though scholars disagree on whether or not Platonism provided any actual esoteric application, being primarily intellectual in nature, there are signs that the Neoplatonic tradition does address esoteric practice.

Neoplatonism arose around the third century and persisted for around two hundred years. Inspired by the work of Plato, the Neoplatonists vary in their approach to Plato's philosophy yet usually agree on the idea of a singular creative principle in the universe. Plotinus is generally considered the founder of Neoplatonism, but his student Iamblichus of Syria is worthy of study in the analysis of psychonautics. Iamblichus's contribution to the occultism of the Western Mystery Tradition cannot be understated; his legacy inspired the Roman Emperor Julian to help ease the threat to pagan shrines in the early Christian world, influenced the Renaissance magical operations of Marsilio Ficino, and even contributed to some of the practices used in the earliest Christian sacraments. The correlations to

Qabalah in Iamblichus's work are profound. In remembering the *Ain Soph Aur*—the Veils of Negative Existence—and their turning point from nothingness into the first Sephirah, Kether, and thus the rest of the Sephiroth, regard the following from Iamblichus's *De Mysteriis*: "God produced matter out of the scission of materiality from substantiality, which the Demiurge, receiving as a living substance, fashioned into simple and impassible spheres and organized the last of this into generated and mortal bodies." [89]

Iamblichus is credited most with concretizing the philosophy and practice of Platonic theurgy. Theurgy is different from theology, which is differentiated by prominent Iamblichan scholar Gregory Shaw: "For theology was merely *logos*, a 'discourse about the gods,' and however exalted, it remained a human activity, as did philosophy. Theurgy, on the other hand, was a *theion ergon*, a 'work of the gods' capable of transforming man to a divine status." [90]

In other words, theurgy dealt with rites and sacraments that executed the Great Work itself. To illustrate the underlying approach to theurgy, I would like to return to Usrula K. Le Guin's *The Dispossessed*, specifically the work of the lead protagonist, Shevek. As stated earlier, Shevek is a physicist who is sent to Urras to develop and share the results of his research, what he calls "Simultaneity Theory." Simultaneity Theory revolves around the idea that time is happening all at once, rather than within a sequence of past, present, and future. During a conversation in the novel, Shevek says,

Within the strict terms of Simultaneity Theory, succession is not considered as a physically objective phenomenon, but as a subjective one.... We think that time 'passes,' flows past us, but what if it is we who move forward, from past to future, always discovering the new? It would be a little like reading a book, you see. The book is all there, all at once, between its covers. But if you want to read the story and understand it, you must begin with the first page, and go forward, always in order. So the universe would be a very great book, and we would be very small readers.[91]

89. Iamblichus, *Iamblichus: The Platonic Commentaries,* trans. John Dillon (Leiden, Netherlands: E. J. Brill, 1973), 141.

90. Gregory Shaw, *Theurgy and the Soul: The Neoplatonism of Iamblichus* (Kettering, OH: Angelico Press, 2014), 5.

91. Le Guin, *The Dispossessed*, 221–22.

Perhaps without knowing it, Le Guin hearkens to the sympathies of tapping into Ka-masqa and the imaginative space in order to grasp the immensity of scope contained in Simultaneity Theory. Regarding the development of his theory, Shevek muses, "It is only in consciousness, it seems, that we experience time at all.... In a dream there is no time, and succession is all changed about, and cause and effect are all mixed together. In myth and legend there is no time." [92]

Neoplatonist philosopher Iamblichus, it just so happens, provides a similar take on the sequence of time and its interplay with consciousness: "Although the cosmos is eternally in being the exigencies of discourse separate the creation from the creator and bring into existence in a time sequence things which are established simultaneously." [93]

How convenient it is that Le Guin introduces in her treatise on anarchism a quantum theory—bordering on mystical illumination—that has to do with time or the lack thereof within human consciousness. Given Le Guin's level of sophistication as an author, we can only assume the overlap of the two themes was intentional. The correlations to Iamblichus's time-space universal framework coming into sequence "simultaneously" cannot be overlooked. So what then can we make of the sacred anarchism she offers in the initiatory revelations of the scientist Shevek? Why the focus on time and its lack of sequence in regard to psychonauticism, specifically within a shamanic Qabalah?

Iamblichan scholar Gregory Shaw, in providing a distinct rationale of theurgic practice, offers an intriguing interpretation:

Thus, although in the *Timaeus* Plato describes creation as a sequence of events, the work of the Demiurge was simultaneous. For Iamblichus this meant that the cosmogony did not take place in a chronological past but always present in *illo tempore*, and was therefore always accessible by means of theurgic ritual. The chronology of the *Timaeus* simply portrayed ontological grades of being simultaneously present in the corporeal world. The separation of corporeality from its principles was an impossibility that could occur only in abstraction, not in actuality. In other words, at the "moment" the Demiurge exists the entire corporeal world exists, and in every sense. There was no spatial or temporal separation between the Forms and their sensible expression.[94]

92. Le Guin, *The Dispossessed*, 222.
93. Shaw, *Theurgy and the Soul*, 30.
94. Shaw, *Theurgy and the Soul*, 39; underlining added.

The purpose then of theurgy is to relive the creative act—the *Kamasqa* principle—within a ritual context. The Tree of Life is itself a map of creation, and walking the Sephiroth becomes the very act of walking the sequence of creation. As a composite symbol, the Tree of Life displays that sequence within a single, simultaneous cosmos.

Pathworking

There are as many ways to be a psychonaut in the cosmos as there are human beings on the planet. Each person is equipped to be the prime expert in their own psychonautica. As an ages-old shamanic tradition, psychonautics is as varied a methodology as there are cultures around the world, each approach with its own individual flavors as information gets passed on, retried, tested, and refined over time.

The great thing about the Tree of Life is that it is not only a symbol but also a composite one that can carry within it an innumerable amount of images from almost any tradition across the planet. It can place these magical images into categories that can then interact through relationships via the paths between the Sephiroth. Psychically and astrally exploring the symbol-systems on the Tree of Life is most generally referred to as *pathworking*.

There is no better way to define pathworking than through the living maestra of pathworking herself, Dolores Ashcroft-Nowicki. In *Highways of the Mind,* she writes,

> A pathworking is a journey between this side of the mental worlds and the other side. One of the most exciting journeys mankind can take because it offers a path, a map through the landscapes of the mind, landscapes that are as yet barely explored and offer one of the last great frontiers. They are Doorways between the known and the physical and the unknown and the non-corporeal. They accomplish their work through the medium of the creative imagination … the seed from which everything made and produced by mankind has sprung. They can and do cause actual physical effects in the everyday world in which we live, which is one of the reasons why they have been held in secret for so long.[95]

Pathworking, in the context of Western esotericism, is the process of journeying with the imagination through the various paths and Sephiroth of the Tree of Life. If the paths are the roads, the Sephiroth are the destinations, and the symbols upon each are the mark-

---

95. Dolores Ashcroft-Nowicki, *Highways of the Mind: The Art and History of Pathworking* (Sechelt, BC, Canada: Twin Eagles Publishing, 2010), 19–20.

ings and road signs pointing the way, allowing passage, and keeping you on the right trail. It is easy to get lost in the imagination. Just because one is able to induce visuals within the mind does not mean one is pathworking. The symbols are very important. One should imagine that the pathways on the Tree of Life are covered in a fog at night, and the symbols are light posts keeping you from veering off into the ditch, your own altar the headlight of your vehicle paving a beam of illumination ahead.

This is why it is very important to follow a ritual process of some sort. These ceremonies have been designed to facilitate an efficient use of these symbols and motions within the subconscious, opening the appropriate doorways of access to the intelligences associated with the tree and its machinations. As our master teacher Dion Fortune says, "It is well known to mystics that if a man meditates upon a symbol around which certain ideas have been associated by past meditation, he will obtain access, to those ideas, even if the glyph has never been elucidated to him by those who have received the oral tradition 'by mouth to ear.'" [96]

Furthermore, these ceremonies have evolved. As evolution progresses, the dross burns away, what no longer works finds its place in obscurity, and the new, more effective methods grow into pristine channels of reception. Dion Fortune herself was no slave to tradition for tradition's sake, especially if it stymied the evolution of a system.

When I was majoring in studio art for my undergraduate degree, the professors expressed time and again that, for now, learn the basics, learn the rules, learn from the masters that came before. Then, when the foundation is set, take off from there, be creative. Take what they did and deconstruct it, bend it to your own will, make it work for you. In essence, experiment. But you can only do that by truly learning the system first. My instructors could spot from a mile away someone who built something new from a foundation of aesthetics and technique, and someone who was just randomly trying to be abstract: there was no substance to the work of those who didn't take the time or energy to school themselves in the masters of old first.

The following pages will provide some sample ritual protocol to follow in order to engage in a pathworking on the Tree of Life. However, your journey is your own, and I cannot define it for you. Ceremonially, you must find what works and what doesn't. But, once you do discover your niche, stick to it, take it seriously, and become as expert as you can at it. It is only through expertise that true results come. So goes the common adage, practice makes perfect.

---

96. Fortune, *Mystical Qabalah*, 6.

Sacred Space

First, create a space in which to perform your work. Ideally, you will want a lodge space that is private and in which you can easily close away the outside world. However, because the modern world doesn't always afford us all with such opportunities, at least carve out for yourself a space within your home: a corner, a cleaned-out closet space, and so on. You need a place that is dedicated solely to the Work itself. This amps up the power of your pathworking and also provides a focal point of concentration that is required for an effective theurgy. There needs to be a clear delineation of the outside world and the inner one.

Add to this sacred space an altar of some sort. I, of course, have recommended the use of a Pachakuti mesa in this book, but you must choose whatever vehicle of ritualistic paradigm works for you, whether Golden Dawn, Wiccan, Lakota, and so on. Whatever altar system you have in place, study it, and study it thoroughly. Make it your life's work. Working an altar is not a trifle matter. It requires attention, love, and care. Immersing yourself in the mythology of the tradition you are practicing is essential, as it adds to the depth of the pathworking experience.

Ideally, in your study and expertise, you will need to immerse yourself in the tradition or lineage of that altar set. Learn how to "turn on" and "turn off" the altar as you would a computer. Learn how to operate it effectively, how to provide the commensurate offerings that will feed its etheric nutritive organism. In the Pachakuti Mesa Tradition, we burn incense like *palo santo* or copal or use scented waters like *agua de florida* to feed the ceremonial grounds. This starts the dialogue, the discourse with the unseen; your altar is the interface, just as the web page you may look at on the internet is the user interface for the unseen code behind the application. Regardless of the altar set in use, incorporating the elemental matrix is vital. From there, it is recommended to carry over certain ritual practices from the Western Mystery Tradition in order to provide the core curriculum of a viable pathworking in the Qabalah Tree of Life.

The Qabalistic Cross

After opening the space, you will want to begin the practice of rituals designed to prepare you for journeywork upon the tree. One specific ritual is typically what any practicing Qabalist uses after opening the ritual space. It is called the Qabalastic Cross. Israel Regardie best describes the purpose of the Qabalistic Cross meditation in *The Middle Pillar*: "The Qabalistic Cross … indicates [an] awareness of other levels of consciousness, and the necessity of bringing them into operation within the human psyche. Not only so, but it recognizes that these newly awakened levels of power and consciousness may be deeply disturbing to the novice who attempts this voyage of discovery. Therefore, what is essential is that not only should they be awakened, but that they should be recognized and equilibrated in a balanced disposition." [97]

One does this by ritualistically and imaginally simulating the coniunctio upon the body, calling forth the balance of the forces of the cosmos from the unconscious. The ritual motions imitate the motion of the cross much like in Roman Catholic ceremonies. When intoning the ritual phrases in the following rituals, it is important to focus more on the vibration than the notes, as in the mesa opening described earlier. The vibration is typically low, with less of a focus on volume than the resonance being generated within the physical body. The usual Western Mystery Tradition paradigm of the Qabalistic Cross goes thus:

1. With your right finger (or a ritual wand) touch your forehead, imagining a white glow of light emanating into your forehead area, and intone, "*Atoh*" (meaning "Thou art").

2. Bring the finger down, drawing an imaginary line of white laser-like light, and touch the breast, intoning, "Malkuth."

3. Now bring the finger up to your right shoulder, imagining a white glow of light emanating into your shoulder area, and intone, "*Ve-Gedulah*" (meaning "glory," another name for the Sephirah Chesed).

4. Bring the finger across your body, again drawing an imaginary line of white laser-like light, and touch your left shoulder imagining a white glow of light emanating into your shoulder area, and intone, "*Ve-Geburah*" (meaning "power").

5. Imagining the laser-like cross of light you have just created over and throughout your body, clasp your hands in a prayer-like fashion over your heart, and intone, "*Le Olahm*, amen" (meaning "forever, so be it").

Those with a Christian upbringing will recognize the doxology—sometimes added at the end of the Lord's Prayer—embedded throughout the intonations of this ritual: "For thine is the kingdom, the power, and the glory, forever and ever. Amen." Whether Christian or not, it is a fine prayer or mantra to emulate the Hermetic axiom "as above (for thine), so below (is the kingdom)." It represents the two Pillars of Manifestation—Chesed

---

97. Israel Regardie, *The Middle Pillar: The Balance Between Mind and Magic,* ed. Chic Cicero and Sandra Tabatha Cicero (St. Paul, MN: Llewellyn Publications, 2000), 50.

and Geburah, masculine and feminine, glory and power—within one's physical form as well.

The Qabalistic Cross can be, more so than any other ritual, one of the most important tools one can use in the process of initiation. It can be utilized, adapted, and meditated upon for lifetimes. So, it is important to find a use for the Qabalistic Cross in such a way that it works and makes sense to you.

Chic and Sandra Tabatha Cicero, adepts of the Golden Dawn Tradition, have created many additions to Israel Regardie's work and offer a Native North American shamanic version of the Qabalistic Cross.[98] The intonations are as follows, with added modifications of my own. A prime addition is that the second step is completed at the stomach. The spiritual stomach is a major energetic center in the body used in shamanic cultures around the world. The Native North American Qabalistic Cross is as follows:

1. With your right finger (or a ritual wand) touch your forehead, imagining a white glow of light emanating into your forehead area, and intone, *"Wakan Tanka"* (Great Spirit, Creator of the Lakota).
2. Bring the finger down, drawing an imaginary line of white laser-like light, and touch the stomach, intoning, *"Michabo"* (Great Hare Trickster god of the Algonquin).
3. Now bring the finger up to your right shoulder, imagining a white glow of light emanating into your shoulder area, and intone, *"Ioskeha"* (human benefactor god of the Iroquis and Huron).
4. Bring the finger across your body, again drawing an imaginary line of white laser-like light, and touch your left shoulder, imagining a white glow of light emanating into your shoulder area, and intone, *"Whope"* (goddess of whom the Lakota White Buffalo Calf Woman is a manifestation).
5. Imagining the laser-like cross of light you have just created over and throughout your body, clasp your hands in a prayer-like fashion over your heart, and intone, *"Aho mitakuye oyasin"* (meaning "All are related, so be it" in Lakota).

In terms of the Pachakuti Mesa Tradition, I have developed a version of the Qabalistic Cross that incorporates the directions and qualities of the mesa. As don Oscar teaches, each direction not only contains an elemental and tutelary as well as healing attributes, they also provide standards of virtue by which to uphold one's character and actions.

---

98. Regardie, *Middle Pillar*, 204.

These virtues provide a template for living one's life in alignment with goals of the Great Work, and are attributed to the mesa thus:

- *Pachamama (South—Earth): Llankay* (pronounced YAHNG-kai), which means hard work, right action, and pragmatic industriousness.
- *Mamakilla (West—Water): Munay* (pronounced MOON-ai), which means compassion and unconditional love.
- *Wiracocha (North—Spirit): Yuyay* (pronounced YOO-yai), which means a nonembodied understanding, a Remembering of who we really are as spiritual beings.
- *Intitayta (East—Fire): Yachay* (pronounced YAH-chai), which means wisdom, knowledge, and mindfulness.
- *K'yuchi (Center—Aether): Huñuy* (pronounced HOO-nooee), which means to join, to unite or reunite, to bring together in harmony.

Taken together, if we were to follow the spiraling of the mesa from south to center, the words themselves form into a sentence that is itself a mantra to be taken into meditative consideration:

Llankay, munay, yuyay, yachay, huñuy.

Bringing these concepts together in English, we have this mantra:

Right action, borne of compassionate spiritual wisdom, unites.

Pulling these attributes into the Qabalistic Cross not only invokes the power of these virtues, but, when aligned accordingly, it also replicates the power of the mesa onto one's very own body. The following steps are considered the Qabalistic Cross of the Pachakuti Mesa Tradition:

1. With your right finger (or a ritual wand) touch your forehead, imagining a white glow of light emanating into your forehead area, and intone, "Yuyay."
2. Bring the finger down, drawing an imaginary line of white laser-like light, and touch the stomach, intoning, "Llankay."

3. Now bring the finger up to your right shoulder, imagining a white glow of light emanating into your shoulder area, and intone, "Yachay."

4. Bring the finger across your body, again drawing an imaginary line of white laser-like light, and touch your left shoulder, imagining a white glow of light emanating into your shoulder area, and intone, "Munay."

5. Imagining the laser-like cross of light you have just created over and throughout your body, clasp your hands in a prayer-like fashion over your heart, and intone, "Huñuy."

As I stated earlier, the function of initiation is to shepherd one into a process of labor. By simulating the virtue of llankay into our stomachs, the area in our bodies most industrious in breaking down what is no longer needed, we make way for the other virtues to manifest within our form.

Figure 26: The Qabalistic Cross for the Pachakuti Mesa Tradition

The LBRP

Although I will not provide as thorough a study for it as for the Qabalistic Cross, the Lesser Banishing Ritual of the Pentagram (LBRP) is nothing to ignore in the slightest. Together with the Qabalistic Cross, it is one of the most basic and preliminary of magical techniques taught in the mystery schools. Donald Michael Kraig, the renowned occultist who authored the best-selling *Modern Magick*, has said, "I cannot overstress the importance of the LBRP. Becoming proficient in Magick is a precarious task, and the LBRP is the rather tiny support. If you are not proficient at the LBRP, the entire system can fall down around you. This is why the LBRP is taught right at the beginning. In fact, other than initiation rituals, it was the only ritual given out to members of the Golden Dawn until they entered the Inner Order. This would take over one year of practice." [99]

Because this book is focused on mysticism and not magic, more focus is devoted to the Qabalistic Cross ritual. However, even though the LBRP leans more toward the magical territory, it is an important one to integrate into your practice. There are many reasons to do this ritual, chief among them being to widen your scope of the celestial presence in preparation for theurgic pathworking. It is also designed to remove (or banish) any influences from the ritual space that could be dangerous or undesired. This is in actuality what the pentagram is for. Although it has been bastardized by popular culture as a symbol of evil or witchcraft, the pentagram in the Western Mystery Tradition serves as a vital tool for protection. The pentagram relates wholly to Geburah, the fifth Sephirah on the Tree of Life, as the pentagram is a symbol for banishing unwanted forces.

The LBRP seals your ceremonial space in preparation for travelling the Tree of Life, ensuring that your sacred intentions remain clean and clear. It acts as a filter, removing any dross that may want to make its way into your ritual. It should be followed thus:

1. After the Qabalistic Cross ritual, ensure you are facing east. Extend your right hand and with your index finger trace a five-pointed star into the air, the line manifesting as a white or blue beam of laser-like light. Start with the lower left point, going to the top, then down to the lower right point, up to the upper left point, over to the upper right, and completing the pentagram by tracing it back down to the lower left point. With the pentagram complete, touch the center of the pentagram you have created in the air, establishing a white point of light in the center. Intone the God name for the east: "YHVH," *Yod-Heh-Vav-Heh.*

2. Then turn to face the south. Complete the tracing of the pentagram the same way as before. Then touch the center of the pentagram you have created in the air, establishing a white point of light in the center. Intone the God name for the south: "ADNI" (ah-DOH-nai).

3. Turn to face the west. Complete the tracing of the pentagram the same way as before. Then touch the center of the pentagram you have created in the air, establishing a

99. Donald Michael Kraig, *Modern Magick: Eleven Lessons in the High Magickal Arts,* 2nd ed. (St. Paul, MN: Llewellyn Publications, 1988), 165–66.

white point of light in the center. Intone the God name for the west: "AHIH" (eh-HEH-yeh).

4. Turn to face the north. Complete the tracing of the pentagram the same way as before. Then touch the center of the pentagram you have created in the air, establishing a white point of light in the center. Intone the God name for the north: "AGLA" (eh-GAH-lah).

5. Return to face the east, holding your arms and hands out horizontally, extending to your left and right. And state clearly, visualizing the pentagrams you have created surrounding you, alive and glowing vibrantly, "Before me Raphael (RAH-fai-el), behind me Gabriel (GAHB-ray-el), on my right hand Michael (MIH-chai-el), and on my left hand Auriel (OHR-ree-el), for about me flame the pentagrams, and in the column stands the six-rayed star."

After this, it is conducive to repeat the Qabalistic Cross a final time. There is plenty of scholarship available on the LBRP in occult literature, and I advise you to study it thoroughly and make it a part of your daily practice, along with the Qabalistic Cross.

Now that you have the space created, turned on, and sealed, and the angelic intelligences of each direction called forth, it is time to begin your pathworking on the Tree of Life.

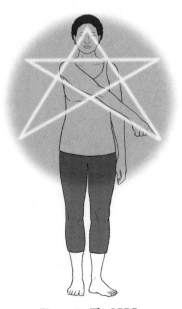

Figure 27: The LBRP

Animal Totems of the Sephiroth

There are various ways to ensure an effective pathworking with the Tree of Life, especially by meditating or journeying with various symbols associated with the Sephiroth and paths, such as the tarot cards, the Hebrew letters, and other provided imagery. Another way can be to deepen one's connection with the natural world … particularly animals. Our animal relatives are great teachers; they are often used in shamanic practice to receive messages from Spirit or assist in healing endeavors. Either in physical reality or in meditative journeywork, animal totems are key allies in interpreting the otherwise misunderstood powers of the universe around us.

The Sephiroth of the Tree of Life are regularly represented in terms of aspects of God or angelic powers. However, this can sometimes usher in a layer of abstraction that is difficult to integrate into the material world. Being our next of kin in consciousness, animal allies provide a relatable translation of perception of the universal powers inherent in the Tree of Life. In the shamanic sense, the late great Ted Andrews wrote, "The image of the animal helps the shaman transcend the normal, waking consciousness so that he or she can more easily attune to the more ethereal realms and beings." [100] An animal totem provides an access point to a specific universal archetype or energy, in much the same way as the other symbols associated with the Sephiroth.

There are many good references for the meaning of various animal totems, but like interpreting a dream, the meaning is mainly subjective to the experience of the receiver. Also, to my knowledge, no one has made animal totem attributions to the Sephiroth of the Tree of Life, so this is my interpretation only. I will provide basic information here and in the individual sections on the Sephiroth in futures chapters, but only you—like for all symbols—can derive its most potent meaning for yourself.

To develop a vital animal totem cosmology for the Sephiroth, we must review the Tree of Life in terms of creation, from top to bottom, Kether to Malkuth. Producing an animal guide for each Sephirah is akin to telling the story of life itself:

1. *Kether—Sponge:* It's surprising to some, but the sea sponge is actually classified as an animal, not a plant. In fact, it is one of the oldest species of animal on the planet, which is why it is the representation of Kether, the fount of all creation. The sponge is our oldest living relative that still resides in the primordial waters of our birth.

---

100. Ted Andrews, *Animal Speak: The Spiritual & Magical Powers of Creatures Great & Small* (St. Paul, MN: Llewellyn Publications, 1993), 8.

2. *Chokmah—Shark:* Still residing within the waters of life, the shark represents the prime masculine concept within the Supernal Triad. The shark is still an ancient being that connects with our archaic origins on the planet.

3. *Binah—Alligator:* A being that lives within the waters but makes its way onto land, the alligator represents the bridging point of Binah as a purveyor of creation into Form. Still, the alligator is an ancient being, like the shark, but with legs to bridge from one state of being into another.

4. *Chesed—Deer:* From the waters, we now evolve onto land for the next three Sephiroth, the Ethical Triad. This is where life really begins to take shape, and the deer represents that elegance and grace that Chesed exudes.

5. *Geburah—Wolf:* The wolf counters the deer, representing those aspects of Binah that organize and break down the aspects of creation that are yearning to become Manifest.

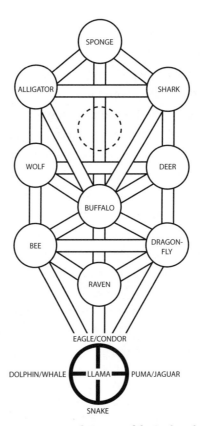

Figure 28: Animal Totems of the Sephiroth

6. *Tiphareth—Buffalo:* A semblance of perfect balance and a reflection of Spirit in many native cultures, the buffalo resides in the center of the Ethical Triad and indeed the entire Tree of Life.

7. *Netzach—Dragonfly:* From land now evolution lifts off the ground, metaphorically, to reach its perfected state of Manifestation in the Astral Triad. The dragonfly perfectly replicates the creative energies of Netzach.

8. *Hod—Bee:* The bee colony is one of the most accomplished organizations in nature, where the bee is a pristine example of the organizing principles of Hod.

9. *Yesod—Raven:* A long-standing symbol of magic and mystery, the raven has often been associated with the powers of the moon, Yesod's prime planetary body.

10. *Malkuth—Snake, Dolphin/Whale, Eagle/Condor, Puma/Jaguar, and Llama:* Even though Malkuth is often associated with the four holy living creatures (explained in chapter 10), the five tutelary animals of the Pachakuti mesa are another shamanic attribution worth considering. Although the animals discussed above corresponded with elements (from water, to ground, and then to air), I propose that these elements are a higher level of archetype; the animal totems in Malkuth are a grounded, tangible depiction of the physical elements here in Manifestation.

This layout, like all the other symbolism in this book, is not meant to be taken literally. The dynamic of the animal totems on the Tree of Life is merely a story, meant to convey a magical image to interact with a certain level of consciousness as a psychonaut. Every animal provides a certain level of medicine for the soul, a teaching that shows us a little bit about our own behaviors and interaction with the world around us. To receive these teachings with open arms is the modus operandi of the shamanic journey.

The Journey

To be truthful, there is actually not much to be written about shamanic journeying itself. If you look, you will find a plethora of books, YouTube videos, workshops, and seminars that will drain thousands of dollars of your money and thousands of minutes of your time, just to teach you all these different steps on "how to journey." But, truth is, journeying is the most simple, primal skill that any conscious being has.

You journey every single day. Frankly, you journey every single moment of every single day, because life itself is journeying, is dreaming. But, to break it down and make it simpler to understand, you journey whenever you dream at night. You journey whenever you are in the car and you zone out for a minute. You journey whenever you are sitting in class or at work and you are thinking of being someplace else. You journey whenever you are in a conversation with someone and you are painting in your mind's eye exactly what they are saying, a visualization of what it is they are describing. One of the more common and creative forms of shamanic journeying that has extended throughout all time is storytelling. Since the inception of fire at human hands back in the Paleolithic or Neopaleolithic era, humans began to gather around the hearth, established community, and devised a way to transmit their dreams. Because before that, they wandered at night, they had to stay quiet, and they had to spend all day foraging, hunting, and gathering. But with the hearth came leisure time. Not only could we cook and eat our food in new and different ways, but the hearth also gave us light and the ability to gather around a central, magical flame to exchange ideas and tell stories of our days, tell stories of our dreams. And we've carried this tradition throughout time.

This tradition has evolved and turned into songs, plays, novels, and nowadays most commonly television and movies. But the novel is an interesting format for journeying because, if you think about it, as once tweeted by British writer Katie Oldham: "Ever realised how fucking surreal reading a book actually is? You stare at marked slices of tree for hours on end, hallucinating vividly." [101] Reading is basically the art of hallucinating, visioning, journeying into the world of words that the writer is painting for you as on a canvas.

The most common format for pathworkings to be transmitted through literary form is through guided meditations or visualizations. And these are wonderful and amazing. Dolores Ashcroft-Nowicki's meditations specifically are the most efficient visualizations for any novice. However, whenever reading a guided visualization, it's almost as if the experience doesn't become one's own, because after guided visualization, Ashcroft-Nowicki, among others, will always recommend to continue the work, to go on your own journeys.

We've all forgotten how to dream for ourselves. Dreaming, in the Aboriginal Australian tradition, is a way of creating one's reality, a way of forming the material world from behind, from the unseen. And we've lost these ways in the modern world. We always start with the material first rather than the concept, and we try to work backward. But we must start any endeavor in the dreaming, in the astral, in the Kamasqa, and formulate the material world from there. Because when we do that, we are essentially simulating the re-

---

101. Katie Oldham (@KatieOldham), Twitter, December 9, 2014, 8:02 a.m., https://twitter.com /KatieOldham/status/542348626711019520.

creation of the universe, over and over and over again. And by that measure, what is created is pure.

So in essence, my practical instruction ends with this:

Sit comfortably. Always have your back straight. Never cross your arms and legs; keep them open, your palms open or resting comfortably in your lap. I personally recommend to not lie down, because it is easy to slip off into sleep, and you want to be in control of the journeying. You want to be able to be in both worlds, this one and the other, and by lying down it is much too easy to give in to sleeping consciousness.

Breathe normally. There are many good breathing methods out there, some that work very efficiently for specific purposes. Just learn to breathe in a normal, comfortable rhythm and to visualize your breath moving in you, through you, throughout your body, as if you can imagine the oxygen flowing to every limb of your body and then the carbon dioxide flowing out with the exhale. This breath and the way that it moves in and out of your body are like the gears and pistons of a great machine, an engine that facilitates your experience.

I recommend spending at least five to ten minutes anytime you sit down for ceremony just to experience your breath. And if other thoughts come in, that's fine … we're not trying for Buddhahood here. Just be patient with yourself, move the thought to the side, and keep your focus on your breath.

And then, working with your altar, use your altar space as your central grounds of operation. Your altar space, your mesa, is your portal into the unseen, your wizard's table in mixing the alchemical formula necessary to do the Great Work. The code for the software of teleportation has already been set within the mesa, which incorporates all the elements of matter.

The simplest of visualizations is to imagine (with just your *pure* imagination, your daydreaming—it doesn't matter if you feel like it is real or not, just *imagine*) a cord of light extending from your crown. Imagine it as if it were an umbilical cord but made out of light. This is traditionally the connector between you and the other realms. It is what mystics throughout the centuries in almost every culture have used to maintain their connection to the material world while traversing other dimensions. And now allow it to extend out to the center of your mesa, your altar, establishing a connection between you and your altar space. Before doing anything and going anywhere, just allow it to be. Just allow that connection to settle between you and your sacred ground.

Then, imagine a simulation of yourself, your body (many traditions call this the astral body or astral form; in the Pachakuti Mesa Tradition it is called the *sombra*), forming inside you and flowing out of your physical body and into the cord of light, almost as if that cord were a tunnel of light you are traveling through. This astral form, this sombra, is nothing more than the reflection of you in the unseen world. Flowing through that tunnel, allow yourself to move into the center of your mesa, into whatever medicine piece resides in the center of the altar space, and as you move through that center piece, imagine that center-piece as a portal that transfers you into the unseen.

As you exit, just imagine pure darkness, just like the darkness that resides behind your eyes. And as the darkness unfolds slowly, you notice that you are in the Temple of Malkuth (described on page 141), which is the gateway into the rest of the Tree of Life. From there your adventures begin. Knowing what you know, allow yourself to go there. Explore. Read other books, gain more knowledge, get training, because it will all help you along the way.

A Final Word

Receive the information as presented and use it as you will, because this narrative is only my personal experience and knowledge base of a shamanic Qabalah. It can only truly belong to me. I could tell you a story, but it will never be your story. You must create your own story and be your own creator. That is how humanity will truly save itself from destruction.

The following section, "Simulacra," is only one of many interpretations of the symbols involved in pathworking and what may lie behind them. They are mysteries, waiting to be unlocked. The Sephiroth and the paths among them act as keys. No one person's interpretation can unlock, or most especially lock, them all. This is your work, the Great Work. You have to exhibit llankay, some industriousness in finding a way unveil the mystery of the tabernacle. That's the whole gig of esotericism, occultism, or shamanism. It's a very individual process in which you do truly own the means of your production. You are the only one who can capitalize on your own efforts, no matter how much you try to sell your ideas or interpretations. The daimonic realm only works at the level of soul, and soul will always find a way to evade detection, banality, and commercialization. Soul is wild, the river of Kamasqa, and will not be tamed by our efforts, no matter what symbols we slap on its visage.

Figure 29: The Journey

Take the information, add it to your brain-space library, and create your own keys. Civil rights activist June Jordan read this reminder, often attributed to a Hopi phrase, from "Poem for South African Women" to the United Nations in 1978: "we are the ones we have been waiting for." [102] In a sense, this is true. One reason humanity seems to feel so lost and chaotic nowadays is because we are lost and chaotic in our minds. The ancients long ago uncovered ways to help us sharpen our wits. I argue that the ancient mysteries must be studied so that we can evolve these archaic symbols and techniques into a new era of simulacra that will support and conduct the consciousness of the next seven generations and beyond.

---

102. June Jordan, "Poem for South African Women," *Directed by Desire: The Collected Poems of June Jordan,* ed. Jan Heller Levi and Sara Miles (Port Townsend, WA: Copper Canyon Press, 2007), line 35.

Part III
SIMULACRA

10

THE ASTRAL FOUNDATION

The next few Sephiroth and paths represent the astral foundation of the universe. Anything manifest actually has its origins here. The astral plane is where the magician does their work in order to effect change in the material world. When the astral plane is mastered, so then is reality. Even though the goal of shamanic Qabalah is to attain a mystic connection with God, rather than trying to manipulate change, one still has to learn of all levels of manifestation in order to gain proper footing in the unseen realms.

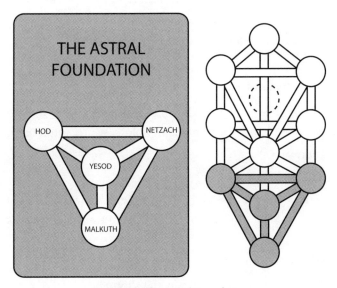

Figure 30: The Astral Foundation

Malkuth: Path 10

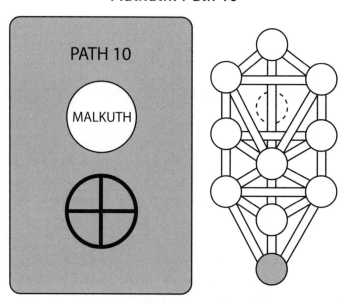

Figure 31: Path 10

God Names: Adonai Malekh, Adonai ha Aretz (Lord of the Earth)

Archangel: Sandalphon

Order of Angels: Ashim, Souls of Fire

Animal Totems: Snake, dolphin / whale, eagle / condor, puma / jaguar, and llama

Colors: Citrine, olive, russet, and black; shamanic colors: white, yellow, red, and black

Virtue: Discrimination

Vices: Avarice, Inertia

Tarot Attributions: Ten of Pentacles, Ten of Cups, Ten of Swords, Ten of Wands, Page / Princess of Pentacles, Page / Princess of Cups, Page / Princess of Swords, Page / Princess of Wands

Spiritual Experience: Vision of the Holy Guardian Angel

Titles: The Gate, the Gate of Death, the Bride, the Virgin

Symbols: Equal-armed cross

Yetziratic Text: "The Tenth Path is the Resplendent Intelligence, because it is exalted above every head, and sits on the throne of Binah (the Intelligence spoke of in the Third Path).

It illuminates the splendour of all lights, and causes a supply of influence to emanate from the Prince of countenances." [103]

So much has already been written about Malkuth in previous chapters, but not even an entire book can cover all there is to know. Many people, while undergoing spiritual work, wish to be floating in the heavens and realms, though they often forget that Malkuth is the only true place where spiritual work begins and ends. As stated earlier, the tenth Sephirah is Malkuth (mahl-KOOT) which means "kingdom" in Hebrew. It resides at the bottom of the tree and is the output of all manifestation, the end result of creation. It is here, this world, this manifest reality all around us in which we participate via our immediate experience of consciousness. It is because of this that Malkuth, unlike any of the other Sephiroth, is broken out into the four primary elements: earth, water, air, and fire. These elements are traditionally depicted in many originating mystical traditions as an equal-armed cross, the symbol of Malkuth.

It is best to try to understand the elements in terms of Malkuth's relationship with the Sephirah Yesod, the astral realm that ensouls the world of matter. Studying the elements in terms of the physical sciences can be helpful, but studying them in terms of the esoteric sciences is a more accurate approach.

Keeping us in contact with the tangible world around us, Malkuth is not typically associated with the spiritual life by one who is not versed in the Mysteries. One that is versed, however, knows that mastering the material world is the essential ingredient in living a true spiritual life. Gareth Knight labels Malkuth as "one of the most important of the whole Tree for it is the Gateway to all further spiritual development, and until the lessons of Malkuth are well and truly learnt, the paths of the higher spheres must be closed to us." [104] I could not agree more. The fact that Malkuth deals with the world of matter does not make it an unspiritual Sephirah—in fact, it may very well be the most spiritual.

Malkuth is the end result of the evolution of all life. It is the product of God's creation; therefore, how could it be unholy, unspiritual? The Gnostics saw matter as evil, and it seems many hold this material existence to be a prison for their spiritual bodies. However, Malkuth is the place in which the soul finds expression. There is, in fact, no other place to be. If we try to escape the hold of matter, we will not be able to achieve the attainment of spiritual mastery. This is the foundation of the Great Work.

103. Westcott, *Sepher Yetzirah*, 2nd ed., 29.
104. Knight, *Qabalistic Symbolism*, vol. 1, 203.

As designated by the *Sepher Yetzirah*, Malkuth (the Bride, the Virgin) has a distinct relationship with Binah (the Supreme Mother). Since Binah is the Sephirah where Form first comes into being in the Supernal sense, and Malkuth is the end result of Form, we can then learn a lot about Malkuth by meditating upon Binah. These are the two feminine designations in the Chemical Marriage, the two *Hehs* of the Tetragrammaton: *Yod-Heh-Vav-Heh*.

However, Malkuth has a more prominent relationship with another Sephirah: Kether, the fount of all creation. MacGrethor Mathers, former head of the Order of the Golden Dawn, has stated that "Kether is the Malkuth of the Unmanifest," and much can be revealed by meditating upon this maxim as a mantra to ingrain in one's consciousness. It carries the same tenet as "as above, so below" and teaches that matter and spirit are the positive and negative within the battery of the cosmos. It is a current, working together in its polarity, to generate what we know of as creation.

Among its titles is the "Gate," and for good reason. Malkuth is the closest Sephirah of the tree to waking consciousness; therefore, it is our entryway into the rest of the tree. It is the base; from here we can then ascend to the higher spheres. It is the gate one must always enter before treading the higher paths and Sephiroth. Hence, ensuring one's altar and sacred space replicates the energetic and symbolic paradigms of Malkuth creates a better gate. As per the example in chapter 5, the Pachakuti mesa makes a fine altar for just such a portal (see figure 13).

True entrance and exit in and out of Malkuth, outside of pathworking, only really comes at the behest of death, which is why it is also referred to as the Gate of Death. As enunciated by Kabbalist Viviane Crowley, "The knowledge of our own existence raises questions about our non-existence. If we can live, we can also cease to live. The created can be uncreated."[105] She continues, "The self-awareness that we acquire at Malkhut remains with us when we shed our bodies with each incarnation. Each death is like a snake shedding its skin. We emerge renewed for another season of our life cycle."[106]

Practical Experience

All Sephiroth are experienced as a temple in which to implement the Great Work; the paths themselves act as experiences between the Sephiroth.

It is good to always begin your experience of pathworking in the Temple of Malkuth and set out on your journeying from there.

---

105. Vivianne Crowley, *A Woman's Kabbalah: Kabbalah for the 21st Century* (London: Thorsons, 2000), 193.

106. Vivianne Crowley, *A Woman's Kabbalah*, 193–94.

The Temple of Malkuth generally manifests as either a ten-sided or four-sided chamber. One enters from the west, facing the east. The flooring is tiled in black and white checkered squares. In the north of the chamber (to one's left) is a stained-glass window with a winged bull. In the west (behind one) is a stained-glass window with an eagle. In the south (to one's right) is a stained-glass window with a winged lion. These are three of the four holy living creatures, as described in Ezekiel's vision from Nevi'im of the Holy Scriptures. In the center of the temple stands a double-cubed altar, with a bowl on top, glowing a blue hue of light. Each temple will have a similar altar—though changed slightly per the significance of that Sephirah—and it must be lit with such a light in order to initiate contact.

Although these are the "totemic" representations of the elemental powers of the world in the Western Mystery Tradition, you can integrate the animal totems of the Pachakuti Mesa Tradition—or any lineage of your choosing—into the temple space as well. As discussed briefly in chapter 9, the animal totems representing Malkuth in the Pachakuti Mesa lineage are:

- *South—Snake:* In the elemental realm of earth, the snake (boa, anaconda, etc.) is the animal closest to Pachamama. The snake teaches us how to honor the physicality of material existence as it slithers limbless directly on the dirt of the world. At the same time, the snake grants the opportunity for transformation, that we can shed our old skins and be rebirthed anew. This is the foundation of physical life and a testament to the possibilities of physical healing in this work.

- *West—Dolphin or Whale:* In the elemental realm of water, the dolphin and whale teach us how to navigate the waters of the emotional realm. Directly connected to the moon, Mamakilla, the dolphin and whale use their abilities to flow within the depths and currents of that pull that emotion can have on us at times. Both highly intelligent species, the dolphin and whale frequently exhibit personalities of compassion in their family units (pods).

- *North—Eagle or Condor:* In the elemental realm of air, the eagle and the condor are the primary totemic allies representing spirit. These animal guides touch the Hanaqpacha daily, and legends say they bring messages to humankind directly from Creator. Additionally, by emulating the eagle or condor's flight in our own lives, rising above the trivialities of the world, we will gain a broader perspective of consciousness.

- *East—Puma or Jaguar:* In the elemental realm of fire, the puma and jaguar represent the fire of consciousness in the realm of mind. As a frequent guide to other worlds in many shamanic traditions, the puma and jaguar illuminate the dark paths of the inner world one must travail when engaging in shamanic journeywork. As the puma and jaguar can saunter easily on tree limbs and see in the dark, so too can we learn their precision of balance and sight within the darkness of our own lives.

- *Center—Llama:* In the Andean tradition, the llama is in many ways much like the buffalo of the Native North American traditions (see chapter 11); it is an animal vital to the survival of the community. Being the center of all the elements—thus representing the center of ourselves, our very awakening soul—the llama is the representation of the four directions unified. In Andean society, the llama is a grazer and pack animal, carrying the load of the farmer. It sacrifices its whole life to service, and even in death the llama's remains are used for clothing, its bones for tools, its fat for offerings to the spirits. In life and death, the llama is a symbol of service, which is the goal of existence itself.

Back to the temple layout, one should imagine two columns directly across from where they have entered, the one on the left made of ebony, the one on the right made of silver. Carved on the tops are gilded pomegranate. Between the two columns stand three oaken doors: the one on the left bearing the Hebrew letter *Shin* for the 31st Path, the one in the center bearing the Hebrew letter *Tau* for the 32nd Path, and the one on the right bearing the Hebrew letter *Qoph* for the 29th Path. These are the three primary entrances into the tree via the Temple of Malkuth.

In Malkuth, one needs to cultivate a relationship with the archangel and order of angels before traversing the rest of the tree.

The archangel for Malkuth is Sandalphon, who is considered the twin of Metatron, the archangel of Kether (again, Kether is the Malkuth of the Unmanifest). In one of the most notable magical tomes in the mystery tradition canon, *The Greater Key of Solomon*, Sandalphon is designated as a feminine presence, but really all angelic intelligences are androgynous at root. Sandalphon is said to be the one responsible for watching over earth directly, and she assists in the growth of crops (metaphorical or otherwise), as well as brings about the differentiation of gender within the embryo of all mothers. Sandalphon, when called upon, will assist in preparing one for the journey throughout the rest of the tree; she is in charge of keeping the Gate ready and clear for one's travels in and out of the temple.

The Ashim are the order of angels known as the Souls of Fire, who normally appear as sparks or flames generally in the shape of the Hebrew letter *Yod*. They are the embodiment of the sacred flame, found in every temple upon the Tree of Life, lighting the way in their ember dance. They are the souls of human beings dedicated to service of the divine light.

The experience of Malkuth is a reflection on the Great Work here in this world, to garner a relationship with the elementals and ready oneself in piety for further journeys on the Tree of Life. The goal of pathworking in Malkuth is to understand that there is no such thing as a "spiritual experience" outside of what is real, what is practical, right here in front of you. Only what is relevant to the real world is what counts, otherwise all else on the mystic path is pointless.

Rabbi Gershon Winkler resolves that the universe "is not secondary to the spiritual, is not dispensable to our soul journey. It is essential. It is a requisite. It is the mean by which we germinate." [107] From here on out, no matter where you travel within the Tree of Life, Malkuth shall be your launching pad. It is the responsibility of the initiate to cultivate a relationship with the Temple of Malkuth, as well as the archangel and order of angels within that Sephirah, before undergoing any further work.

Tau: Path 32

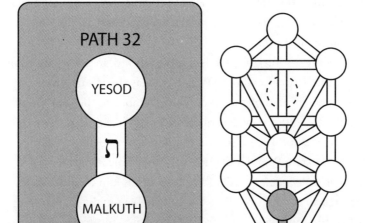

Figure 31: Path 32

Path: Path 32, Malkuth to Yesod

Hebrew Letter: Tau

---

107. Winkler, *Magic of the Ordinary*, 20.

Hebrew Letter Meaning: Cross

Tarot Attribution: XXI, the World

Astrological Sign: Saturn

Yetziratic Text: "The Thirty-second Path is the Administrative Intelligence, and it is so
  called because it directs and associates, in all their operations, the seven planets, even all
  of them in their own due courses."[108]

If Malkuth is the Gate, then Path 32 is the first (and last) opening. Knowing the path of
initiation as both a beginning and an end lends to the ouroboric nature of all things. Com-
forting and terrifying all at the same time.

This is the first path on any initiatory pathworking with the Tree of Life. It is the path
between Malkuth (the Kingdom) and Yesod (the Foundation). As Malkuth is the earth,
Yesod is symbolized by the moon, so this path corresponds to the relationship between
the two as the basis for initiation: before exploring the rest of the universe, we must first
spring from the earth to the moon. This is not just an outer (exoteric) experience but also
an inner (esoteric) one. This path is the primary passageway to the inner world, which is
the true key to the Great Work.

The tarot key representing this path is the World card. In a way, the figure in the tarot
card is a more cosmic vision of *Alice in Wonderland*, as she is surrounded by the four holy
living creatures at the corners of the card, which symbolize the four elemental attributes
of the earth (Malkuth). Originally described as cherub-like beings in the book of Ezekiel,
the four holy living creatures are also noted in Judaism as being attributes of each of the
four winds. Rabbi Gershon Winkler describes the four holy living creatures in regard to the
Four Winds of shamanic Judaism: "All of the four winds join together to form the singular
spirit that animates all of creation. The ancient rabbis taught that the human is created
from the spirit of the four winds and from the earth taken from all four corners of the
planet."[109]

The four holy living creatures are described by Rabbi Winkler as:

• *The Eagle:* Representing the north wind, the eagle signifies the human being's connection to spirit, to God.

---

108. Westcott, *Sepher Yetzirah*, 2nd ed., 31.
109. Winkler, *Magic of the Ordinary*, 42.

- *The Lion:* Representing the east wind, the lion signifies the divine spark within us that stimulates creativity, individuality, and warriorship.
- *The Human:* Representing the south wind, the human signifies us in our most basic and banal form, the opposite of the eagle.
- *The Bull:* Representing the west wind, the bull is a herd animal that signifies our merging into family, community, and even death (the greater herd of the unseen).[110]

So the woman in the card is in descent from spirit, surrounded by four attributes of the earth. The woman (in actuality a hermaphrodite, the genitalia traditionally covered by a floating sash) further signifies spirit entering Malkuth as shown through the two rods she holds in her hands: the positive and negative attributes of spirit joining to descend into material form. The fact that she is hermaphroditic is another signal of the conjoining of positive and negative, male and female, in order to create the unity of form, of matter. She is surrounded by a wreath, another symbol of her enclosure by the World around her. It's meaning: material reality is always dual in nature and exists by the harmonization of the two opposing forces.

This is further illustrated through the Hebrew letter *Tau* (pronounced TAHV). Its primary attribute stems from the way in which the letter was originally written: a three-armed cross, a cross without the upper vertical bar. Like the World card, it signifies two forces interacting on a higher level, their impact producing a form on a denser level below. This is illustrated by the two high bars of the *Tau* cross intersecting in the middle and a chute of their interaction descending below them. This is another representation of how the Unmanifest influences the Manifest, which is the prime lesson of the Mysteries.

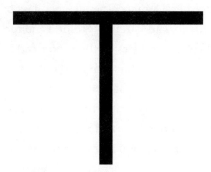

Figure 33: Three-Armed Cross

110. Winkler, *Magic of the Ordinary*, 44.

To work this path, it is vital to understand the two-way nature of it: spirit ascending and matter descending. If we are to engage with Path 32 ascending the Tree of Life, we can see that all things from the material world do indeed come from the immaterial; matter is caused by the astral realm's influence upon it. To descend the tree, the route of creation into the Manifest, it is apparent that the spirit becomes limited—compacted and dense—into Form. The cyclic nature of these two actions is again apparent in the World card of the tarot: the woman represents the essence of spirit itself, but she is bound by a wreath circling her form, bound by matter.

To accept this truth in body, heart, and mind is the first step in devotional mysticism. To be an initiate in the Mysteries, acceptance of all that is (both positive and negative) has to not only be just a posture of the intellect, but the attitude of one's whole being.

Practical Experience

One of the prime methodologies for experiencing a path on the Tree of Life is to dive into the stories and characters of the mythologies associated with each path. The Greek myths especially were designed for this task. These myths are in actuality archetypes of our own consciousness and help us understand the relationship between the Sephiroth that they link to.

The myth associated with this path is the Greek myth of Persephone. This myth was the foundational teaching of initiation for the Eleusinian Mysteries (and still is for modern mystery schools). Persephone is the daughter of Zeus and Demeter, who is the goddess of harvest and agriculture. In essence, Persephone is the mascot for Path 32. Her story revolves around being kidnapped by Hades, god of the underworld, and he whisks her away to the lower realms to marry her. Demeter (being a goddess of the earth, she represents Malkuth) is heartbroken at the loss and journeys to find and reclaim her daughter. During her quest, she encounters Hecate, goddess of the moon and magic (which is an obvious symbol of Yesod). Hecate guides Demeter with her lamp (moonlight) into the depths of the underworld, and then Persephone is discovered. Demeter and Persephone return to the surface world. Persephone then becomes the deity of vegetation, for it is said she returns to the underworld after every harvest and returns again in the spring.

The key here is that Path 32 is twofold: a descent to the interior realms and then a return (resurrection). The Great Work is performed and then the initiate returns to Malkuth, where the results of the Work can be put to action. It is important to understand that any descent into the Lower Realms, the Ukhupacha, is an opportunity to look into the mirror at one's true nature. This is the medicine of Hades—he pulls us down into the depths of our own darkness so that we may come to terms with who and what we really are to ourselves, as well as to others. It is only through Hecate's light (the light of the moon, itself a reflection of the sun) that the darkness is pierced and we can see in the dark and find our way back to Malkuth to plant our own seeds so that the fruit we bear into the world will grow aplenty.

Yesod: Path 9

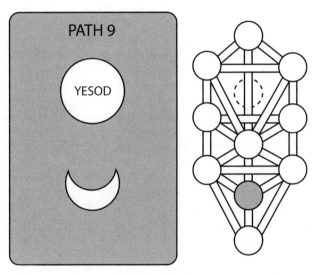

Figure 34: Path 9

God Name: Shaddai El Chai

Archangel: Gabriel

Order of Angels: Cherubim

Animal Totem: Raven

Colors: Indigo, violet

Virtue: Independence

Vice: Idleness

Tarot Attributions: Nine of Pentacles, Nine of Cups, Nine of Swords, Nine of Wands

Spiritual Experience: Vision of the Machinery of the Universe

Title: Storehouse of Images

Symbols: Perfumes, sandals

Yetziratic Text: "The Ninth Path is the Pure Intelligence so called because it purifies the Numerations, it proves and corrects the designing of their representation, and disposes their unity with which they are combined without diminution or division."[111]

Known as the Storehouse of Images, Yesod in Hebrew means "foundation," and by this it is meant the "astral foundation or matrix on which all manifested forms in the physical universe are based and built on."[112] As all matter, all Form is manifest fully into Malkuth, it must first come via the Sephirah Yesod. Any idea, Force or Form, that has spilled down from all preceding Sephiroth must pass through Yesod in order to materialize into corporeality. This is why the Yeztiratic text calls Yesod the Pure Intelligence, because it "purifies the Numerations."

Thus, Yesod operates as a filter for creation. When the power of creation descends from above, Yesod is the emanation which dilutes that power so as not to overwhelm physical reality. A direct encounter of the Supernal and Ethical Triads is too much for material reality and can only truly be experienced in death. For those who have sought to bypass the filtration offered by Yesod and ascend directly to the higher spheres, a breakdown occurs in the mind … it is too intense. Yesod absorbs the full power of the Supernal Light before material reality fully manifests in Malkuth.

Yesod is the lower point of the inverted triangle that makes up the Astral Triad on the Tree, of which Hod and Netzach are a part. It is the seat of the astral/etheric plane of existence. This is most important to those who are interested in magic and in causing change within Malkuth, because it is the astral/etheric plane where every form in Malkuth originates. Thus, in order to cause change in the Manifest, one has to go to Yesod, where the images of the Manifest are stored.

In the mythology of the Star Wars franchise, the Force is an invisible energy field connected to all living things. With it, those sensitive to the Force (the Jedi) can tap into it and manipulate the living world, for good or ill. The astral field is very similar, as it integrates and coordinates the molecules in the physical world. Without the astral organization of Yesod, cells would not be able to arrange themselves into fully functioning organisms such as the human body. It is a network, like the internet in computer technology, in which the disparate parts of material reality can communicate and organize into a singular purpose.

---

111. Westcott, *Sepher Yetzirah*, 2nd ed., 29.
112. Regardie, *Garden of Pomegranates*, 241.

As Yesod is titled the Storehouse of Images, sages throughout time have practiced the art of interacting with the images within the astral—where all material forms are rooted—to change physical reality. This is the infrastructure of the healing arts, including shamanic healing: to change the image from the storehouse itself, rather than treating the symptom in Malkuth.

The moon is the primary planetary body of Yesod, and the dreamtime is its primary location within human consciousness. The moon is a crucial factor in all magical workings, its light waxing and waning, its pull on the oceans ebbing and flowing. Dreams are equally fluid and in flux, which is a significant quality of Yesod, and it is in the dreamtime that we have some of our greatest connections with the astral plane. Although, one would be wise to be highly discerning of any experience with dreams as being a definitive message from Yesod or the astral plane, as confirmed by esoteric scholar Tau Malachi: "Schools of thought are mistaken that propose that all dreams inherently convey deeper wisdom or that all dreams represent the communication of the inner light or higher self. Rather, dreams reflect the state of the soul or the state of consciousness." [113]

Not all dreams are visions; not all visions are dreams. The oceans of dreamtime are like the oceans of reality: they are illusory and not always trustworthy. Part of the accumulation of wisdom comes with learning what is indeed coming from higher spheres and what is just imaginary fancy.

Because Malkuth is a reflection of Yesod, we can then see the mirroring of that relationship with the other Sephiroth on the middle pillar of the Tree of Life. Remember, in the mystery traditions everything resides within a duality. Specifically, the earth (Malkuth) is the negative circuit to the positive circuit of the moon (Yesod). The earth is a receptor of universal creative energy coming from the moon. Likewise, the moon reflects the light of the sun, which is symbolized by Tiphareth on the Tree of Life. In turn, Tiphareth receives its light only through Kether.

As Kether is the apex of the Supernal Triad, so Tiphareth is the reflected apex of the Ethical Triad, and Yesod the re-reflected one of the Astral Triad. This shows how manifest reality is driven by the forces above it. If we can, according to Fortune, "liken the kingdom of earth to a great ship, then Yesod would be the engine-room." [114]

113. Tau Malachi, *Gnosis of the Cosmic Christ: A Gnostic Christian Kabbalah* (St. Paul, MN: Llewellyn Publications, 2005), 290.

114. Fortune, *Mystical Qabalah*, 236.

Practical Experience

The Temple of Yesod is, like all the other temples within the Sephiroth of the tree, a mere reflection of the Temple of Malkuth. There are variations to how the temples of the other Sephiroth manifest (minus Malkuth). Studying the attributes of the Sephiroth, one should be able to build one's own perspective of the temples of the individual Sephirah. Take for instance that the Temple of Yesod would indeed be a moon temple, since its astrological attribution is the moon, so it may be round instead of being square like the Temple of Malkuth. The walls may be silver, and the phases of the moon depicted visually on the floor instead of black-and-white checkered tile. Regardless, every temple should have the altar in the middle, with a flame rising from its bowl. This attribute will provide a continuity throughout the spheres that will anchor one's theurgic experiences. Further, ensure that the doorways to the other paths are visible, in this case Paths 30, 28, and 25, as well as Path 32, of course.

The archangel for Yesod is Gabriel. Gabriel is known as the archangel of the Annunciation, the messenger who provides the power of visions, one of the highest ranking angels in the heavenly lore. In Islam, his importance is considerable: "Mohammed claimed it was Gabriel (Jibril in Islamic) of the '140 pairs of wings' who dictated to him the Koran, *sura by sura*." [115]

It is befitting to imagine Gabriel in terms of the colors associated with the moon and the sea: blues, greens, silvers. As with most angels and archangels, his true form is not anthropomorphic. Our minds cannot conceive of these intelligences as they actually are. It is encouraged to cultivate a truer form of Gabriel over time, such as a magnificent pillar of silver light. In developing a relationship with Gabriel, learning about the designated symbols of Yesod is vital to initiation: perfumes contain an understanding of the ethereal vibratory quality inherent in the material world, and their aroma can emit a change in consciousness; sandals are a symbol that allows one to walk easily within the Storehouse of the astral realms.

The Cherubim (or Kerubim) are the order of angels known as the Strong. They are depicted as huge winged beings. In Genesis, they guarded the Tree of Life in the Garden of Eden with the Flaming Sword, the symbology of which can be easily deciphered. The benefit of interacting with the Cherubim centers on harnessing astral force, specifically through the use of symbols. As discussed before, this is integral to understanding the depths of the subconscious mind, which is the gateway to the astral fabric.

---

115. Gustav Davidson, *A Dictionary of Angels: Including the Fallen Angels* (New York: The Free Press, 1967), 117.

The Cherubim assist one in learning to use the Storehouse (or Treasurehouse) of Images in order to affect the material world. This is the basis of all magical, as well as mystical, aspirations. All engagement with Yesod should center on building a relationship with the moon, the astral realm, and the framework (foundation) behind magical imagery.

Finally, facilitating connection with the animal totem of the raven is a beneficial endeavor in Yesod. In many cultures the raven is a symbol for magic, divination, and psychic power—prime attributes of Yesod. In Norse belief, there were two ravens that acted as messengers for Odin: one's name was Hugin, which means thought (Hod), and the other's name was Munin, which means memory (Netzach). Through the ages, the raven has frequently been noted as a messenger of the unseen realm, especially associated with omens. Yesod being the primary entry point into the Astral Foundation, into the unseen itself, the raven can teach us to become empowered with our own magical abilities. It is our divine right to be in relationship with the sacred, and the raven is our reminder that we are our own best tools to achieve that right.

Shin: Path 31

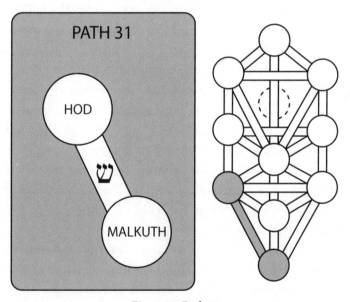

Figure 35: Path 31

Path: Path 31, Malkuth to Hod

Hebrew Letter: Shin

Hebrew Letter Meaning: Tooth

Tarot Attribution: XX, Judgment

Elemental Sign: Fire

Yetziratic Text: "The Thirty-first Path is the Perpetual Intelligence; but why is it so-called? Because it regulates the motions of the Sun and Moon in their proper order, each in an orbit convenient for it." [116]

Delving into the underworld—via Path 32—can dredge up a lot of surly stuff from the murk of one's subconscious. This is not meant to make you suffer but merely to recognize those things in your life walk (whether they be habits, addictions, situations, or even people) that do not serve you. It is now time to begin to formulate how you want your religion, your relationship with God, your psychonautica to be implemented here on Malkuth. This is a difficult task. Formulating your spirit walk is not as easy as it first may seem, because many of us *think* we are walking our true spiritual walk, but the Path of Judgment will reveal to you how that walk *really* looks. Path 31 will show you whether or not you truly walk the talk, as it were.

Path 32 is definitely compelling and an excellent start to pathworking for any proper initiation into the Mysteries. Path 31 also launches from Malkuth, another reminder that all true esoteric work takes place here on earth, not elsewhere. But now this path leads to Hod, the more intellectual, numbers-based Sephirah of the Tree of Life.

With Hod's planetary body being that of Mercury, the primary element for this path then is fire. But, it is not wild fire for the purging of things; it is a controlled fire, a flame of the Perpetual Intelligence. To understand Path 31 is to understand the origins of man. The discovery of fire led to man's evolutionary leap from being at the mercy of the elements to controlling one's environment. Fire stimulated the intellect, inspired the pursuit of knowledge. Fire domesticated the wild mind of the primitive human. With fire came focus in our evolutionary heritage. As we were able to focus our thoughts, so too were we able to better fashion our ideas into physical form.

The Greek Goddess Hestia (whose name means "hearth") is a perfect symbol for this experience, as she presided over the fires of domestication that sat in every home of the family unit as well as the community. Therefore, she is the hub of the wheel of civilization, and the Mystery traditions have titled this path the Path of the Hearth Fire. Its purpose is to domesticate the wild inclinations of man through the aegis of home and family, all in accordance with spiritual principle.

---

116. Westcott, *Sepher Yetzirah*, 2nd ed., 31.

Another myth associated with this path is that of Prometheus, whose name means "foresight." Prometheus is most famous for defying the Gods by bringing the secret of fire to mankind. Again, fire denotes the higher, spiritual Will of consciousness, the awakening of true identity and individuality. Fire not only protected man from the elements but is also the element of the blacksmith, leading to the development and forging of tools and weapons. This suggests the honing of our spiritual Will applied in real life: the path ascends from Malkuth to Hod, but let us not forget it also descends from Hod to Malkuth. Therefore, how can we best apply our spiritual principles in this world? Again, we look to Ashcroft-Nowicki for an answer to this question: "This path is one of learning passed from a higher level. Fire was man's liberator from the inertia that grips when one is hungry and cold. Inertia is also the vice of Malkuth our starting point." [117]

The Hebrew Letter for this path is *Shin*, which means "tooth," its own shape very much resembling the flames of a flickering fire. The tooth is a symbol for creativity or cutting and grinding one's way through any endeavor in order achieve one's desired result. Goals are not attained by wish alone; it takes hard work and self-mastery. The discipline of experience is what assists a soul in its growth to individuality.

Practical Experience

The tarot trump is the Judgment card. Judgment in esoteric work is not associated with the negative connotations of condemnation but rather is associated with the wisdom of Solomon. True judgment denotes discernment or adjustment. This again implies the ability to refine one's works, communications, and actions to conform to the spiritual Will of one's higher self/individuality/Neschamah.

The illustration of the Judgment card depicts three figures rising from the ground: a man, a woman, and a child. In some older decks the child is the only one rising from what appears to be a sarcophagus; in more recent decks all three may be rising from their own. Above them is a glorious angel in the skies—in some cases descending from a great mountain—blowing a trumpet. It is generally agreed that the angel is a symbol for the Neschamah, the higher self. Jungian scholar Dr. Irene Gad elucidates the meaning of the angel's bearing and blowing of the trumpet at the three figures below: "The horn means vibration, movement, penetration into interstitial spaces. It evokes the experience of being immersed in music and in deeply felt emotion; it evokes consonance of existence and time, of

---

117. Ashcroft-Nowicki, *Shining Paths*, 30.

development and regression. The spiritual strength of human beings helps them to escape the grave of the ego complex, to come to terms with evil, and to integrate the shadow." [118]

The horn is the spiritual strength, as emitted from the individuality. The three figures are us in our three parts: the feminine on the left, the masculine on the right, and the child as the potential for the equilibrated middle. The child is the birthing of the two sides and, again, it is the potential for spiritual growth. The Great Work is a task that must be cultivated with discipline and tenacity but overall must be a balancing act of duality, between the positive and negative forces of nature.

Hod: Path 8

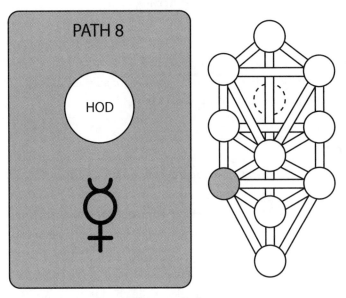

Figure 36: Path 8

God Name: Elohim Tseva'oth

Archangel: Michael

Order of Angels: Bene Elohim

Animal Totem: Bee

Colors: Orange, yellowish-black

118. Irene Gad, *Tarot and Individuation: Correspondences with Cabala and Alchemy* (York Beach, Maine: Nicolas-Hays, 1994), 300.

Virtue: Truthfulness

Vices: Falsehood, dishonesty

Tarot Attributions: Eight of Pentacles, Eight of Cups, Eight of Swords, Eight of Wands

Spiritual Experience: Vision of Splendor

Title: N/A

Symbol: Apron

Yetziratic Text: "The Eighth Path is called Absolute or Perfect, because it is the means of the primordial, which has no root by which it can cleave, nor rest, except in the hidden places of *Gedulah*, Magnificence, which emanates from its own proper essence." [119]

As stated many times before, to understand one Sephirah is to understand its relationship with the paths and Sephiroth around it. Hod is the receiving pole of the Astral Triad, of which Netzach is its active opposite. Yesod is the true center of this triad, representing the astral plane of existence; Hod and Netzach are the representations of Form and Force respectively that comprise the emanation of Yesod.

When the power of creation flows down through the tree and passes through Netzach (the lowest Sephirah of the Pillar of Mercy and Force), it then enters Hod (the lowest Sephirah on the Pillar of Severity and Form) before moving to Yesod and thus manifesting into material reality. Being the Lightning Flash's last interaction with the Pillar of Severity, it is in Hod where the last vestiges of creation are constrained into Form—into images—before they are brought into being. Where Netzach concerns itself with the emotional aspects of being, it is in Hod where those forces are tempered, so that the astral body of Yesod may be balanced. It is important to understand that this is a pole of the dualistic nature of the astral realm (Yesod). Netzach tends to be the more emotional and intuitive aspect of astral consciousness, whereas Hod is the more logical component.

Hod is, then, the waking consciousness of the logical mind. Logic exists so that we may communicate with thoughts and ideas in a clear, rational way. Writer and magician Alan Moore's comic book epic *Promethea* (a pristine treatise on magic and esotericism) relays why Hod means "splendor" and how that impacts being a sphere of the logical mind through the titular character, Promethea: "I suppose communication is how minds reveal themselves. Language gives a shape to the splendours of the intellect…. Language, it

---

119. Westcott, *Sepher Yetzirah*, 2nd ed., 29.

shapes our whole consciousness, how we put ideas together. Even our concepts of time. Before we had command of language, we couldn't record events in the past." [120]

Therefore, written language and mathematics are the primary achievements of Hod. Hod is a realm of intellect, its planet Mercury; thus, it is associated with the Greek Hermes. Hermes was the messenger of the gods, therefore the deity of communication and language. His name was also inherited by the arcane figure—and some say originator—of the Western Mystery Tradition, Hermes Trismegistus. The purported author of the influential *Corpus Hermeticum*, the Thrice-Great Hermes is known to be the founder of the Hermetic tradition, responsible for the prime occult axiom "as above, so below." He was a great esoteric philosopher and alchemist as well as the master of all magic.

Hod, then, is the Sephirah of the magician. It is in Hod where the constructions of Form are fashioned to manifest in Malkuth, such as language and mathematics. Therefore, it is Hod where these Forms are retrieved for magical work … for if magic is the modification of reality, are language and math not the building blocks of reality itself?

Through the mental Sephirah of Hod, the astral energies of Yesod can be refined, polished into clarity. It will be noted that the symbol of Hod is the Masonic Apron, which is typically imagined as the apron of a blacksmith forging his weapon; this echoes the idea of God as architect, building and formulating reality. When worn, the apron conceals the area of the body in which Yesod is located (the gut). Therefore, Hod's forms are best worked when the astral realm is veiled. The daimonic realm cannot ever be fully understood. That being said, considering that logic and intellect are the center of Hod's attributes and Truthfulness is its highest virtue, it is something to meditate upon regarding the concealment of Truth's expression.

Practical Experience

It is prudent to first interact with Hod before Netzach because it is in Hod that the emotive inhibitions of Netzach are tempered by the rational mind. Emotion is a good thing, but not when it is out of control. Esoteric initiation with the Tree of Life can often lead one down emotional labyrinths in which one can get lost; emotional upheavals will prevent ascension of the paths by knocking one down completely from the Tower (Path 27). One of the things we can learn most from Hod is the usage of symbols, where the chaotic nature of emotion can be constrained and focused in accordance with one's Will.

---

120. Alan Moore, J. H. Williams III, Mick Gray, and Jeromy Cox, *Promethea*, collected edition, bk. 3, issue 15 (La Jolla, CA: Wildstorm, 2013), 4–5.

The Temple of Hod will, of course, be logical and numerical, as the Sephirah designates. It is not just the planet but also the chemical element of mercury that pervades over the structure of this sphere. Therefore, it is likely that various themes in the environment of Hod will be mercurial. This is an excellent opportunity to begin to astrally experiment with mercury as a builder of forms. Further, because this is a Sephirah whose primary element is fire does not mean to take that literally, necessarily. Remember, these are all symbols. Some depictions of the Temple of Hod manifest as structures made of ice (that the Sephirah of fire could be constructed of frozen water is evidence of a pristine alchemical meditation). Again, the doorways to the other paths, Paths 31, 30, 26, and 23, should be visible.

The archangel for Hod, Michael, is known in biblical lore as being one of the more powerful angels in the celestial hierarchy, along with Gabriel. The Chaldeans worshipped him as a god. Being chief of the order of virtues, Truth is his magnate (which is the primary virtue of Hod). In most depictions, Michael sports wings and brandishes an unsheathed sword. The sword is an important aspect for this Sephirah—especially as the base Sephirah of the Pillar of Severity—in the symbolism of discipline pertaining to esoteric craft. This is the Sephirah of magic, and the exercise thereof must not be treaded lightly or carelessly; magic is less about muttering spells and gestures than it is about having a precise understanding of how things are constructed.

In this, the sword compels us to slice through illusion by refining our intellectual capacities. Science, mathematics, and philosophy are the tools of the trade for the ancient occultists; they were in fact the first scientists, and it is only in the last couple of centuries that the logical competencies of the mind have become secularized. Mysticism should go hand in hand with reason and critical analysis.

The order of angels is the Bene Elohim, who will assist in the mercurial arrangement and manipulation of forms. *Bene Elohim* is translated sometimes as "sons of God" or "sons of man," of which there is considerable debate in rabbinical academia. Much knowledge can be gained by meditating on either translation.

The bee is the animal totem of Hod. As Hod is the "Perfect Intelligence," it is no surprise that the bee—in its highly structured society—would represent this Sephirah. The bee colony is one of the most well-organized systems in nature, with a distinct role for every member in order to attain the most effective means of production. Much can be learned from observing the bee's example in order to produce our own manifestations in the world. Although the bee has a sting, it is good to remember that this rigidly mechanical lifestyle does indeed produce sweetness into the world that can be enjoyed by all. Through its perfect system, the bee's life is integral to the entire ecosystem of the planet. Likewise, it would be good for us to remember our own impact.

Resh: Path 30

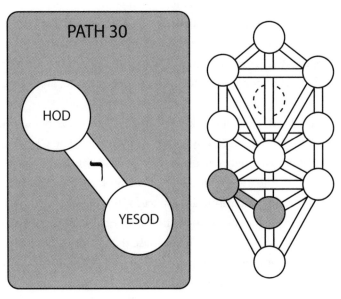

Figure 37: Path 30

Path: Yesod to Hod

Hebrew Letter: Resh

Hebrew Letter Meaning: Head

Tarot Card: XIX, the Sun

Astrological Sign: The sun

Yetziratic Text: "The Thirtieth Path is the Collecting Intelligence, and is so-called because Astrologers deduce from it the judgment of the Stars, and of the celestial signs, and the perfections of their science, according to the rules of their resolutions." [121]

After working Paths 32 and 31, you should have a distinct realization of what no longer serves you, and thus it has been revealed how you want to truly walk the talk of the Great

---

121. Westcott, *Sepher Yetzirah*, 2nd ed., 31.

Work. Path 30 is the path where the opportunity to give it a shot comes from. This is a good path to concretize one's daily spiritual regimen, if so inclined. A spiritual ethic should be outlined, a craft formulized and ready to execute: Will it be used wisely for humankind? Or will your gift become the next A-bomb? Will you abuse the knowledge of the sacred arts? Although this path has its highs—a great lesson in the tarot card is that you will dance in the Sun—be ready to fall and land back on the earth with a thud at any time. Pick up and move on.

Path 30 completes a triad of pathworking among Malkuth, Yesod, and Hod. The primary symbol of this path, as denoted by the tarot trump, is the sun. In Path 32 one has delved into the underworld of the subconscious. In Path 31 those unconscious aspects found in the underworld were called to be regarded and integrated into conscious awareness. Now, in Path 30, we are tasked to fully realize the spiritual with the material. The sun, of course, represents our highest attribute of spirit in this path.

The *Sefer Yetzirah* refers to this path as the Collective Intelligence, and in its description it is indeed heralding true enlightenment. Not the "enlightenment" most assume comes from yogic meditations or Buddhist transcendentalism, but one more closely associated with the Age of Enlightenment beginning in the late seventeenth century, which signaled an age of science and reason, pulling us out of the depths of the dark ages and into a time of philosophy, comfort, and technological progress. As with every aspect of being on the tree (and thus life), there is a virtue to these attributes as well as a vice. The sun's light brings life, but too much sunlight can cause withering death. Reason is no different when out of balance.

The Hebrew letter *Resh* is the "head." This is the seat of the mind, of intelligence. Through this symbolism, it becomes apparent that this path consists of improving the relationship between Hod (the sun, mind) and Yesod (the moon, dream). The aim of pathworking the Tree of Life is to balance these two opposing forces, to harmonize the rational and intuitive minds with us.

Practical Experience

The most informative teaching of this path comes from its tarot card, the Sun. A common image is of two children dancing in a garden under the sun, enclosed by a garden wall. Another is a single child on a horse, the garden wall in the background. The card normally signifies illumination, inspiration, the sun outpouring the forces of light and love upon humankind below (by "below" it is meant the manifest world).

The card also represents the popular meaning of spiritual liberation. However, unlike what it may seem, spiritual liberation is not about unhindered freedom, left unchecked. The wall, as articulated by Gareth Knight, represents restriction and discernment; it is "an enclosure, the limitation which is a protection, the cultivated growth within a garden which is sealed off from wild nature. This has its higher implications on a Cosmic level, for it is by limitation only that growth can be attained." [122]

This stems directly from the Judgment trump, from which we learned discernment, what needs disciplining in our lives; and now the Sun is a refinement of this discipline to allow our Great Work to continue pristine.

There is an infectious tendency in our modern spiritual culture to believe that one's belief is all that is required for self-liberation—a common goal in modern spiritual movements. There is a yearning for the spiritualist to be free from limitation, most particularly in their yearnings to liberate themselves from traditional upbringings. But that is all hubris.

It is only by limitation—by the concrescence of boundaries—that we understand our place in the world and develop our understanding of it. It is by understanding that "spiritual attainment" (whatever that means) is only reached through discipline and hard work, not just by "feeling" and "intuition" alone. A thorough study of the tarot illumines this, as the traditional Sun card, as well as every card in the major arcana, is a replication of the balance between male and female—the masculine and the feminine—to portray the path to knowledge. These depictions of the masculine (mind) and feminine (emotion) represent the two Pillars of Manifestation in the Mysteries, as seen in the Temple of Apollo and in the Judaic traditions of Qabalah. These two pillars stem from the highest supremacy of the feminine and the masculine principles of the universe. It is within the uniting of these dualities that we experience the limitations of form, but also the harmony of true singularity. This unity is likened to Nirvana in Buddhism as well as Moksha in the Hindu traditions. It is the closest attainment one can have to union with the Source of All Being, with God, or with what we in the shamanic circles often call the Great Originating Mystery.

The universe isn't limitless. It has rules, boundaries, limitations. And tarot, among other methodologies such as Qabalah, shamanism, and Hermeticism, help us understand those rules and learn how to utilize them for our own potential growth.

---

122. Knight, *Qabalistic Symbolism*, vol. 2, 52.

Qoph: Path 29

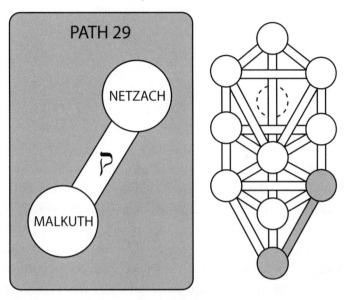

Figure 38: Path 29

Path: Malkuth to Netzach

Hebrew Letter: Qoph

Hebrew Letter Meaning: Back of head

Tarot Card: XVIII, the Moon

Astrological Sign: Pisces

Yetziratic Text: "The Twenty-ninth Path is the Corporeal Intelligence, so-called because it forms every body which is formed beneath the whole set of worlds and the increment of them." [123]

In the same way that the farmer plants a seed and allows it to germinate in the soil, so Path 29 germinates our spiritual ethic before it fully comes into fruition. Path 29 is all about subtlety and letting data settle underneath the surface of the waters; it will take effect over time. As the phases of the moon wax and wane, we can watch the effects of time and its attenuated pulls on us. This path is so subtle that in fact it is very hard to register the conscious outlines of it. The common image of the iceberg comes to mind: 90 percent of

---

123. Westcott, *Sepher Yetzirah*, 2nd ed., 31.

it is under the surface of the water, and that 90 percent is actually what's driving the direction of the 10 percent that we are aware of above the surface. This is exactly how the astral realm affects the Manifest, and this is the prime teaching of this path.

"If any of the Paths should have a sign marked 'CAUTION,'" says Dolores Ashcroft-Nowicki, "the twenty-ninth is the one I would choose." [124]

This is one of those paths that are difficult to describe. It can now be seen that this is the final exit from Malkuth in the pathworking, as the other two have led to Hod and Yesod, and now a connection with Netzach is made. While we have been working with the calculation and exactitude of Hod—the logical side of the astral fabric—we now dive into the Venusian waters of Netzach—the emotional side. This is most definitely a path of intuition. It is a path of flux and reflux, like the tides of the waters being drawn by the moon.

In the previous path, 30, the Hebrew letter acting as the gate was *Resh*, the head, where one can travel into the intellectual auspices of consciousness. Now, in Path 29, the gate is *Qoph*, "the back of the head." The visual portrayal of the letter itself resembles the cerebellum, which links to the spinal column, the wilder, more primal part of the brain. The initiate understands that no matter how much of a path of reason we may tread, we can never escape the primitive. The astrological sign is Pisces, the two interlocking fish, and we again acquire this connection with water as well as seeing the male-female duality inherent in all symbols upon this path (see info below on the next page on the tarot trump). Indeed, this path is primarily about sex; not necessarily in terms of reproduction, but in the utter primal connection between Self and Other, man and woman, human and nature.

"Nature is red in tooth and claw" is the primary axiom for Path 29. The raw, unbridled brutality of nature in this path is what one must encounter. This is not an experience of frolicking in a field of flowers, prancing with the fluttery butterflies. This is an experience of watching a lioness tear the flesh off her own children due to starvation. The Black Isis, in her ugliest and most grotesque form, must be accepted before the White Isis, in her glorious beauty, can be experienced.

Nature is not only a thing of refined beauty; she is also terrible. To love nature is not only to appreciate her glorious qualities, but also to confront her and accept the harsh and brutal realities she has to offer us.

---

124. Ashcroft-Nowicki, *Shining Paths*, 45.

Practical Experience

The tarot trump is the Moon. It is normally illustrated as two towers on either side of a body of water, the moon in the sky between them. The towers of course stand for the Pillars of Manifestation (this symbolism should actually be inherent, in one way or another, in every card of the major arcana). An animal resides at the base of each tower: a wolf on one side and a dog on the other. A very distinct dialectic of duality can be noted here, as both are the same type of animal, but one domesticated and one wild. Through this, we can begin to gain an understanding between our civilized selves and primal selves. A crustacean crawls out of the primordial waters, like we once did hundreds of millions of years ago in our evolutionary cycle. Thus, this card is like a beeline into our evolutionary origins. "Knowing thyself" goes as deep as knowing our biological ancestry as just another organism on this great planet.

In the card, we can see how the moon is the primary deity that moves us, like the tides, even pulling on the blood in our very own bodies. It is well known to science how much the moon phases affect our mood and behavior. However subtle the moon's impact may be, the effects can be extreme.

Connecting with the Egyptian deity Anubis can be beneficial in this path. Anubis is commonly known as the jackal-headed god of mummification and the afterlife, and sometimes the dog and wolf are depicted as Egyptian-style jackals in the tarot trump. My own teacher in the Western Mystery Tradition, John Nichols, is quite the Egyptologist himself and once explained that Anubis (in reality the hieroglyph should be transliterated as *Anpu*) is actually referred to as the "Neter of the Horizon." The horizon is the place between worlds; the horizon is not really there because you cannot ever actually get to it or touch it … However, it seemingly still separates two realms: the above and the below. This idea is a worthy meditation for Path 29.

Netzach: Path 7

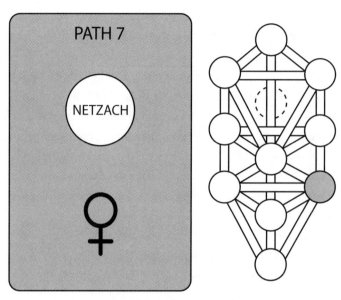

Figure 39: Path 7—Netzach

God Name: Jehovah Tzabaoth, "The Lord of Hosts"

Archangel: Haneal

Order of Angels: Elohim

Animal Totem: Dragonfly

Colors: Emerald, olive

Virtue: Unselfishness

Vices: Unchastity, lust

Tarot Attributions: Seven of Pentacles, Seven of Cups, Seven of Swords, Seven of Wands

Spiritual Experience: Vision of Beauty Triumphant

Titles: Firmness, Valor

Symbols: Lamp and girdle, rose

Yetziratic Text: "The Seventh Path is the Occult Intelligence, because it is the Refulgent Splendour of all the Intellectual virtues which are perceived by the eyes of intellect, and by the contemplation of faith." [125]

---

125. Westcott, *Sepher Yetzirah*, 2nd ed., 29.

The seventh Sephirah on the Tree of Life, *Netzach*, means "victory." This victory is the victory of achievement, and one can trace the seven days it took God to create the world in Genesis to Netzach as the seventh Sephirah. Netzach is God's victory in creation's achievement, the victory of life to overcome inertia and blossom into being.

Of course, like all other Sephiroth, Netzach cannot accurately be understood without its relationship to the Sephiroth surrounding it, specifically Hod. Again, Netzach sits at the base of the Pillar of Mercy (Force) and Hod sits and the base of the Pillar of Severity (Form). We must understand its function within the Astral Triad, the lowest level of manifestation in creation, as described by Tau Malachi: "Netzach represents the imagination, feelings, and emotions of the mind; Hod represents the thoughts of the mind. Yesod, which is the union of Netzach and Hod, represents desires that come into being by way of the activity of the mind." [126] Therefore, from Yesod the activities of the mind become manifest in Malkuth.

Aphrodite or Venus, the goddess of love from the Greek and Roman mythologies, is the main deity of Netzach. But, of course, in Greek life love was so much more than the idea of romance between the sexes. Aphrodite's reign held sway over the love and kinship among friends and pupils and even facilitated the comradeship between fighting men (remember, one of Aphrodite's lovers in the myths is Ares, god of war). Aphrodite's presence within Netzach is a reminder that the Sephirah provides a reflection on the magnetism of human exchange and how the needs of the soul may be met.

This was the job of the mystery school Cult of Aphrodite in ancient Greece: the management of polarities. It is through this management that that achievement of victory is experienced, in the harmony of both force and form. Netzach facilitates unity, a perfected state of interrelationship; in essence, the Quechua term *huñuy* as used in the Pachakuti Mesa version of the Qabalistic Cross in chapter 9.

Netzach's victory is the full potential of beauty inherent in all manifest things. It is the Creator's achievement in ensuring the Divine exists within all of creation. This realization of divinity within all things is the signature pallette of the poet. Where connection with Hod is sought through philosophy and mathematics, connection with Netzach can be attained through the arts: painting, music, dance, poetry, or any activity that taps one into the instinctual aspects of creative and passionate expression. The realm of inspiration is where Netzach bears its fruit.

In this light, the victory of Netzach is also revealed as the valor and resolve needed in the battle every great artist must fight in order to breach the threshold of new ideas on the

---

126. Malachi, *Gnosis of the Cosmic Christ*, 238.

mass culture. All pioneers are at first rejected and sometimes resented. But the greatest among them will eventually have their works accepted and embraced into the fold of the mainstream. After that, it is up to the next generation to break that mold. The victory of Netzach is theirs if they persist.

Practical Experience

To make the most effective use of Netzach is to spend an abundant amount of time in communion with nature but also to utilize one's creative faculties. Indeed, Netzach is the place in consciousness where our creativity is derived. Painting, music, poetry, dance, pottery—whatever it is that stimulates the imagination fully into the creative flow is Netzach's playground. This is the Sephiroth of the muses, where we receive our inspiration for things which eventually become formed in Hod.

In connecting with nature, the symbol of Netzach—the rose—and the shamanic animal totem—the dragonfly—are suggested items of focus.

The rose as an esoteric symbol gets its roots from the Rosicrucian movement of Christian mysticism, dating back to as early as the thirteenth century. Normally in conjunction with a cross, the Rose Cross represented the evolution of man's spiritual climb to connect to God, the rose being that blossoming moment of enlightenment. A primarily feminine symbol, the rose is the perfected representation of the spiritual experience. Rose water, rose petals, and incense reflect Netzach's characteristics of purity, passion, and perfection.

Likewise, the dragonfly is often found around water, a feminine element that embodies the chaotic waters of emotion, a prime attribute of Netzach. Starting off early life within water itself, the dragonfly undergoes metamorphosis—mastering the waters—and then inhabits the air. The dragonfly's movement is precise and dazzling with its aerial stunts, becoming a master of the air. The medicine offered by the dragonfly within Netzach is harnessing the creative and emotional waters, mastering them so that they can become focused intentions to carry out in honor of spirit.

Tzaddi: Path 28

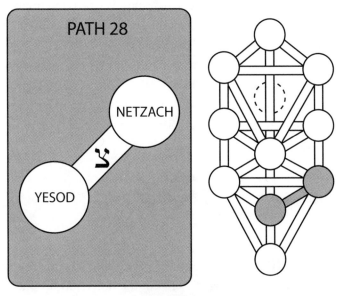

Figure 40: Path 28

Path: Yesod to Netzach

Hebrew Letter: Tzaddi

Hebrew Letter Meaning: Fishhook

Tarot Card: XVII, the Star

Astrological Sign: Aquarius

Yetziratic Text: "The Twenty-eighth Path is called the Natural Intelligence; by it is completed and perfected the nature of all that exists beneath the Sun." [127]

Path 28 ignites the implementation of one's spiritual path fully by their own hands. This path is about manifesting the dreams created on the previous paths; they are all working consecutively in perfect alignment.

To support this execution of manifestation, this path highly distinguishes the importance of knowledge regarding the individuality and personality, which have specific definitions in

---

127. William Wynn Wescott, trans., *Sepher Yetzirah,* 3rd ed. (London: J. M. Watkins, 1911), electronic reproduction by John B. Hare for the Internet Sacred Text Archive, http://www.sacred-texts.com/jud/sephir.htm.

occult philosophy that we discussed earlier. The correlations of individuality and personality have also been made to Neschamah and Ruach, respectively. It is important to note that the Sephiroth within the triad of the Astral relate to the personality, the Ethical to the individuality, and the Supernal to the Source of All Creation.

The point of this path, and of course all initiation, is to get in touch with the individuality, recognizing the mirroring quality of the personality on the lower planes, as represented by the astrological symbol for this path, Aquarius. The zigzags reflect one another, as the surface of the water reflecting one's image. This is an important image to consider when engaging with Path 28.

Figure 41: Aquarius

We are not to fall short and succumb to the personality. The lower self should be the reflection—a simulacrum—of the higher self, not the other way around. This path takes everything we have learned so far and seeks to implement it into action with balance. As above, so below; but also as below, so above.

As a follow-up to Path 29 (which was primarily about sexual union), this path yearns to integrate the symbols of the Holy Naked Man of Yesod and the Holy Naked Woman of Netzach into a union that is less about the horizontal (physically sexual) conjunction of bodies and more about the vertical (God-centered) synchronization of harmony between two poles: positive and negative, like a battery. *Tzaddi* is a fitting Hebrew letter for this path, as it is the fishhook: the dancing between these poles for balance is much like a fisherman teasing the fish along with his hook skipping along the water, being reeled in to the Source. And so is our yearning for the Divine.

This is done under the sun, as the *Yetzirah* suggests. It may seem like this would be referring to Path 30 of the Sun tarot trump, but in this case the sun being referred to is the Sephirah of Tiphareth as the guiding principle. There is a great risk of falling into vice regarding sexual work on this path, so be prepared for tests to your commitment to Truth, to Beauty, and to the Great Work. Do not mistake the symbols of sexuality as literal interpretations of male-female copulation. Further, do not fall into the guise of believing you can produce supernatural effects to change the natural laws of the universe. As Gareth Knight has stated, there is truly is no such thing as the *"super*natural." For instance, per Gareth's example, if one is falling off a cliff, a magic wand will do you no good. The magical tool for this issue is a parachute. Be practical and utilize the established laws of the universe.

Being tested is a primary component of this path, which is why Lucifer, the Light-Bringer, is an excellent angelic source to tap into. His role exemplifies the testing of one's spiritual identity, for one cannot truly grow and evolve without the temptation of glamour, power, and perfection, such as the fall from Eden. Only through mistakes can growth be allowed to occur.

Practical Experience

There can be confusion regarding the major arcana to be used for Path 28. As we have been following the sequence of the tarot trumps in reverse order, it would naturally seem to befall the trump of the Star, being the twenty-seventh card of the major arcana. However, many mystery schools switch this trump for the fourth card, the Emperor. Each magical system has its purposes for this switch, but it is up to the initiate to do the work in figuring out which card works for them on this path and why. I have chosen to keep in natural sequence of the major arcana in reverse, aligning with the paths on the Tree of Life.

The tarot trump of the Star depicts a naked woman pouring two jars of water, one on the ground, and one in a body of water, each symbolizing the balancing of polarities. Stars reign in the heavens above, along with at least one major one that normally stands out among the others. This can usually be seen as a representation of Tiphareth, which sits above this path on the Tree of Life. According to Dr. Gad, "The Star(s) represents the beginning of true initiation. The light of the Star(s) gives direction in the night as do position lights, beacons, milestones, and timers. This card expresses a yearning for that world that goes beyond recognition, conflict, and separation.... The mystic's soul is guided by the stars; inspired by the heart, he or she surrenders to their heavenly influences, which leads to mystical enlightenment."[128]

The Star signifies the capacity of the higher self, the individuality, to awaken the sleeper, to come alive within the human personality. Aleister Crowley calls the Star the "the goddess...shown in manifestation....personified as a human-seeming figure."[129] The Star awakens these sleeping energies within us as the goddess pours that which is above into the waters of the subconscious below.

---

128. Gad, *Tarot and Individuation*, 271.

129. Aleister Crowley, *The Book of Thoth: A Short Essay on the Tarot of the Egyptians* (Boston: Red Wheel/Weiser, 1969), 109.

Peh: Path 27

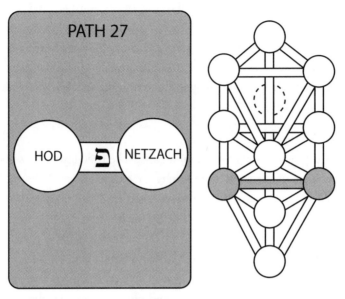

Figure 42: Path 27

Path: Netzach to Hod

Hebrew Letter: Peh

Hebrew Letter Meaning: Mouth

Tarot Card: XVI, the Tower

Astrological Sign: Mars

Yetziratic Text: "The Twenty-seventh Path is the Exciting Intelligence, and it is so called because through it is consummated and perfected the nature of every existent being under the orb of the Sun, in perfection." [130]

Path 27 completes the bottom inverted triangle on the Tree of Life: the Astral Triad, what I call the Astral Fabric. This triad is the etheric framework that is the foundation of physical matter, where the Lady of Nature (Netzach) and the Lord of Books (Hod) have been equilibrated by the Mistress of Witchcraft (Yesod). Path 27 seals our work on this triad, and through it, as initiates, we must be tested for purity in order to continue on to the higher aspects of the tree. It must be ensured one's character and intentions are pris-

---

130. Westcott, *Sepher Yetzirah*, 2nd ed., 31.

tine. This is a huge accomplishment, and anyone who has committed to the Work thus far should be proud of themselves—but not too proud, for hubris is one of the prime vices that will make us crash, and failure will ensue.

There is something to be said for this path being the first horizontal path encountered on the Tree of Life, directly connecting the two Pillars of Manifestation. It is the first of only three paths that do this, so the energies produced can be extremely powerful, potent, and jarring for the unprepared. The lateral paths are the extreme polarities of the tree, so if one is not ready for these extremities, then the effects can be likened to being bounced around inside a pinball machine. A call to being grounded—rooted with the principles of reason—is essential for experiencing this path in balance and not chaos.

As it is important to understand a Sephirah based upon its relations to another, it is also imperative to study a triad based upon the other triads on the tree. The Ethical Triad (in the next chapter, "the Ethical Machine") is the place where the individuality resides, and the Astral Triad is home to the personality. Path 27 creates the division between the two and offers an opportunity to sever aspects of the personality that no longer serve the Great Work. This path, according to mystic Ted Andrews, "brings to life circumstances that offer the chance to survey our entire personality." [131]

What is experienced throughout the Astral Triad, if the pathworking is authentic and true, is an alchemical change that transmutes the personality in preparation for the individuality (higher self) to become the driving force in one's life. The personality does not go away, but its interests become sidelined. Investment in the higher self, the Will of the Divine, becomes more and more paramount in a person's life. Within the Astral Triad, this initiatory process acts more as a seed, which will be nurtured into growth further along the pathworking process as one climbs the higher spheres of the Tree of Life. Over time, a person's motivations transmute into being less about the Self and more about the Other, the greater whole of all being.

This is alchemy in its purest form. Prime examples to more deeply understand this "distillation" process can be read in the fifteenth-century text *The Chymical Wedding of Christian Rosenkreutz* or seen in Alejandro Jodorowsky's surrealist film *The Holy Mountain*.

We can then begin to understand the Hebrew letter for this path, *Peh*, the "mouth." The mouth both gives and receives, a perfect gateway between the Astral and Ethical Triads. The mouth takes in nourishment and utters speech. In terms of the personality,

---

131. Ted Andrews, *Pathworking: A Qabala Guide to Empowerment and Initiation* (Jackson, TN: Dragonhawk Publishing, 2009), 153.

and the rightful utilization thereof in the Great Work, the mouth teaches us that incarnation into life truly is like entering a buffet. Life experiences represent the varieties of food, and so we partake of these blessings given to us. Conversely, we also use these mouths in which we have received nourishment to also give, to express into the manifest world the Divine Word of the Creator. It is through the physical mouth that the Word of God can be expressed into the densest level of creation, Malkuth.

In the history of mystery school training, pathworking is like building a relationship with these various levels and intelligences of consciousness. It is well advised to take a break from the pathworking after mastering the paths and Sephiroth from Malkuth to Path 27 and allow time to integrate the experiences thus far. This is where self-discipline as an initiate can be practiced, for there are those who would love to charge on through the paths in anticipation of ascending the tree. However, caution is advised.

Esoteric practices facilitate intimate touchpoints with the human psyche; therefore, time and patience are allies in processing information. The genuine initiate will take the respite—for a recommended lunar month—and take the pathworking back up again. One may even want to revisit the entirety of the Astral Foundation before moving onward to the other levels of the Tree of Life. Mastery over one's foundation is essential before exploring the ethical and supernal faculties of the universe.

Pushing onward without ample time to rest and assimilate all the work done thus far will cause one to collapse, like the builders of the Tower of Babel experiencing hubris, which brings us to the practical experience …

Practical Experience

The tarot trump for Path 27 is the Tower. Though the biblical story of the Tower of Babel was just referenced as a sign of hubris, the primary significance of this tarot image it is not the traditional fundamental notions that cause man's Tower (personality) to collapse and shatter from the lightning (the Lightning Flash / Flaming Sword / Initiation), which is what man seeks to become godlike or one with God. To become the gods we are is our birthright; that is Creator's design. As Yeshua (Jesus) said in the book of John, "I have said 'Ye are gods.'" [132]

In truth, it is man's personality retaining its separation from divinity, building the Tower prematurely, or wrongly, that causes its collapse (its rise denoting our rise from the Astral Triad to the Ethical, and then eventually the Supernal). We are reminded of the story of

---

132. Psalm 82:6.

the Tower of Babel in the Book of Genesis: hubris will be one's downfall if our foundations are not sound. This is an indication that not only should our worldly endeavors be secured before embarking upon spiritual work, but we should also be fit in faith and humility to ready ourselves for the Ethical, and thus Supernal, expressions of universal experience. If we are not ready, the universe will certainly knock down our towers of ascent in order to teach a vital lesson.

In the card, a bolt of lightning—the Lightning Flash of Initiation coming from the highest Source—strikes the Tower toward the upper half, causing it to crumble. People fall from the blast, flailing to their deaths. It may seem gruesome, but this Path is designed to compel one toward success. Our desire to receive the Lightning Flash of Initiation will surely knock us on our asses, but will our individuality (higher self) reign supreme and continue onward?

Lightning is truly a symbol of true initiation. In the Quechua tradition, to be struck by lightning—called the *hanaqpachaqaqyarayu*—is the highest form of initiation possible, likened to being touched by God. It is a cleanser, burning out the aspects of our personalities that no longer serve our higher good. This sort of cleansing only hurts if one resists the current.

However, if one accepts the bolt of initiation, ready to learn its lessons, then one is touched by the finger of creation. The source of the lightning bolt is Kether, the divine spark of all that is. To accept that level of download fully and without reserve is akin to what the Quechua refer to as an *altomesayaoq*, a high priesthood. This is the goal of the mystic path and the purpose of what Path 27—and, in fact, the entirety of the Astral Foundation—has to teach us all.

11

THE ETHICAL MACHINE

The next phase to traverse on the Tree of Life represents the area of the Ethical Triad, which—included with its paths—I refer to as the Ethical Machine. As the spiritual experience of Yesod represents the vision of the machinery of the universe, the following paths and Sephiroth make up those machinations that build the constructs of the universe. It is the scaffolding that the Astral Foundation fills as the cement of existence.

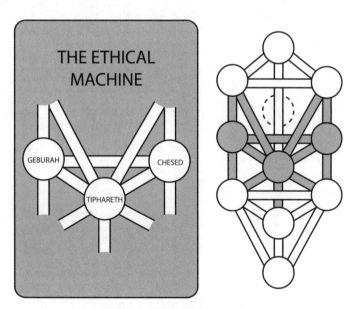

Figure 43: The Ethical Machine

Indeed, being the skeletal framework, the Ethical Machine teaches us about the inner workings of creation, how ideas get from the Unmanifest to the Manifest. From here on out (and especially once the Supernals are reached), descriptions of the paths and Sephiroth may become more and more abstract. This is because when one travels up the tree, one draws closer and closer to the Great Unknown … our human minds are not capable of handling the vast realities behind the veil. Therefore, the practical experience subsections will be omitted. If pathworking difficulties arise, a psychonaut is always best fitted to anchor onto the tarot imagery for focus and meditation.

Ayin: Path 26

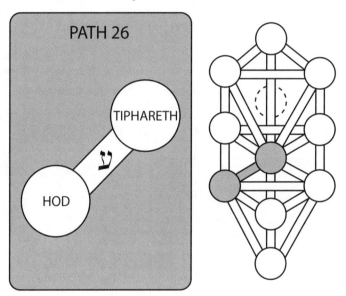

Figure 44: Path 26

Path: Path 26, Hod to Tiphareth

Hebrew Letter: Ayin

Hebrew Letter Meaning: Eye

Tarot Attribution: XV, the Devil

Astrological Sign: Capricorn

Yetziratic Text: "The Twenty-sixth Path is called the Renovating Intelligence, because the Holy God renews by it all the changing things which are renewed by the creation of the world."[133]

Hopefully, one will have taken a quality holiday from pathworking before engaging the following series of gates on the Tree of Life, for the next few paths set up a very specific trilogy that can be quite daunting if one is not sufficiently prepared. In many mystery traditions, the following three paths refer to the spiritual experience known as the dark night of the soul.

The *dark night of the soul* is a common term to denote a spiritual crisis. However, this experience doesn't have to be a "crisis" per se, as long as one faces the Work head-on. Although in some cases resistance can prove beneficial for revolutionary change, this is one of those Zen moments in a spiritual walk when surrendering to the experience will assist you in gaining far more ground than an antagonistic approach. A more competent means of understanding success for the next three paths can be found in St. John of the Cross's "Dark Night of the Soul" ("La noche oscura del alma"). This poem embodies mystic achievement in the Christian paradigm but can be applied to any spiritual framework. The dark night has normally been understood as an experience of meaninglessness that comes from spiritual depression, but this is an incorrect assertion when referring to the poem by St. John of the Cross.[134] "Dark Night of the Soul" outlines the necessary series of purifications one must go through in order to achieve union with God. It can almost be seen as a sort of purgatory state in one's spiritual path, where the remnants of the personality are faced with being stripped away so that the individuality can be the guiding force of one's thoughts and actions. So, again, this can, during the experience, seem like a spiritual crisis. Always remember, though, that it is a purging of what no longer serves the human vessel in order to receive the full benefits of initiation. The crisis only persists when you resist stripping away the parts of the personality that weigh you down.

For the next three paths, pieces of the poem will be presented as meditative pieces, beginning with the first three stanzas:

---

133. Westcott, *Sepher Yetzirah,* 2nd ed., 31.

134. Eckhart Tolle, "Eckhart on the Dark Night of the Soul," Eckhart Teachings, October 2011, https://www.eckharttolle.com/newsletter/october-2011.

On a dark night,
Kindled in love with yearnings
—oh, happy chance!
I went forth without being observed,
My house being now at rest.

In darkness and secure,
By the secret ladder, disguised
—oh, happy chance!
In darkness and in concealment,
My house being now at rest.

In the happy night,
In secret, when none saw me,
Nor I beheld aught,
Without light or guide,
Save that which burned in my heart.[135]

So, the test begins, the serpent crawling up from the lower Sephiroth—the personality—to the higher spheres, which will now be centered on Tiphareth, the focal point of the individuality. Thus begins our process of the alchemical marriage between the conscious and subconscious mind. Various aspects of the human psyche and soul are tested throughout these three paths. According to Gareth Knight, "the 24th Path tests the driving emotions, the 25th Path the devotional aspirations, and the 26th Path the intellect." [136] Therefore, these three paths truly work in concert to ready the soul for the higher Sephiroth on the Tree of Life.

It may seem absurd at first, but it is perfectly fitting that our first touchpoint with Tiphareth, the Sephirah that represents the consciousness of the Christ, is represented by the Devil tarot card. The devil, unfortunately, has had a bad rap over the centuries.

It is unfortunate that the mythological significance of the devil has been taken literally by the throng of religious fervor over the centuries. It must be clearly stated that the sym-

---

135. John of the Cross, *Dark Night of the Soul,* trans. E. Allison Peers, Dover Thrift Editions (Mineola, NY: Dover, 2003), 1–2.

136. Knight, *Qabalistic Symbolism,* vol. 2, 78.

bol of the devil is indeed that: a symbol! We are not referring to a literal demonic being of evil that is intent on defying God and torturing humanity. The devil is merely a symbol for an illusion. At the same time, so are all man's ideas of what "God" is: an illusion. We indeed become caught up in our own personal perceptions of God, rather than the *reality* of God.

We get so wrapped up—and become slave to—our ideas and notions of what we *think* God is to us, just like the two chained persons in the tarot card. They are slave not to the literal creature "the devil"; they are slave to the established orthodoxy of their own ideas. The devil is merely a scapegoat for their own shortcomings. Too often we blame this invisible adversary for the sins which are, frankly, our own responsibility. The devil was invented by man in order to escape blame. Facing the devil, facing this illusion, is the first step in the dark night to receive the truth of Tiphareth, of the individuality.

Moving further into the Great Work, our notions of what we perceive God to be are likely to change, to be turned completely upside down. We need to be ready, as we strive further and further to uncover the veil of the Mysteries, for Truth with a capital *T*. Based upon our current understanding of the world, this Truth can seem more like paradox than logic. Yet, the world of spirit is often irrational to the world of the nonspiritual.

This takes an intuitive leap past the logical framework of Hod in order to reach new frontiers of understanding that will often seem downright scary because of their illogical nature. We must be constantly aware of everything around us as illusion. The Hebrew letter for this Path, *Ayin*, means "eye," which aligns with the optical nature of this theme. The eye can be easily tricked. *Ayin* is a reminder of the paradox between the physical eye and one's intuition. The initiate must understand that the material world is illusion and take great care not to confuse outer forms with inner reflection. One may relate to another in some way, but they are not the same thing. As always, discernment is your ally.

As the Yetziractic text calls this path the "Renewing Intelligence," we are being provided here an opportunity to face these aspects of ourselves and renew them, let them go, which the two people in the tarot trump could do if they allowed themselves. They are responsible for their own freedom, because being chained is an illusion: the devil doesn't *actually* exist! We rarely allow ourselves that opportunity, so here is our chance. In order to experience the higher levels of the Tree of Life, our current notions of "God," of a spiritual life, must be challenged.

Samech: Path 25

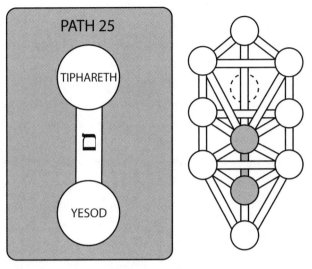

Figure 45: Path 25

Path: Path 25, Yesod to Tiphareth

Hebrew Letter: Samech

Hebrew Letter Meaning: Prop

Tarot Attribution: XIV, Temperance

Astrological Sign: Sagittarius

Yetziratic Text: "The Twenty-fifth Path is the Intelligence of Probation, or is Tentative, and is so called because it is the primary temptation, by which the Creator trieth all righteous persons." [137]

Path 25 is part two of three of "Dark Night of the Soul." The next couple of stanzas of the poem by St. John of the Cross:

This light guided me
More surely than the light of noonday
To the place where he (well I knew who!) was awaiting me
—A place where none appeared.

---

137. Westcott, *Sepher Yetzirah,* 2nd ed., 31.

Oh, night that guided me,
Oh, night more lovely than the dawn,
Oh, night that joined Beloved with lover,
Lover transformed in the Beloved![138]

Here we begin to reach the phase of the dark night where the paths begin to defy description, much to the dismay of writers throughout history. Although we live in an age when an individual is defined by their opinion, in the Great Work, when one delves deeper into initiation, the less there is to say. This is because the higher we ascend on the tree, the greater the impact on the human soul, which is a construct beyond human language.

Thus, symbols become all that more important. Although, remember the aim of a symbol is its own destruction. It cannot be taken literally; what matters is *behind* the symbol. We have learned that lesson most with the devil.

While Path 26 was a test of illusion, this path is a test of temptation. Devotion to one's faith is most important here, for if that faith fails you, then finding comfort in the denser levels of experience becomes way too easy. The story of Jesus being tempted in the desert is a perfect theme associated with Path 25, including all stories of visioning into the wilderness. To test one's faith and senses in exchange for a high connection with the upper worlds … those familiar with Native American shamanic vision questing will understand the nuance, which is why I believe a shamanic approach to Qabalah is vital. Temptation is Creator's way of strengthening the soul.

The Hebrew letter *Samech* means "prop" or "crutch," implying a support from the divine in the face of temptation. It should be noted this prop also forms a T cross (*Tau*, see figure 33 on page 145) on the Tree of Life with Path 27, Hod to Netzach. This closely aligns this path with Path 32, given that they both form the lower half of the Middle Pillar of Manifestation on the tree.

That being noted, *Samech*, the prop, resembles both a means of supporting life and of taking it away. This paradox is one of the more important ideas in occult training that must be understood. As mystics throughout the ages have noted, the truest formula of life comes from the decay and breaking down of old life (death) and the formulation of something new (birth).

Sagittarius, the zodiac of the archer, is the astrological influence. It should be noted that Sagittarius is a centaur, and in occult work the symbol of a half-man, half-animal

---

138. John of the Cross, *Dark Night of the Soul*, 2.

shows the struggle between the lower self (personality) and the higher self (individuality). If the man half is on top (like the centaur), the higher self is winning over this struggle; if the animal half is on top, (like a minotaur or Baphomet, in the Devil tarot card) then the lower self is in control. In this light, the arrow of Sagittarius can be taken in two ways. If the archer's arrow is pointing upward, the archer's aims are toward the heavens and he has forsaken the baser parts of himself. If the arrow is pointing downward, it could be seen as the individuality taking aim toward what needs purging in the personality. It is either a precise ascension to the Divine or the Divine's descent into the lower worlds. The arrow is the symbol of directed Will—not the will (lowercase) of the human being, but the Will (uppercase) of God.

The tarot trump Temperance shows an angel (assumed by most esoteric scholars to be Raphael) pouring the waters of life from a golden cup (symbolizing the sun, Tiphareth) into a silver cup (symbolizing the moon, Yesod). This imagery shows the alchemical process of "the tempering of souls, as with metals, to make them fit to be used as tools in the Great Works of God," according to Knight.[139]

Aleister Crowley, of course, has his own interpretation. Changing the title of the card to "Art," the angel of the card in the Thoth Tarot is instead represented as an amalgamation of the king and queen who have been married from the Lovers card (Path 17); they are fused into one androgynous being. Since the duality has become obsolete and now unified, Crowley references this symbolism as being a foreshadowing of the result of the Great Work.[140]

We can see then his reasoning for the name change, as this is the symbol of the True Art, the arrow piercing the rainbow. The rainbow, hearkening back to the story of Noah and the Flood, is the divine promise kept. The rainbow—*K'yuchi* in Quechua—is the bridge between God and man. Its promise is that despite the dark age of the Flood (the dark night of the soul), we will overcome our tribulations to achieve union with the Source of Creation.

---

139. Knight, *Qabalistic Symbolism*, vol. 2, 75.
140. Crowley, *Book of Thoth*, 103.

Nun: Path 24

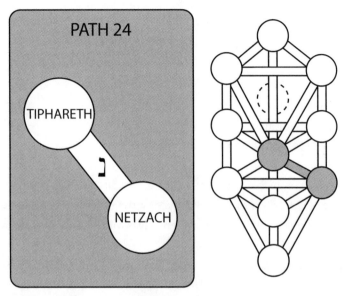

Figure 46: Path 24

Path: Path 24, Netzach to Tiphareth

Hebrew Letter: Nun

Hebrew Letter Meaning: Fish

Tarot Attribution: XIII, Death

Astrological Sign: Scorpio

Yetziratic Text: "The Twenty-fourth Path is the Imaginative Intelligence, and it is so called because it gives a likeness to all the similitudes, which are created in like manner similar to its harmonious elegancies."[141]

These are the final three stanzas of "Dark Night of the Soul" by St. John of the Cross:

Upon my flowery breast,
Kept wholly for himself alone,
There he stayed sleeping, and I caressed him,
And the fanning of the cedars made a breeze.

---

141. Westcott, *Sepher Yetzirah*, 2nd ed., 31.

The breeze blew from the turret
As I parted his locks;
With his gentle hand he wounded my neck
And caused all my senses to be suspended.

I remained, lost in oblivion;
My face I reclined on the Beloved.
All ceased and I abandoned myself,
Leaving my cares forgotten among the lilies.[142]

The previous two paths have perfectly set up the initiate's Work ahead. For this final installment of the "Dark Night of the Soul" trilogy, the task of the initiate is to finally shed the old skins of the Personality and ready themselves for the unknown ahead. Full trust in God's love is crucial at this point.

The primary symbol of this path is the tarot trump of Death. Before rebirth into higher levels of consciousness, one must die to who they are today. It is the fear of change that must be faced, transmuting that fear into a full acceptance of what is, what has been, and what will be.

Dion Fortune, in her occult masterpiece *The Cosmic Doctrine*, recounts seven different types of death that are important to study not just for this path, but for all prospects of initiation:

- *First Death:* Two separate forces cease to exist independently but become a single, entirely new manifestation.
- *Second Death:* The evolution of a lower form into a higher form takes place.
- *Third Death:* The death of the physical body, synonymous with Path 32.
- *Fourth Death:* Essentially, sleep; this is actually a lesser form of the Third Death.
- *Fifth Death:* A death of the personality, the process represented by this, the 24th Path.
- *Sixth Death:* Trance, which is an induced sleep, akin to the Fourth Death.
- *Seventh Death:* Illumination; a death wherein any lingering remnants of the personality are burned away for good. All paths below Tiphareth are still subject to the whims of the personality, but from Tiphareth and above, only the individuality can prevail.

---

142. John of the Cross, *Dark Night of the Soul*, 2.

In this path we are concerned with the Fifth Death, in that it will eventually lead to the Seventh Death. The aim of the path is to tap into one's true spiritual Will, which in fact is the Will of Creator, and to have the courage and discipline to act on it. Therefore, death is a necessity for the higher spheres of consciousness to work appropriately: the lower animal mind will distort whatever information is coming in through Tiphareth … so the animal mind (the personality) must die.

The Hebrew letter of this path is *Nun*, the "fish" (obviously representative of water), and its astrological sign is Scorpio, ruled by Mars (a planet of fiery presence). So, these two energies together could be shown to mimic a First Death, the blending of fire and water to make steam (the essence of Spirit).

As the Abyss is the gulf between the Supernal states of the godhood and the Ethical Triad (the higher spiritual centers of man), so we are also experiencing a similar gulf here with the dark night of the soul, separating the individuality and the personality. According to Knight, "The Gulf is something that has to be leaped, and leaped alone, stripped of all hindering burdens, in faith.… It is thus one of the crisis points of spiritual progress because of the great temptation to turn back from the unknown to the apparent safety of known things, and to succumb to this temptation is to lose all the fruits of past endeavour." [143]

Sometimes, in order to not surrender to these temptations, we must allow ourselves to be devoured completely by the death offered by spirit. A helpful image to meditate on is that of the Hebrew letter for this path, *Nun*, the fish, and its mirroring of Path 28, *Tzaddi*, the fishhook (from the Star). Is the hook catching the fish or is the fish swallowing the hook? One may recall the story of Jonah and the whale, in which Jonah is swallowed whole by the fish and by God's Will.

This path is a renewal, regeneration into a new form of being. This is the goal of initiation. All gods and myths centered in Tiphareth are gods and myths that have died to become reborn: Christ, Osiris, and so on. It is our aim, as initiates, to follow in their footsteps. As the song goes, "Merrily, merrily, merrily, merrily, life is but a dream." Tricksters throughout time have asked, if life is the dream, then who is the dreamer? Well, death is the dreamer of life. Life and death are truly the embodiment of the yin and yang, a marriage of two fundamental expressions of the universe that are both natural and essential to the growth and development of the soul. Indeed, to ignore death in life is the worst death of all; for without the threat of our ultimate end permeating our waking consciousness, the human mind is liable to squander the limited time we have available to live.

---

143. Knight, *Qabalistic Symbolism*, vol. 2, 98–99.

Tiphareth: Path 6

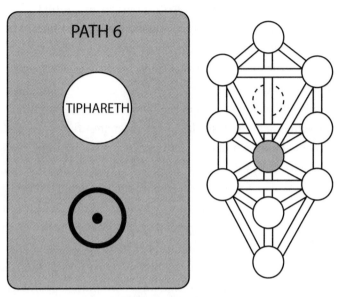

Figure 47: Path 6

God Name: Jehovah Aloah Va Daath, "God Made Manifest in the Sphere of Mind"

Archangel: Raphael

Order of Angels: Malachim

Animal Totem: Buffalo

Color: Gold, yellow, or pink

Virtue: Devotion to the Great Work

Vice: Pride

Tarot Attributions: Six of Pentacles, Six of Cups, Six of Swords, Six of Wands, Knight/ Prince of Pentacles, Knight/Prince of Cups, Knight/Prince of Swords, Knight/Prince of Wands

Spiritual Experience: Vision of the Harmony of Things

Titles: Zoar Anpin, the Lesser Countenance

Symbols: Calvary cross, rose cross, the cube

Yetziratic Text: "The Sixth Path is called the Intelligence of the Mediating Influence, because in it are multiplied the influxes of the emanations; for it causes that affluence to flow into all reservoirs of the Blessings, with which these themselves are united." [144]

Tiphareth, the sixth Sephirah on the Tree of Life, is the goal of illumination sought by initiates. It is the inspiration for the name of the Order of the Golden Dawn; Tiphareth *is* the Golden Dawn. It is the source of the higher self, Neschamah, the individuality. Known as the "Mediating Influence" from the *Sepher Yetzirah*, human consciousness cannot truly ascend past the sphere of Tiphareth. Beyond this Sephirah, there can only be speculation or the intimations of experience, but not experience itself. It is the highest point of evolution a human soul can reach while alive. Tiphareth means, and *is*, beauty: the Divine Plan coming into fruition as it should be. It is the central Sephirah and holds all the others around it in balance—the *axis mundi,* as it were. Taken into context of the three triads on the Tree of Life, it is the apex of the Ethical Triad where the machinations of the universe construct the "rules" or "ideas" of what Form will be in the Manifest before it is then moved on to the Astral Triad to be, in actuality, *formed.* In a nutshell, Tiphareth is where above and below meet.

Again, writer and occultist Alan Moore explains in his graphic novel masterpiece *Promethea*, as relayed by the titular character: "Tiphareth's mankind's highest point, and God's lowest, where the two connect…. Absolute God's the highest sphere, above existence. Tiphareth's God born into existence, as man. As his own Son. Humanity's highest point." [145] This is the gold the alchemists sought—not the literal mineral, but the beauty and perfection of the eternal soul.

There are many symbols and associations attributed to Tiphareth, one of them being the symbol of Christ as the Son, which is why the princes (or knights, depending on the deck) of the tarot are the primary correlation (along with the sixes), as well as the planetary body of our own sun. Kether represents the Father, and Yesod the Holy Spirit; thus, Tiphareth is the Son in the Holy Trinity upon the Tree of Life. Therefore, we can see again how the Bible can actually be a vital Qabalistic text in understanding the tree and especially Tiphareth and its symbolism. This Holy Trinity creates a direct vertical line of the three primary Sephiroth on the tree, upon the Pillar of Mildness, thus forming the backbone of mystic Initiation.

---

144. Westcott, *Sepher Yetzirah,* 2nd ed., 28–29.
145. Moore et al., *Promethea,* bk. 3, issue 17, 9.

Akin to Christ in the Abrahamic traditions is White Buffalo Calf Woman in the Native North American traditions, specifically the Lakota Nation. White Buffalo Calf Woman came to the Lakota people to deliver the messages of how to conduct ceremonies to connect earth (Malkuth) to spirit (Kether), which is the very axis mundi represented in Tiphareth. Like the llama in the Andes, the buffalo provided sustenance, such as food, clothing, and shelter, to the people of the plains. It is the most sacred animal to many of the First Nations peoples still to this day, representing a benediction from spirit to all humanity. Buffalo is a messenger of illumination, a bridge of every person's potential to intimately connect with Creator.

It should be no surprise, then, that Tiphareth is often referred to as the "Giver of Illumination," which can also be associated with the Greek god Apollo. As discussed previously, this illumination, according to the entire aim of the Great Work as described within the Golden Dawn system, is delivered by means of a ray of light—*lux*—whose beams of brilliance really come from Tiphareth, not actually from Kether (the Source) as most may assume.

As initiates, this *must* be understood, because illumination is so often *mis*understood. The human mind cannot take the illumination offered from Kether, which is why Tiphareth is the "Mediating Intelligence." A direct transmission from the Supernal levels of consciousness simply overwhelm the human mind. A buffer is needed to cushion the impact of information readily flowing from the higher levels.

Therefore, absolute devotion to the Great Work is imperative. If we do not train ourselves sufficiently, slowly, patiently, and humbly to befit even the illumination from Tiphareth, then this flash of illumination is nothing more than a blast of light that will leave us blind. We will be left with more mystery and darkness than when we first began the mystical experience.

Luckily, Dion Fortune rarely leaves her students without a remedy to counter such a predicament. The story, miracles, and parables of Christ as an adult provide a crucial locus to this Sephirah. At the same time, Fortune offers a compelling case to meditate upon concerning the Christ as Child, as well: "We must accept the fact that the Child-Christ does not spring like Minerva, full-armed from the head of the God-Father, but starts as a small thing, humbly laid among the beasts and not even housed in the inn with the humans. The first glimpses of mystical experience must perforce be very limited because we have not had time to build up through experience a body of images and ideas that shall serve to represent them." [146]

These images and ideas can only be compiled into the conscious mind through time, through study, patience, and discipline. We must always remember the lessons of the Child-Christ in Tiphareth, whose lesson unveils to us a process of growth and evolution to understand the illumination waiting for us. The Christ story, the Christmas story especially, can teach us more than we may assume. Too many in the circles of alternative spirituality have forsaken the lessons of the Christian Holy Bible in an act of rebellion from years of persecution. However, the sins of the Church should not override the treasure trove of esoteric knowledge that resides in the Holy Book, despite how much that knowledge has been abused (another prime lesson for this Sephirah). We must always begin each foray into knowledge completely anew, every day starting from the place of the Fool, the beginner.

Following this, a developed initiate engaged with this Sephirah will then henceforth be capable of engaging in that culmination of the Great Work as prescribed by Abramelin the Mage: the knowledge of and conversation with one's Holy Guardian Angel (HGA). Normally called the Abramelin Operation, the process of conjuring and communicating with one's HGA is typically an excruciating course which takes months of prayer and ritual to implement. To gain access to your HGA is a rare and honoring occasion. The Holy Guardian Angel is not some cherub that flits around you, catching you when you trip; it is most typically understood as an aspect of the higher self, that state of the individuality that resides in Tiphareth. It is an intelligence that acts as an emissary between you and God.

Even though the pathworking process is not equipped to evoke one's HGA, it is a good idea to become familiar with its presence. The Holy Guardian Angel is rarely experienced through visions but is rather a mode of pure consciousness. This level of consciousness is less of a psychic phenomenon and more of an intuitive state of awareness and presence. Hence, any mystical experience still operating out of a visionary state is still operating in the Astral Triad, rather than the Ethical Triad, where mystical experience is more of a highly matured perceptivity of the universe. This type of consciousness prepares one's senses to be able to interact with the higher realms, most specifically with the unknown.

This leads to a final lesson on Tiphareth—which contains enough material to fill tons of books—which centers on Christ again. The crucifixion of Jesus Christ is an integral moment in the history of humanity, revered by billions of Earth's citizens the world over. Whether one is Christian or not, the significance of the Christ's life and miracles, as well

---

146. Fortune, *Mystical Qabalah*, 180.

as his death, cannot be underestimated. It may be shocking for some to know that occultism in fact finds many of its core roots in early Christian Hermeticism. Much of the symbology inherent in Hermetic Qabalah stems from Christian doctrine. So, it is perhaps fitting to finish our notes on Tiphareth with the final living act of the Christ as human flesh, before the Resurrection as a new being of light.

In Alan Moore's *Promethea*, the two main characters—Sophie and Barb—are acting as vessels for the Promethea deity (a goddess of the imagination) and literally traveling the spheres of the Tree of Life in search for Barb's dead husband. Upon entering Tiphareth, they meet Barb's Holy Guardian Angel, who just so happens to be a cigarette-smoking, foul-mouthed, younger version of Barb herself. As the Holy Guardian Angel walks them through the golden realm of Tiphareth—which is basically our closest conception to what heaven really is—she teaches them about the various god-forms throughout history that had died and risen, like Osiris. They then stumble upon a mighty image of Christ on the cross and the mood darkens. Sophie and Barb find themselves stunned and sobbing at the sight, their hearts crushed. Barb's Holy Guardian Angel comments as she fixes her gaze upon the dying, suffering Christ, "The best in us. The gold. And it's nailed writhing on the cross of the world. That's us up there, man. But even down here, at the lowest Auschwitz ass-end of what humans are, and what humans do … our highest point is still here with us. There's light. Always remember that. There's light at the bottom." [147]

Tiphareth is our highest connection to our soul's potential, but we must always remember the banality of our own flawed humanity for the true beauty of the Sephiroth to flourish. We are a paradox: both divine and mundane, good and evil. Christ—a divine being who walks in the flesh, who gave up his life to be beaten, battered, and crucified—is the essence of beauty.

147. Moore et al., *Promethea*, bk. 3, issue 17, 20.

Mem: Path 23

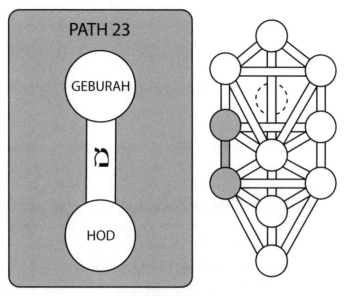

Figure 48: Path 23

Path: Path 23, Hod to Geburah

Hebrew Letter: Mem

Hebrew Letter Meaning: Water

Tarot Attribution: XII, the Hanged Man

Elemental Sign: Water

Yetziratic Text: "The Twenty-third Path is the Stable Intelligence, and it is so called because it has the virtue of consistency among all numerations."[148]

In Path 23, we are engaging in first contact with Geburah. Whereas Hod is the sphere of mental forms and communication, Geburah is the sphere of breaking down those forms before entering the Astral Triad so that creation remains pristine. Geburah is a sphere of fire as purifier, remover of dross. The Hebrew letter for this path, *Mem*, means "water." So, what we have is a type of spiritual technology where fire and water come together to produce an immense alchemical power.

---

148. Westcott, *Sepher Yetzirah*, 2nd ed., 30–31.

No better analogy can be used for this path than a machinery of higher consciousness, which helps us understand the chosen moniker of the Ethical Machine. Geburah contracts while Hod expands. Geburah restricts any forms from ascending the tree that are not clean and pure, while forms descending the tree are molded to fit the restrictors of the Manifest. The opposing energies of Hod and Geburah are forced to comply, which, according to the Yetziratic text, creates a stability between polarities. Through the fusion of these two opposites, a universal stability is formed.

The lesson in this path is taught sufficiently by the trump of the Hanged Man, a personal favorite. The Hanged Man is one of the better teachers of all the trumps on how to train the human mind (Hod) to work from the spiritual perspective. Since the figure on the card is being hung upside down, this indicates that the values of the higher world are most often the reverse of the lower. The Hanged Man gives an indication of serenity through chaos, as his face is placid despite being strung up and his head about to be submerged in a body of water (again, *Mem*) in the Thoth Tarot. This explains why most mystics throughout time have been thought to be insane: their ideas and values are normally at odds with dogma and culture, and they are revolutionaries and radicals. Most often, when engaging with the higher spheres of consciousness, one encounters realities that far surpass culture's understanding of what is and is not acceptable. The Hanged Man encapsulates the expression of mystic action, which is rarely understood in conventional culture. When these spiritual ideas and values are expressed, the prevailing mindset of society often misinterprets these expressions, becomes afraid, and retaliates either through crucifixion, persecution, or banishment. Hence, the secrecy of occultism.

Again, a deeper understanding of the Sephiroth denotes a more intimate understanding of this path's place in terms of our relationship with the individuality (higher self). Geburah is the action of the individuality. It assesses and then corrects the energy moving through it, either ascending or descending. To interact with Geburah is to see a situation for what it currently is and then to see how it should be. Geburah's function is to adjust conditions to correct the course.

Crowley calls this path and trump the "card of the Dying God," and perhaps he has a point.[149] Path 23 is the roadway where old ideas are purged to make way for a new, higher perspective in accordance with the spiritual Will of the universe. Ascending the tree, the fiery heart of Geburah tests the purity of forms to discern what is useful and what isn't.

Another principle of water to be considered is its ability to reflect like a mirror. If the Hanged Man were placed directly on the model of the Tree of Life on this path, his head

---

149. Crowley, *Book of Thoth*, 97.

would be immersed in Hod. It is in Hod that the principles of the higher mind (via Geburah) should be reflected. In order for us to be a mirror of the Divine, we must be pristine, like a placid lake reflecting the stars in the heavens. Being a reflection of God, we can beget an understanding of God as a reflection of itself. We then remember that each Sephirah is merely a chalice receiving the pouring waters of the one preceding it, all originating from the Unmanifest. It is sufficient then to inherit the symbol of the cup for the mystic way of being. A true mystic should be able to be a clear vessel to receive the fruits of spirit, composed and unperturbed in the face of social pressures and norms.

Turning one's point of view upside down, in reverse, a *pachakuti*, is the magical formula of seeing the world via the perspective of spirit. It is the prime elixir of alchemy. Further, in the obvious attributions of self-sacrifice, of surrender, as seen in the tarot trump, we can understand that the result of this formula rests in the absolute relinquishing of one's personal will for the Will of the God.

Geburah: Path 5

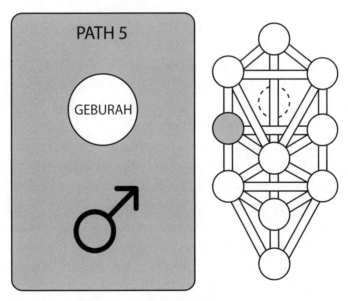

Figure 49: Path 5

God Name: Elohim Gebor, "Almighty God"
Archangel: Khamael
Order of Angels: Seraphim

Animal Totem: Wolf

Color: Scarlet red

Virtues: Energy, courage

Vices: Cruelty, destruction

Tarot Attributions: Five of Pentacles, Five of Cups, Five of Swords, Five of Wands

Spiritual Experience: Vision of Power

Titles: Pachad, "Fear"; Din, "Justice"

Symbols: Pentagon, pentagram, sword

Yetziratic Text: "The Fifth Path is called the Radical Intelligence, because it is itself the essence equal to the Unity, uniting itself to the Binah, or Intelligence which emanates from the Primordial depths of Wisdom or Chokmah." [150]

Destruction, especially in spiritual circles, is often perceived as a negative thing. In the mystery traditions, it is an often-necessary means in order to transmute into finer states of being.

This is the crux of the experience of the Sephirah of Geburah, which means "severity." It is sometimes the least understood Sephirah of the Tree of Life. Geburah has been referred to as a "negative" Sephirah, but that reference is entirely wrong. In reality, Geburah represents the center of the Pillar of Severity, the counterbalance to Chesed in the center of the Pillar of Mercy. The universe, and thus the truth of beauty (Tiphareth), cannot exist without either of these poles.

Geburah is the holy, purging fire of God that burns away the counterproductive aspects of any Force or Form. This works both ways: when descending the tree, the Universe is purifying forms in order for it to become manifest; when ascending the tree, the soul is purified of its dross before climbing to the higher spheres. The archangel of Geburah, Khamael (whose name literally means "burner/fire of God"), represents a purifying presence whose sole purpose is to remove obstacles that prevent the flow of grace.

Geburah is a Sephirah of adjustment; another name for it is "Judgment" (much like the tarot card Justice). It is an assessment of the powers that exist which flow through it. Change is always necessary in the orientation of the soul. As I have discussed before, if change is resisted, then the resulting chaos of that resistance can be unpleasant. In fact, some mystics and magicians have stated that to deny the adjustment of Geburah is to risk possible mental breakdown, sickness, or even worse. Not even good intentions guarantee passage at this level of pathworking; everyone will have to face these adjustments, whether

---

150. Westcott, *Sepher Yetzirah*, 2nd ed., 28.

alive and implementing the Great Work or in the realms of death as a soul traversing the planes to make their way home.

It is at this stage in pathworking, also, when sacrifice is necessary. There are parts of ourselves—the way we may treat others, our addictions, and so on—that must be given up for the sake of devotion. True sacrifice is about making a clear and deliberate choice for the greater good. A pianist must give up other priorities to make time at the keyboard. A sculptor must choose to spend their resources on clay and kilns. An athlete would rather push their limits in a gym than sit on the couch. These are examples of individuals who generate the conditions necessary for their success, and they give up Friday nights out and the latest TV shows in order to make it happen.

Breaking away from anything that separates one from the Great Work is the essence of the magical act, which really is just the transmutation of Force. This is a place where conflict is almost a necessary (if misunderstood) phenomenon in the mystical process. In the curanderismo traditions, swords are often used to battle and cut away aspects of a person's lower self that no longer serve their highest good. The cut must be clean, precise, and exact. The recipient must be ready to be rid of that aspect forever. If the lower inhibition is merely repressed and denied expression, they are setting themselves up for failure. The base desires of the personality will always come back to haunt, unless they are placed on the altar of sacrifice and sliced away as a commitment or contract with the Divine Will.

This may seem contrary to the common spiritual nomenclature of modern mystical philosophy, but it is a theme as timeless as the mystery traditions and beyond. Fortune writes, "There is a place where patience becomes weakness and wastes the time of better men, and when mercy becomes folly and exposes the innocent to danger." [151] Not that patience and mercy don't have their place in the Great Work, but those virtues reside in Chesed, not in Geburah.

So then may we learn from the wolf as the primary totem of Geburah. The wolf is keen, is strong, and can destroy most anything with its sharp maw. The wolf pack is one of the strongest family bonds in the mammal kingdom, precisely designed with definitive rituals and rules to ensure survival. Thus, it is with Geburah that whatever energy may pass through its sphere of influence—either ascending or descending—is adjusted by the laws that govern the Ethical Machinery of the universe. It is with ritual that the wolf adjusts the chaos that may exist, that each member of the pack may know its own place. Geburah is the prime Sephirah of esoteric ritual—the five points of the pentagram, the five directions of the mesa—and likewise exists to help us adjust our own bearings, to understand our role in the cosmic scheme.

---

151. Fortune, *Mystical Qabalah*, 164.

Lamed: Path 22

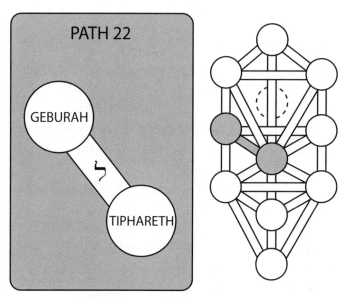

Figure 50: Path 22

Path: Path 22, Tiphareth to Geburah

Hebrew Letter: Lamed

Hebrew Letter Meaning: Ox-goad

Tarot Attribution: XI, Justice

Astrological Sign: Libra

Yetziratic Text: "The Twenty-second Path is the Faithful Intelligence and is so called because by it spiritual virtues are increased, and all dwellers on earth are nearly under its
shadow." [152]

The first time I underwent a pathworking on the Tree of Life, I had just completed
Path 23 (which had upturned my life) and then soon after read in Dolores Ashcroft-
Nowicki's *The Shining Paths* that this next path, Path 22, "can be the nearest thing to spir-
itual agony." My heart sank. She continues, that for the student of Qabalah, an initiate,

---

152. Westcott, *Sepher Yetzirah,* 2nd ed., 30.

"it can be the point at which a crossroads is reached in his decision to go on, or remain where he is."[153]

I nearly threw the book across the room. I was about done.

But then I took a deep breath and continued onward; the Yetziratic text shows a way through, as this path is the "Faithful Intelligence." It promises that through faith, one's spiritual virtues will be "increased."

This is the place where we really, truly begin to meet our mettle in true integration of the individuality (the higher self), where the personality (lower self) no longer has influence. The Hebrew letter *Lamed* is the "ox-goad," the instrument that guides the ox down its path. Seeing as the first Hebrew letter, *Aleph* (Path 11), means "ox," we see an obvious reciprocal relationship here. An ox moves slowly, but it is persistent. The whole gist of the Mysteries is that the subtle enigmas of life are the goad of Creator, urging us back into the arms of the Universal Mother and Father.

Generally known in esoteric circles as the Path of Karmic Adjustment, this is where the lords of karma operate upon us like surgeons in order to restore cosmic balance within our soul. This path is connected to Geburah, and while that Sephirah specifically calls us to banish our dross, this path is also connected to Tiphareth and so beseeches redemption. This means we must face ourselves—our entire life circumstance—as it really is and be ready and willing to change what is necessary in order keep our devotion intact. This requires brutal honesty, discernment, and a lot of courage.

The best way to understand this path is from the Egyptian Book of the Dead. The Judgment Hall where the dead go is also referred to as the Hall of the Double Maat. Maat is the Egyptian goddess of truth and law. When the dead arrive at the hall, their hearts are weighed against Maat's feather, an emblem of truth. That the heart is another symbol for Tiphareth bears mentioning, as this path is directly connected to the Sephirah.

We also see the obvious connection to the astrological sign Libra (the scales) as well as the symbology of the tarot trump Justice. It must be noted that a feather often represents air in the shamanic traditions, which translates into a sword in the Western Mystery Tradition, as carried by the figure of Justice in the card.

Aleister Crowley refers to his version of the tarot card for this path as Adjustment. He compares the Harlequin (his figure starring in the Justice from his Thoth deck) and the Fool (from Path 11, *Aleph*):

---

153. Ashcroft-Nowicki, *Shining Paths*, 102.

In the greatest symbolism of all, however, the symbolism beyond all planetary and Zodiacal considerations, this card is the feminine compliment to The Fool.... This woman-goddess is Harlequin; she is the partner and fulfillment of The Fool. She is the ultimate illusion which is manifestation; she is the dance, many-coloured, many-wiled, of Life itself. Constantly whirling, all possibilities are enjoyed, under the phantom show of Space and Time: all things are real, the soul is the surface, precisely because they are instantly compensated by this Adjustment. All things are harmony and beauty; all things are Truth: because they cancel out.[154]

Justice is about finding the Truth. And in this seeking of the Truth, we can understand that the universe will always mask itself as the Harlequin does. In the typical Justice card, Lady Justice is of course blinded. The scales of what is right and what is wrong are always subject to relativity, but that is why Lady Justice stays concealed behind the blindfold: the scales will remain balanced when the senses are directed to the mysteries of creation.

Kaph: Path 21

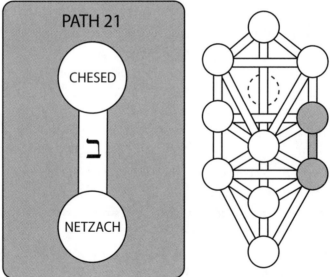

Figure 51: Path 21

154. Crowley, *Book of Thoth*, 86–87.

Path: Path 21, Netzach to Chesed

Hebrew Letter: Kaph

Hebrew Letter Meaning: Palm of the hand

Tarot Attribution: X, Wheel of Fortune

Astrological Sign: Jupiter

Yetziratic Text: "The Twenty-first Path is the Intelligence of Conciliation, and is so called because it receives the divine influence which flows into it from its benediction upon all and each existence." [155]

The key to this path is of course the tarot card the Wheel of Fortune, which implies the process of the cycles of life—the ups, the downs—in one continuous loop. Like a Möbius strip, the infinite loop can seem as a maze at times. Our patterns will turn back in on themselves over and over if we don't recognize them. Conversely, as emblematic of the seasons of the year and the orbit of the planet, the card also represents the universe itself as an expression of change.

This is our first touchpoint with Chesed, the sphere of mercy, which is the polar opposite of Geburah. Chesed is the Sephirah where the image of the individuality is contained. Because of the connection to Netzach, this path then is responsible for generating the true aspirations of our imaginative minds.

Because of this, it is the idea of the quest, and most especially the spiritual quest for the Holy Grail, that is one of the driving myths of this path. The grail is obviously a symbol for the individuality (higher self), but the notion of a "quest"—wherein one embarks upon a journey to find the treasure and defeat dragons—gives the assurance you will not retrieve the grail too easily … It is often a task taking multiple lifetimes. The grail is one of the prime sources of inspiration and imagination in the Western world.

The process of this quest is clarified by the Yetziratic text and its reference to this path as the "Intelligence of Conciliation." Conciliation is about overcoming adversity in order to gain understanding (a clear reference to the victory of Netzach). In the context of the tarot card, this means the disparate parts of the wheel actually work in harmony in order to allow the Divine Spirit to flow into creation.

The Hebrew letter *Kaph* is the "palm of the hand." The hand is a highly mystical symbol through the ages, representing the use of spiritual power: divination, scrying, palmistry,

---

155. Westcott, *Sepher Yetzirah*, 2nd ed., 30.

and so on. "The hand of *kaph* is the hand of opportunity," writes Ashcroft-Nowicki.[156] *Kaph* provides for us an opportunity and an avenue, leading us through the maze, which is the continual state of change in the universe. It is by action we keep with the flow of the turning of the wheel, rather than getting stuck in the cog. Staying the course of this path on our quest is apparent in the virtues of each of the Sephiroth we have touched upon so far: the discrimination of Malkuth, the independence of Yesod, the truthfulness of Hod, the unselfishness of Netzach, as well as the devotion of Tiphareth.

This path teaches us how to receive the benediction of the divine influence of Chesed, where all new forms are created, where the "fatherly" images of the Godhead reside. By being open to receiving the blessing from the Upperworld, the Hanaqpacha, the flow of destiny will come down. A father operates life in service to the family; therefore, the initiate acts accordingly: utilizing their own talents and possessions in service to the greater good. The resources of the universe will thus be at one's disposal.

Chesed: Path 4

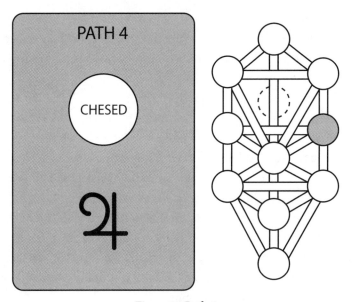

Figure 52: Path 4

God Name: El

Archangel: Tzadkiel

---

156. Ashcroft-Nowicki, *Shining Paths*, 112.

Order of Angels: Chasmalim

Animal Totem: Deer

Color: Blue or deep purple

Virtue: Obedience

Vices: Bigotry, hypocrisy, gluttony, tyranny

Tarot Attributions: Four of Pentacles, Four of Cups, Four of Swords, Four of Wands

Spiritual Experience: Vision of Love

Titles: Gedulah; Love, Majesty, Magnificence

Symbols: Tetrahedron, wand, or scepter

Yetziratic Text: "The Fourth Path is named Measuring, Cohesive, Receptacular; and is so called because it contains all the holy powers, and from it emanate all the spiritual virtues with the most exalted essences: they emanate one from the other by the power of the primordial emanation. (The Highest Crown.)" [157]

The deer is a fitting totem for the fourth Sephirah, Chesed; it is graceful in its stride, regal with its crown of antlers, and in mythology is harkened as the bearer of great adventure. In many tales of old it is normally the deer or stag that inspires the spirit of the quest; so it is that Chesed represents that spirit of why we engage in Great Work.

One of the earliest depictions of a shamanic figure comes from a cave painting in Trois-Frères, France, called the Sorcerer. This image is of an antlered man—half beast, half human—and not only reveals the ancient dependency humankind once had on the natural world, but also unveils the shape-shifting tendency of the shamanic method. Assuming the form of an animal was a common staple of indigenous shamanic practices in order to fully tap into the healing potencies of that spirit. Likewise, we come to the place in the Tree of Life where we shed our own identity in order to allow ourselves to be fully encompassed by spirit above.

Another name for Chesed is *Gedulah,* the opposing force on the Qabalistic Cross from Geburah. To understand Chesed is to understand Geburah, just as we need to gain knowledge of any opposing Sephirah in order to understand the designated sphere of influence. Whereas Geburah is the center of the Pillar of Severity (and thus its meaning and title), Chesed is the center of the Pillar of Mercy. Where Geburah breaks down energy, Chesed uplifts. One of the designated symbols is a scepter, denoting the presence of a king on his throne, ruling his kingdom in peace. Geburah, on the other hand, is the Sephirah of war.

---

157. Westcott, *Sepher Yetzirah,* 2nd ed., 28.

In Geburah we understand when using the sword is called for. In Chesed, however, we understand when to use compassion.

As the Tree of Life is a symbol representing the creation of the universe, Chesed is the first place in which true manifestation begins. When descending from the first three Sephiroth, the gulf created by the Abyss (Daath) separates the Supernal Triad from the rest of the tree. This makes Chesed the first sphere of influence on our physical world. While the forces of the Supernals are abstract, the first interaction of this Sephirah builds the archetypal images that will later determine how the Divine is perceived and received in the material, Malkuth.

Because of its placement beneath the Abyss, Chesed is the place where the highest entities of known consciousness reside (as anything above the Abyss is truly unknowable). These highest entities, otherwise known as the ascended masters or Inner Plane Adepti, are the human souls who have evolved beyond the cycle of life and death (karma) and choose to interact with and guide humanity, such as Jesus, Kuan Yin, Paul the Venetian, Sanat Kumara, or even Buddha (coincidentally, there are many ancient depictions of Buddha with a deer). They do not interact directly with humanity but by proxy via Tiphareth and then Yesod. Therefore, when an initiate is interacting with one of these Adepti, they are interacting with an abstract force that is representative of that master, whose center of force resides in Tiphareth. However, their point of origin or location (if ever that concept could be imagined in the cosmos) is in the dimensional intelligence of Chesed.

As divisive as the opinions on the man are, we do gain much from Aleister Crowley's philosophy in the case of Chesed, for he coined the phrases "Do what thou wilt shall be the whole of the Law" and "Love is the law, love under will." These statements are often misinterpreted as being a spiritual justification for doing whatever it is you desire, but they are certainly *not* about that. In actuality, they promote Chesed's highest virtue: obedience. According to Gareth Knight (a frequent critic of Crowley, actually, but he gives him credit where it's due), these phrases "apply well to Chesed, for at the level of this Sephirah the will of the individual is completely in harmony with the Will of God. Thus Obedience … does not mean the willingness to take orders. What is implied is that the soul who has achieved the grade of the Chesed initiation is so aligned with the Will of God that his own will is the same as the Will of God and so he can do no evil—it is completely foreign to his nature." [158]

---

158. Knight, *Qabalistic Symbolism*, vol. 1, 119.

This is the Sephirah where the individuality (as described by Dion Fortune) is in full play and the personality is no more. We can learn much from Chesed and Geburah's relationship and their interplay with each other in how to achieve this full-on individuality. This interplay is reflected in all life. Life is rhythm. It is a balancing act, as one might achieve motion by playing with the pull of gravity to ride a bike or fluctuating with the winds of the sea while sailing a boat. By giving in to one pull or the other, one is likely to collapse or capsize. Initiation involves establishing a rhythm with these forces and riding along with it. The personality loses its sway and one submits to the full authority of the higher self, the individuality.

Yod: Path 20

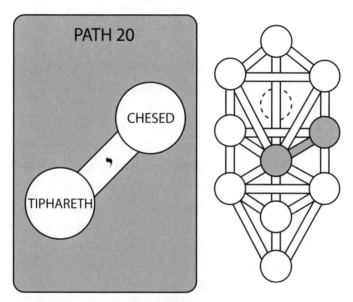

Figure 53: Path 20

Path: Path 20, Tiphareth to Chesed

Hebrew Leter: Yod

Hebrew Letter Meaning: Hand

Tarot Attribution: IX, the Hermit

Astrological Sign: Virgo

Yetziratic Text: "The Twentieth Path is the Intelligence of the Will, and is so called because it is the means of preparation of all and each created being, and by this intelligence the existence of the Primordial Wisdom becomes known." [159]

According to the Yeztiratic text, this path is called the "Intelligence of Will" because this is the path where we initiated into the Primordial Wisdom: the Divine Will of Creator.

This is made clear by the Hebrew Letter *Yod*, which is the first letter of the God-name YHVH, the tetragrammaton. It is the seed of wisdom sprouting forth to grow into the created form. Imagining this seed in terms of sperm fertilizing an egg, take into account the astrological sign of the path, as relayed by Virgo, which is the virgin, the recipient of the Immaculate Conception.

We are the virgins, ripe to become impregnated with the seed of spirit.

Yod means "hand" and represents the Hand of God leading the soul on its evolutionary path. Because the hand can both give and receive, this path is the perfect conduit of balance for both giving and receiving the wisdom of the spirit. For this path is connected to Chesed and as such is connected to the master teachers of humankind. This includes Jesus, the Buddha, Enoch, Moses, Black Elk, and the list goes on. When one engages in contact with these ascended masters, it is in Chesed that are they are receiving this contact (via the intercession of Tiphareth, of course).

The major arcana card for Chesed is the Hermit, who holds the staff of faith and bears a lantern of light, which (depending on the deck) is often sourced by either the sun or the geometric figure of the tetrahedron. Knight explains, "This Light-bearer of the Tarot may be equated with the hidden, or unrevealed cosmic mind of man, which serves to guide and inspire the soul in all its ways." [160] The Hermit sits in the darkness, quiet and still, ready to receive the fullness of spirit from Chesed. From Chesed is where the individuality (which is always centered in Tiphareth, both Chesed and Geburah being two poles thereof) first takes its form. However, it is well noted that even though the individuality is the higher self, it is still not perfect, for the only perfection resides in Kether. The individuality is the first deviation from the Supernal realm of being … so know that the journey does not end here. The Hermit represents a higher level of spiritual commitment.

---

159. Westcott, *Sepher Yetzirah,* 2nd ed., 30.
160. Knight, *Qabalistic Symbolism,* 105.

Teth: Path 19

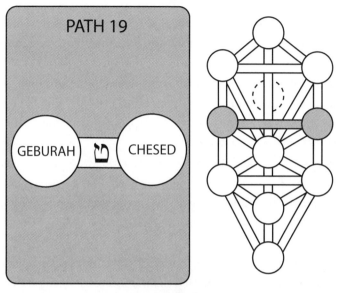

Figure 54: Path 19

Path: Path 19, Geburah to Chesed

Hebrew Letter: Teth

Hebrew Letter Meaning: Serpent

Tarot Attribution: VIII, Strength

Astrological Sign: Leo

Yetziratic Text: "The Nineteenth Path is the Intelligence of all activities of the spiritual beings, and is so called because of the affluence diffused by it from the most high blessing and most exalted sublime glory."[161]

One of the first things to know about this path is the correlation with Path 27, *Peh*, the Tower (also called the Mouth), which was the first lateral path on the Tree of Life encountered in this pathworking. There is a similarity in the distribution of energy here, from Force to Form, the Pillars of Mercy and Severity linked together. An understanding of this power comes from insight into the zodiacal sign, Leo, which teaches us about pride. Too much of it, of course, will get in the way of Divine Will and be our downfall. Yet the

---

161. Westcott, *Sepher Yetzirah,* 2nd ed., 30.

symbol of the lion in the mystery traditions is a symbol of true dignity, where hubris has no sway.

The lion, in the case of the major arcana, has other meanings as well. In alchemy, the lion represents the uncontrolled forces of nature. So, immediately we can see the process of the woman holding open the mouth (another reference to Path 27) of the wild lion in order to control and subdue it. The woman of course signifies our highest connection to spirit, the individuality. The subduing of the lion is not just subduing the lower, primal self (personality), but it also is a test to see if we are capable of utilizing all the knowledge we have collected on the journey of initiation thus far.

Traveling this path, we should see and be able to strip away the last illusion keeping us confined to the whims of our personality, our lower self. Our personality can often act as a mask (or series of masks) that hides our truest selves from the world. True strength comes from shedding theses masks, becoming vulnerable, and standing firm as the beings we truly are.

The key to this strength can be found within the mysteries of the Hebrew letter *Teth*. *Teth* means the "serpent," and those with a shamanic knowledgebase should understand the serpent as a teacher of transformation from one state of being to another. In Jewish mysticism, unlike in modern Christianity, it is a symbol of wisdom. In the Western Mystery Tradition, Chic and Sandra Tabatha Cicero explain that the serpent "also represents a type of electromagnetic energy not unlike that of the Eastern Kundalini. This 'serpent power' is used by mystics to activate the body's energy centers to cause a kind of divine rapture. The 19th Path connects the Sephiroth of Chesed and Geburah, the primary spheres of water and fire on the Tree. Between these two polarities a natural electrical circuit is formed that generates this vitalizing 'serpent power,' which is part of the magnetic current that powers the entire universe. The ability to direct and regulate this power is the basis for all occult work." [162]

Crowley, of course, changed the title of this tarot card to Lust, and even though I generally don't agree with all of his changes to the major arcana, I do understand his reasoning. Lust in this context is vigor in which strength is being exercised. In traditional decks the lion is straining to overcome the woman with its maw, the woman serenely holding back the primal instincts of the beast with ease; whereas in the Thoth arcana she is riding atop the lion with reins in one hand and a cup in the other, celebrating her rapturous victory.

162. Regardie, *Garden of Pomegranates*, 395.

The cup, even though it is not in the traditional imagery of the card, is another prime symbol for this path. It is a key symbol in esotercism for *full* acceptance of one's thoughts, words, and actions, as well as taking *full* responsibility for them. This is the *elixir vitae*, the universal solvent of alchemy. To drink from this cup is strength in its highest form.

Cheth: Path 18

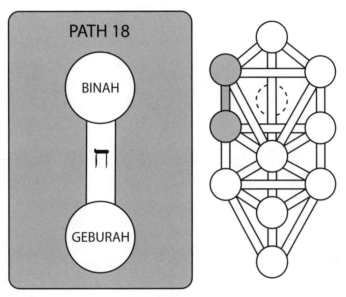

Figure 55: Path 18

Path: Path 18, Geburah to Binah

Hebrew Letter: Cheth

Hebrew Letter Meaning: Fence, enclosure

Tarot Attribution: VII, the Chariot

Astrological Sign: Cancer

Yetziratic Text: "The Eighteenth Path is called the House of Influence (by the greatness of whose abundance the influx of good things upon created beings is increased), and from the midst of the investigation the arcana and hidden senses are drawn forth, which dwell in its shade and which cling to it, from the cause of all causes." [163]

163. Westcott, *Sepher Yetzirah,* 2nd ed., 11.

Even though we still remain within the auspices of the Ethical Triad, this path begins the first interaction point with the Sephiroth of the Supernal Triad, which means we are crossing the space between the Unmanifest and the Manifest: the Abyss. Because of this, language breaks down, and as the occultist Colonel C. R. F. Seymour said, this condition is "utterly beyond our comprehension. It could be given a name, but no attributes." [164] For this chapter outlining the Ethical Machine, the Sephiroth will not be covered, only the paths, for these Sephiroth belong specifically on the Supernal side of the Abyss, which we will not yet cross.

Path 18 enables the ability to regain some balance after such a tumultuous turn around Tiphareth from the previous paths. This path is one of stability, the quiet after a storm. It is designed to be a channel of "Influence" (as stated in the Yetziratic text) for the individuality. Binah is the Sephiroth of understanding, the sphere where faith has its origins. The individuality must keep this channel open and clear so that one's destiny can flow down through the spheres and into the physical planes of manifestation.

The Hebrew letter, *Cheth*, means "fence" or "enclosure," which gives an indication that this path is one of protection and containment. Just as the wall in the Sun card refers to the containment necessary for precise growth, so here *Cheth* refers to the necessary enclosure required for consciousness (descending from above) to be organized into discernable Forms that can be understood at the level of the Manifest (for who can understand the consciousness of the Unmanifest?). This is where words begin to fail at describing the processes at this level of the tree. Again, an enclosure hides what is inside from the outside; therefore, any attempt of the human mind to try to grasp what goes on inside the enclosure becomes futile. This is the crux of the occult arts.

The tarot card of the Chariot more represents a mobile throne rather than a *Ben-Hur*–style chariot. It must be duly noted that the angelic order for Binah is the Aralim, meaning "thrones." The charioteer sits aloft, surveying his kingdom, which he has already set in motion; he no longer needs to conduct it (as per the reins on the Lust lion from Path 19). At this point, after the struggle with the lion (personality) on the previous path, a milestone should have been achieved. One should be able to bear the fruit of the Holy Grail, which is in no way an end result to illumination but merely a significant stage of acquisition or triumph in the ever-cyclic, never-ending path of initiation.

The astrological sign is Cancer, the crab. This provides another symbol of the enclosure, an outer shell for protection of the inner body. We are reminded of the correlation

164. Seymour, *Forgotten Mage*, 32.

to the crustacean crawling out of the waters in the Moon card. The crustacean is a primal creature, crawling out from the archaic waters and influences of the Great Mother. This is indeed our first touchpoint with Binah. The charioteer is one who is ready to receive the first impressions of creation from the Supernals.

In essence, this path is where the hard work and discipleship should be rewarded before the mystic continues on the journey. It is far from a respite. An outer shell (armor) is acquired and from here on out the knowledge and discipline of the initiate should be put to productive use. The aim of the initiate is to be master of the inner world. The previous paths set about conquering the lower influences of the personality, the Ruach and Nephesch. Now, this path is a proclamation on what has been conquered. In Native American traditions, a warrior would put his stake in the ground and hold his position, never to return to whence he came until the battle was complete. Path 18 is the act of putting one's stake in the ground and never returning to those things that pull one way away from the Great Work.

Zain: Path 17

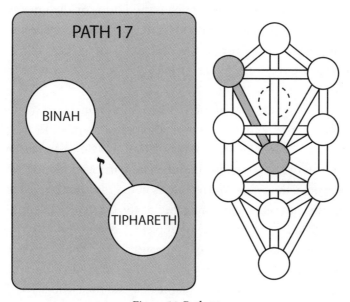

Figure 56: Path 17

Path: Path 17, Tiphareth to Binah

Hebrew Letter: Zain

Hebrew Letter Meaning: Sword

Tarot Attribution: VI, the Lovers

Astrological Sign: Gemini

Yetziratic Text: "The Seventeenth Path is the Disposing Intelligence, which provides Faith to the Righteous, and they are clothed with the Holy Spirit by it, and it is called the Foundation of Excellence in the state of higher things."[165]

Much like the paths of the Devil and Death, Path 17 is an often misunderstood path. This is due to students of the tarot taking the symbols at literal or face value. Many take the tarot card of the Lovers to represent the love between two people, "true love," marriage, and so on when, in fact, it is more closely related to the previously cited Hermetic allegory of *The Chymical Marriage of Christian Rosenkreutz*, which is itself a metaphor for the uniting of spirit (God) and matter (humankind). This duality—as represented by the Lovers—is in us all. When descending the tree from Kether in the process of creation, it is the first of the major arcana to represent more than one figure as the prime symbol.

From this we must understand and pay attention to the Sephiroth connecting this path: Binah, the Great Mother, breaking down the Forms of the universe into the Son of Tiphareth, matter in its highest form. This is the path where creation transitions from a singular to a dual experience. However, while ascending the tree, our duality becomes harmonized. Unity of being is the initiatory quality that will allow us to traverse into the Supernal realms.

This is, in actuality, what the gurus have spoken of as non-dual awareness. That being said, the Hebrew letter of *Zain* (or *Zayen*) is the perfect symbol for this path since its meaning is "sword." As stated before, the sword both cuts down and defends. The sword separates, and it is in this separateness that the two parts can become whole. Once this separation is overcome, the figures of the Lovers in the card are received back into Binah, representative of the innocence and nonduality of the Garden of Eden. Again, this takes place within the individual, not among two people; the division is of us from the Divine, if you will, and the reunification of the two is the reward of reception to the Divine.

Though some may not like to admit it, the universe is based upon the principle of duality: there must be a separation between the Self and the Divine. The Taoist yin-yang symbol is a perfect example of this, as black is defined by the virtue of not being white and white is characterized by not being black. Creator is separate from creation in order that creation can exist; however, it is this divide that causes relationship. Since there is separa-

---

165. Westcott, *Sepher Yetzirah*, 2nd ed., 30.

tion, interaction can occur. Without separation, love has no way to demonstrate itself in manifestation.

Regarding the sword, any meanings can be derived from the legends of King Arthur and Excalibur, especially within the Western Mystery Tradition (as has already been discussed via the Holy Grail). Most especially of note for this path is the tale of the mystical sword that came from and eventually returned to the Lady of the Lake, which could be seen as a manifestation of Binah. The sword of note in the story is Excalibur, which is an expression of polarity because, according to Merlin, the sword itself was not even worth as much as its scabbard, which represented the knowledge and application of the sword's power.

The most crucial experience to take from this path is Binah's particular connection to the Holy Guardian Angel, of which the "Knowledge and Conversation of" is one of the holiest endeavors to embark upon in esotericism. As discussed earlier, the Holy Guardian Angel is a sort of divine emissary connected to one's individuality. As God begat creation, all life was split into a multitude of divine sparks, each one attaching to an individual in manifestation. This divine spark is intended to guide one on one's path in the Great Work. The astrological sign for this path being Gemini, the twins, we can see how the relationship with the Holy Guardian Angel should exist with our higher self: one is the reflection of another, but they are not the same thing.

The Hebrew letter *Zain* also reflects this relationship with one's Holy Guardian Angel. The *Yod* shape at the top indicates the highest conception of God, the rod extending beneath it through the levels of creation and into the manifested universe. This is the vertical purpose of the Holy Guardian Angel and of this path: to provide a direct channel to one's own sacred purpose on the earth.

Vav: Path 16

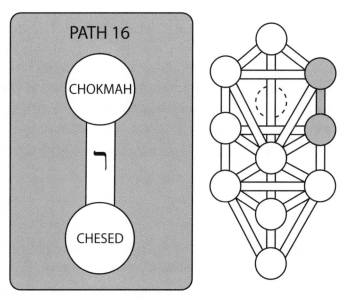

Figure 57: Path 16

Path: Path 16, Chesed to Chokmah

Hebrew Letter: Vav

Hebrew Letter Meaning: Nail

Tarot Attribution: V, the Hierophant

Astrological Sign: Taurus

Yetziratic Text: "The Sixteenth Path is the Triumphal or Eternal Intelligence, so called because it is the pleasure of the Glory, beyond which is no other Glory like to it, and it is
called also the Paradise prepared for the Righteous." [166]

This path is our first connection to Chokmah, the prime masculine Godhead of the
universe, Binah's counterpart. The title of Chokmah is Wisdom, the title of Chesed being
Mercy. However, another title in the esoteric literature granted to Chesed is Glory. Path
16 reflects the true "pleasure of the Glory," as referenced in the Yetziratic text, because it

---

166. Westcott., *Sepher Yetzirah*, 2nd ed., 30.

is the harmonious energy of Divine Will passed from the Great Father, Chokmah, to the merciful influence of Chesed.

This harmonious influx can first be realized through the Hebrew letter *Vav* (or *Vau*), which is the "nail." The nail is the tool that fastens or joins, the conjunction between the wisdom of Chokmah and the glory of Chesed, the Divine Will's influence over the individuality. When looking at this path's parallel counterpart on the Tree of Life, Path 18 (Binah to Geburah), the Hebrew letter being represented there is *Cheth*, the fence.

The dove (a representation of Venus) is another symbol with equal weight and is the manifestation of the Holy Spirit filling the womb of the Virgin Mary with the Christ Consciousness. Please forgive the pun, but the goal of mysticism is that we must be like Mary and open ourselves to being impregnated with the seed from Chokmah, or rather (in the case of *Vav*) to get *nailed!*

Another aspect of *Vav* to consider is its place in the name of God, the Tetragrammaton, YHVH (*Yod-Heh-Vav-Heh*). Explained by Gareth Knight, *Vav* is in essence the "active manifestation in Form, the result of the union of opposites of Yod and Heh.... From an esoteric Christian standpoint the Nail is a significant symbol, being (in triplicity) that which nails the Spirit to the Cross of Matter."[167]

The astrological attribution, Taurus, has perhaps more written about it for Path 16 than any other in esoteric literature. There is far too much to get into here, but further study is recommended. In short, Taurus represents the bull kerub of the four holy living creatures, which is a strong connector to the earth. The figure in Crowley's Thoth card is enraptured by the bull kerub, as well as sentried by elephants, another representation of the Taurus nature. Further, in terms of the body/chakra system, Taurus operates via the throat. The throat is our primary vehicle for speech, the utterance of Will into the physical world.

The major arcana card for this path is the Hierophant, who is the emissary of the Primal Source, also called the Magus of the Eternal. A magus is one who has the ability to mediate power from one level of being to another. Therefore, the Hierophant is one who can conjure the power of the higher realms and transmit them to the lower levels of earthly existence, from the above to the below.

Hence the Hierophant is also the priest officiating the alchemical wedding between the two halves of the self: the higher self (individuality) and the lower self (personality).

---

167. Knight, *Qabalistic Symbolism*, 179.

The two kneeling figures before him (their sex is moot) are receiving the teaching from the priest. Knowledge is being passed down from on high to the two dual selves: the Lovers.

With this, this path calls us to still our monkey minds so that wisdom from the higher worlds can be received. The ability to listen, to truly open ourselves to the unseen, is the primary faculty that must be utilized. This is done less with the physical ears and more with the heart.

Heh: Path 15

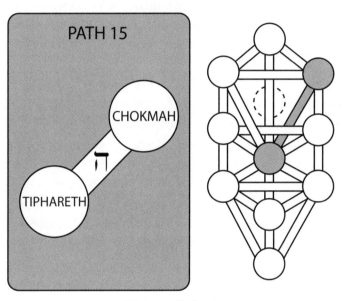

Figure 58: Path 15

Path: Path 15, Tiphareth to Chokmah

Hebrew Letter: Heh

Hebrew Letter Meaning: Window

Tarot Attributino: IV, the Emperor

Astrological Sign: Aries

Yetziratic Text: "The Fifteenth Path is the Constituting Intelligence, so called because it constitutes the substance of creation in pure darkness, and men have spoken of these contemplations; it is that darkness spoken of in Scripture, Job xxxviii. 9, 'and thick darkness a swaddling band for it.' "[168]

In many mystery schools, the major arcana card associated with this path is normally the Star, whereas the Emperor is attributed to Path 28. Dolores Ashcroft-Nowicki suggests either will work, and I agree, though I chose to keep to the sequential order of the tarot corresponding to the sequential ordering of the paths on the Tree of Life. Therefore, for Path 15, the Emperor is the suitable symbol.

The Emperor is, without a doubt, the primary masculine energy of the tarot. The other cards that come before it either are feminine or can be interpreted as androgynous. The Emperor is the first card in the major arcana in which the fiery male aspect of the godhood shines through, which makes sense considering its touchpoint with Chokmah. The energy generated here is swift and creative, the paternal potencies of power reigning into Tiphareth.

The Emperor deals with the governance of such power, as represented by the rams on the throne as well as the scepter. The ram is wild by nature but can be tamed to be a docile beast. This is the goal of governance. A king's (or the Emperor's) scepter is the symbol of the governance issued successfully, a firm hold on the banal nature of the personality established.

Descending, this path leads from Chokmah, the "Giver of Life," to Tiphareth. The *Sepher Yetzirah* calls this path the "Constituting Intelligence," and we can understand that through the governance of the Emperor. This intelligence orders and constructs the life force of the Divine out of the womb of darkness. Therefore, just as the force of creation brought order into the darkness through the spark of divine light, so our relationship to the stabilization and ordering of power and energy, in accordance to the self, can be explored.

The Yeztiratic text also refers to the darkness as a sea. Many creation stories from cultures around the planet speak of the primordial waters of chaos from whence all creation sprang, the Unmanifest. It should be understood that all that has come from the dark seas of the Unmanifest has done so because it has been ordained; it is within divine order.

The Hebrew letter *Heh* means "window." A window's sole purpose is to act as an opening for light to pass through. More importantly, this Hebrew letter appears twice in the tetragrammaton, the Name of God: *Yod-Heh-Vav-Heh*. It is the symbol of incoming life, best represented through the story of Abraham. Before the conception of their child, Isaac

---

168. Westcott, *Sepher Yetzirah,* 2nd ed., 30.

(a symbol of their covenant with God), Abraham and his wife Sarah were known respectively as only Abram and Sarai. Once this covenant was sealed, the *Heh* was added to their names, making them a clear window for God's promise to shine through the roots of their lineage: God's chosen people. This doesn't mean only the "Jews" are God's chosen few; it is an expression of a promise to those dedicated to the Great Work as clear windows for the divine light.

Heh has to do with perception, the perception of consciousness on a cosmic scale. Humanity is limited in our perception. We cannot hope to fully comprehend the divine image, the Majesty of the Great Originating Mystery. The window of *Heh* is that aperture of sight our own vista cannot contain when gazing upon the starry expanse of the heavens, but that our hearts hope to capture.

Thus, one can understand the case for the Star being the primary major arcana card for this path, but the auspices of the Emperor can also fit well.

12

THE SUPERNAL FIRMAMENT

Here we are now working strictly with the Supernals, the highest regions of archetypal consciousness. These vistas cannot ever truly be known. This is the plight of the mystic human: to reach for the unattainable, to try—however impossible it may be—to unveil the Great Originating Mystery. The Supernal Triad is the Great Firmament, the heavenly spheres where we understand the origins of what we call God to be. This is the holiest of holies, and it can only ever really be understood through symbols, metaphor, or poetry. So, take any words hereafter with a grain salt, for no language can truly ascertain the enigma of divinity.

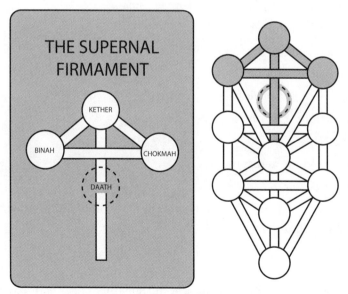

Figure 59: The Supernal Firmament

Daath: Path 0

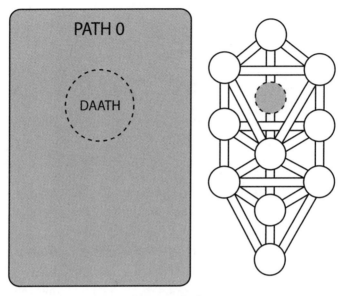

Figure 60: Path 0

God Name: A conjunction of *Jehovah* and *Jehovah Elohim*

Archangel: Archangels of the Cardinal Points

Order of Angels: Serpents

Color: Lavender, silver-gray, violet

Virtue: Detachment of Personality

Vice: Doubt of the future, apathy, inertia

Tarot Attribution: N/A

Spiritual Experience: Vision across the Abyss

Title: The Invisible Sephirah

Symbols: The condemned cell, the empty room, the cloud-hidden peak of the Sacred Mountain of any culture

Yetziratic Text: N/A

There is a chasm that separates the Ethical and Supernal Triads and is sometimes called the Abyss but often referred to as the Invisible Sephirah, the Eleventh Sephirah, or the

Missing Sephirah: Daath. Daath is not considered a Sephirah. The Abyss is a gulf astride the Tree of Life that separates the Supernal Triad from the rest of the Sephiroth. Much has been stated about Daath already in chapter 6, though a little more could be expanded upon.

Crossing the Abyss is noted in the Mysteries as being wrought with peril. However, it is also the most important journey for any magician. Graduation of this degree usually lands a magician the label of Master of the Temple. This is the gap, the opening where God's energy enters the universe. Therefore, only magicians and mystics of the highest order can truly interact with Daath and survive with their psyche intact.

Aleister Crowley wrote many interesting notions about the Abyss and seems to be one of the few magicians in the Western Mystery Tradition who mapped the endeavor in their literary canon. In his autobiography, *The Confessions of Aleister Crowley,* he lays out how crossing the Abyss is truly about sacrificing one's identity completely:

> To penetrate beyond the Abyss, where iniquity cannot exist, my personal self-hood must be annihilated.... My being must be dissolved in that of the infinite.... I may say that the essence of the matter was that I had hitherto clung to certain conceptions of conduct which, while perfectly proper from the standpoint of my human nature, were impertinent to initiation. I could not cross the Abyss till I had torn them out of my heart.... I knew that even my holiest, mine inmost self, might not protect me from the grim abominations of the Abyss.[169]

In essence, Daath is the representative region associated with Nirvana. In Nirvana, the sense of self is lost; there is no ego left in the human psyche. Before Daath, the soul yearns to become one with spirit. Once that soul is initiated into Daath, there is no more sense of trying to become anything—that soul is home. Self-identity is lost. This is the true purpose of mysticism.

This is an experience mapped in many shamanic initiations, in which the identity—or self—is shattered in order to reconstruct the persona into a more dynamic being in union with the natural world. As don Oscar Miro-Quesada states in his own autobiographical account, "Like most shamanic apprentices, I was taken to the brink of complete annihilation as a prerequisite to being able to serve others."[170] Don Oscar was driven to that brink

---

169. Aleister Crowley, *The Confessions of Aleister* Crowley (New York: Penguin, 1989), 620–21.

170. Glass-Coffin and Miro-Quesada, *Lessons in Courage,* 73.

by teacher don Celso, who submitted Oscar to the initiatory process of being buried alive. While lying in a grave covered in wet sand, Oscar's experience of being unable to free himself gripped him in panic. All he could do was surrender his identity completely in order to survive the experience. When his ego was sufficiently dead, don Celso exhumed Oscar and he emerged into the world anew.

Ethnopsychologist Holger Kalweit has studied shamanic initiations and apprenticeship from many cultures around the globe. It can be seen through his observations how the Daath experience of shattering the identity is prevalent through shamanic dismemberment:

> The period of initiation strips the shaman of all his social and mental habits as well as his religious and philosophical ideas. To use a more graphic expression: he is skinned, his bowels are torn out, and as happened to Saint Theresa, the flesh is cut from his bones. He is literally chopped into pieces, cooked, grilled, or fried....
>
> In many traditions the spirits of the underworld not only take the body of the initiate apart in a most gruesome way—they also put it together again, but in a curious manner which endows the person subjected to such a dismemberment with superhuman powers.[171]

It is then apparent that one of the symbols is the cloud-hidden peak of the Sacred Mountain of any culture, as we can understand the cross-cultural tale associated with scaling the mountain in order to find the face of God.

Daath is Hebrew for "knowledge," and because of the intensity of experience regarding the death of one's identity, we can assume this is a knowledge not to be given lightly. It is earned by fear and hardship of falling into the Abyss, the bottomless pit. Legend has it that Daath used to be an actual Sephirah on the Tree of Life; associated with it were the paths of the Beggar and the Fountain (which are now known as the missing tarot cards). But there was a great cataclysm, Daath ruptured into an Abyss, and God (the Supernals) was separated from the rest of the universe. If one were to look at the Tree of Life in planetary terms (Earth as Malkuth, the moon as Yesod, Netzach as Venus, Hod as Mercury, etc.), then Daath would be the asteroid belt, the remnants of the long-lost planet of the solar system.

The knowledge of Daath brings forth the realization that the universe was broken in half, as is replayed in the story of Genesis, when Adam and Eve ate of the fruit from the

---

171. Holger Kalweit, *Dreamtime & Inner Space: The World of the Shaman* (Boston: Shambhala, 1988), 95.

Tree of the Knowledge of Good and Evil. Since this fall, we have—in an almost Gnostic sense—been living in a broken cosmos.

In this we see the true purpose of initiation: that the knowledge we seek is truly unknowable and can only be known by its unknowable state. In Alan Moore's magical epic *Promethea*, the character based on magician Austin Spare notes, "Daath is that knowledge knowable only by its absence. It is the neither-neither.... No light is here emitted." [172] We can understand here why esotericism has survived through the auspices of "occult" or "secret" societies, why many initiatory experiences from all cultures are generally done either in the dark or in private. This is an emulation of Daath's presence—or lack thereof—upon the tree as an invisible, but necessary, division between this world and the other, between the seen and the unseen, between the human and God.

Binah: Path 3

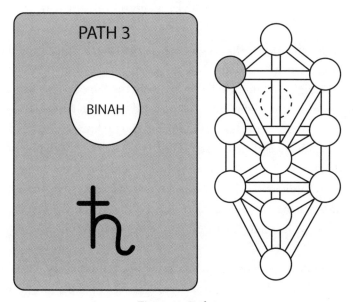

Figure 61: Path 3

God Name: Jehovah Elohim

Archangel: Tzaphkiel

---

172. Alan Moore, J. H. Williams III, Mick Gray, and Jeromy Cox, *Promethea*, collected edition, bk. 4, issue 20 (La Jolla, CA: Wildstorm, 2013), 17.

Order of Angels: Aralim

Animal Totem: Alligator

Color: Black or dark brown

Virtue: Silence

Vice: Avarice

Tarot Attribution: Three of Pentacles, Three of Cups, Three of Swords, Three of Wands, Queen of Pentacles, Queen of Cups, Queen of Swords, Queen of Wands

Spiritual Experience: Vision of the Sorrow

Titles: Ama, the dark, sterile Mother; Aima, the bright, fertile Mother

Symbols: Yoni, vesica piscis; cup or chalice

Yetziratic Text: "The Third Path is the Sanctifying Intelligence, and is the basis of foundation of Primordial Wisdom, which is called the Former of Faith, and its roots, Amen; and it is the parent of Faith, from which virtues doth Faith emanate." [173]

Now that Daath—the Abyss—has been crossed, the realms of the Supernal Firmament can truly be explored. Since Knowledge has broken down the human psyche, only symbolism can provide the slightest hint of relationship with the Supernal Sephiroth.

Binah, which means "understanding," is the third Sephirah on the Tree of Life. When one considers the Creation of the universe, Binah is the first manifestation of the Goddess, and thus the first semblance of manifestation of Form. All forms that exist get their root in Binah. Her titles are Ama, the dark, sterile Mother, and Aima, the bright, fertile Mother; she is Babylon, both Virgin and Whore. She is known in the Mysteries as Sophia. She is the original formulation of the feminine in all of existence. Binah is the first container (Form) of which Chokmah lays its seed (Force). She is the first primal principle of the feminine in the universe.

Whether or not God or Goddess is higher up or lower on the tree, or which came first, is irrelevant: the chicken or the egg. The Supernals, as all of the Sephiroth, are not numerically in sequence as we understand them. Binah being the third Sephirah does not make her third in line in the assembly of creation. It is merely a model in order to understand how Form comes into being. One (the monad, the singularity of Source) plus two (Chokmah, the reflection of the monad) equals three, thus creating a triangle, the first geometric shape that can be created with the minimal amount of lines (other than a circle). As Alan

---

173. Westcott, *Sepher Yetzirah,* 2nd ed., 28.

Moore demonstrates in *Promethea*, through the character of John Dee, "With three points, we may enclose a space in two dimensions. We may plot a triangle. Seen thus [inverted], the triangle is a symbol of water. It is here at Binah that all water, all compassion, has its origin. At Binah is the cup that overfloweth." [174]

It is important to keep engaging with the Tree of Life as a *model* for creation, rather than an exact replica. In this, Binah is regarded as the Great Mother, the archetypal womb of all life. In a womb, life is confined; but, through that limitation, an environment is created that facilitates the evolution of the organism. As Dion Fortune has stated, "Form checks life, thwarts it, and yet enables it to organise. Seen from the point of view of free-moving force, incarceration in a form is extinction." [175] Being the first inclination of Form, Binah constricts the Force from Chokmah and regulates it. Putting the Force through death, Form eventually cultivates it into a useful structure for the Ethical realms to eventually model into manifestation.

The misunderstanding we have discussed many times regarding the role of the feminine in a spiritual context must be finally clarified in this Sephirah. As Dion stated, and I have reiterated many times throughout this book, the feminine principle of the universe is not synonymous with the female gender. The principle of the feminine resides in both man *and* woman, but it must be understood what this energy truly means if we are to herald the return of the Goddess in the modern world.

Binah being the Mother and associated greatly with the womb, we can also understand its reference as the "Great Sea" in esoteric literature. This makes sense for the totemic attribution as we have traveled up the tree and into the Supernal Firmament. The alligator connects us back to the prehistoric origins on this planet, to the primal core of what Binah represents. Alligators and crocodiles, revered by the Egyptians as well as other peoples, have often been associated with the unbridled feminine potencies of the world. Patrolling the shoreline of the waters—the great horizon between birth and death—they are the protectors of all knowledge, which Binah is the first keeper of:

$$\text{Binah (understanding)} + \text{Chokmah (wisdom)} = \text{Daath (knowledge)}$$

The spiritual experience of Binah is the Vision of Sorrow. Within this Sephirah, one is to have a vision of the holistic picture of all that is, all that was, why it was, what it is now,

---

174. Moore et al., *Promethea*, bk. 4, issue 21, 10–11.
175. Fortune, *Mystical Qabalah*, 132.

why it is, and what it is to become. In essence, true and total *understanding* of all existence. The Great Mother sees all. She sees our joys but also our pains and our sins. And, in all that she sees, she is indeed in sorrow.

We are a very stubborn species. Binah watches as all too often we neglect our children's future, poison our air and seas, enslave each other, and go to war. We are at home in our own addictions, and unfortunately it frequently takes a major trauma to wake us up from our unhealthy habits or anosognosia. Take for instance the terrorist attacks of 9/11. How many citizens paid attention to US foreign policy before this tragic event? Even though it would be best to not need these tragedies, human beings are unfortunately thick-headed and need a push in order to evolve.

Regrettably, this is another aspect of the mystical experience not taken into consideration by some. It is not all bliss and rainbows. It is not just a possibility, but a necessity, to assimilate the Vision of the Sorrow that compels the Goddess into her eternal cry for her children. The Tree of Life will simply not allow you to proceed unless this is done.

Therefore, managing the Vision of Sorrow is best achieved through Binah's primary virtue: silence. It is necessary to still the noise and the raging waters to Understand all things in their truest vision. By stilling the clamor can the sparkling stars of the Heavens accurately reflect on the mirroring surface of the body of water below.

As the archetypal Temple, she is the root of all temples in manifestation, the Inner Church, the sacred space of all sacred spaces. Because of this, Binah truly is the womb of life, the container from which all has been embodied. Approach the Dark Mother's temple in silence, approach the temple in sorrow, and the vision shall be received.

The experience of Binah should be practiced through acts of complete silence. As has been taught to me by don Oscar and my other teachers many times, silence is the greatest virtue in all esoteric work. Talking about these things too much is rife to ruin the experience. The Temple of Binah is a pure silence, so deep and piercing it is liable to make one mad. So, when you engage in your ritual work, remember that silencing your mind and tongue is essential to progressing into the Supernal reaches of the Great Work.

Daleth: Path 14

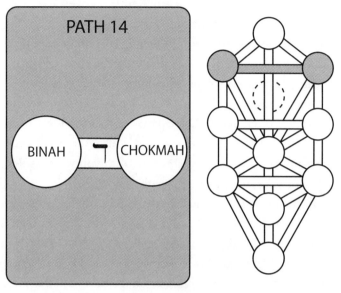

Figure 62: Path 14

Path: Path 14, Binah to Chokmah

Hebrew Letter: Daleth

Hebrew Letter Meaning: Door

Tarot Attribution: III, the Empress

Astrological Sign: Venus

Yetziratic Text: "The Fourteenth Path is the Illuminating Intelligence, and is so called because it is itself that *Chashmal* which is the founder of the concealed and fundamental ideas of holiness and of their stages of preparation." [176]

Path 14 is the final lateral path on the Tree of Life. This path represents the primordial connection between the Great Mother (Binah) and the Great Father (Chokmah). It is important to note the vast amount of symbolism of this path and to not get lost in it. This path has sometimes been called the Gate of Heaven because it is the lateral path that separates the Supernals from the rest of the tree and also because of the beauty represented in its symbolism.

---

176. Westcott, *Sepher Yetzirah*, 2nd ed., 30–31.

To understand this, we must also reflect on the path in its descending nature as well. The Source of All Being, all existence, is above in Kether. However, creation requires polarity in order to stabilize itself in manifestation. It is here on this path, via the dual Sephiroth of Binah and Chokmah, where the prime Principles of Polarity are brought into effect. This is the path in which the Force of Chokmah enters the Form of Binah. This is the fundamental path of the great universal copulation between opposites.

The Hebrew letter *Daleth* means "door." It is not only the doorway into the Supernals, but it is also the portal through which the life force of creation is born into existence. It is here where energies (Force) of Chokmah are passed into Binah, the originator of Form. We see here the first inclinations of a sexual nature of the universe, as this path represents our birth canal into existence; thus, this is the path of fertility.

This fertility is highly representative in the tarot card of the Empress, normally depicted in a natural setting with abundant floral and vegetal growth. She is called Daughter of the Mighty Ones (Binah and Chokmah) and is also referred to as the Isis of Nature. She is both virgin and pregnant with life, a paradox which is set in motion on this path and reflected throughout the rest of the tree. Paradox requires one to believe in the absurd and unimaginable, which is exactly how the door (*Daleth*) to true esoteric knowledge will be opened.

Venus is the astrological sign, which of course has connections to all symbolic attributions to the Goddess, but also, according to Crowley, it is "the only one of the planetary symbols which comprises all the Sephiroth of the Tree of Life." [177] (See figure 63.) So, it is our understanding that this path—the Empress, the representative of the ultimate fertilization and nurturing of the Earth Mother—helps us understand that love, in all its ways of expression, is the most important expression in all existence.

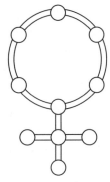

Figure 63: Venus as the Tree of Life

---

177. Crowley, *Book of Thoth*, 75.

Chokmah: Path 2

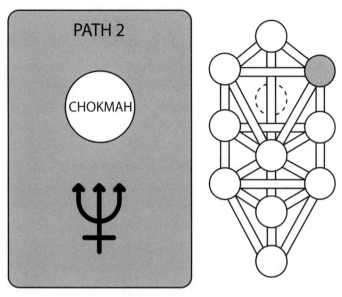

Figure 64: Path 2

God Name: Jehovah (YHVH)

Archangel: Raziel

Order of Angels: Ophannim

Animal Totem: Shark

Color: Gray, sometimes soft blue

Virtue: Devotion

Vice: N/A

Tarot Attributions: Two of Pentacles, Two of Cups, Two of Swords, Two of Wands, King of Pentacles, King of Cups, King of Swords, King of Wands

Spiritual Experience: The Vision of God Face-to-Face

Titles: Abba, the Supernal Father

Symbols: Phallus, tower, straight line

Yetziratic Text: "The Second Path is that of the Illuminating Intelligence it is the Crown of Creation, the Splendor of the Unity, equaling it, and it is exalted above every head, and named by the Kabbalists the Second Glory."[178]

As stated before, the key to pathworking in the Qabalah is understanding (via Binah) the Tree of Life as not just a map of consciousness but also a sort of guiding post for the process of creation itself. In pathworking, we are essentially tracing the path of creation in reverse—backward through time, as it were—to the very beginning of all Manifestation. So, as always, to interpret Chokmah we must understand the Sephiroth surrounding it.

Kether, the first Sephirah, is the originating point of creation. I use the term *point* deliberately, as it can be best understood as a singularity, a one-dimensional point represented by a single dot. Imagine the cosmic egg before the big bang. All that ever was or will be has not yet been made manifest or conceived. However, all its potential is contained within this one-dimensional emanation, a blip of "light" from the Unmanifest. This is God in pure unity; there is nothing "other." But then, God *moved*. An idea was brought into being, the idea of imagining something other than itself. That idea, that movement, formed a line—from one dimension of existence to two dimensions.

When Chokmah was formed, it was merely a reflection of the original Sephirah: a mirror. As illustrated by Gareth Knight, "it therefore reflects upon itself and this reflection causes an image of itself to be formed, and as the Mind of god is so powerful, this image takes on an objective existence—anything that God thinks, is. Thus the whole of manifestation could be conceived of as the thought process of God. 'We are such stuff as dreams are made on.' … It is this first projection of an idea of itself that is what we call the Sephirah Chokmah."[179]

Chokmah is Kether in a lesser emanation, though it is recognized as the purest idea of Force, the first force of movement: a line. It is from here that we then beget Force being contained within its limitations, eventually establishing the venerable rhythm of the Universe via Form in Binah. And here we see the inception of all duality in the universe, according to Israel Regardie: "If we try for a moment to think what is the ultimate differentiation of existence, we shall find that so far as we can grasp it, it is a plus and minus, positive and negative, male and female, and so we should expect on the Tree of Life to find

178. Westcott, *Sepher Yetzirah,* 2nd ed., 28.
179. Knight, *Qabalistic Symbolism,* 77–78.

that the two emanations succeeding Kether partake of these characteristics." [180] And thus we have the Supernal Triad. The cadence of universal manifestation is set: Force and Form in an infinite tango like the tides of the ocean.

Speaking of which, the animal totem for Chokmah is the shark, one of the oldest living species on the planet. Given that the primary symbol for Chokmah in the mystery schools is a phallus, tower, or straight line, the shark perfectly represents this movement of creation thrust from the Source. A shark is in perpetual motion, its entire existence spent careening through space getting what it wants, as does the Force of Chokmah. Sharks are masters of survival, masters of the sea. In them, we learn to drive onward, without fear, into the great Supernals. Because fear, if we hold onto it, will prevent our connection with the individuality and beyond. Stripping ourselves of fear and barreling through with our task is sometimes the only option an initiate may have when travailing the unknown vistas of consciousness.

Chokmah means "wisdom," and it is the ultimate All-father, the primal male expression of the universe. Of the two poles of manifestation, it is the head of the Pillar of Mercy, whereas the feminine principle is the head of the Pillar of Severity. As can be obvious so far in this description, it is nearly impossible to discuss Chokmah without Binah and Binah without Chokmah. It is apparent that through this sexual interchange, the universe is thus known.

Chokmah is the stimulator of life, as has been described throughout the tree as Force. Binah is the builder and organizer of that life, as Form. As forms are built, decisions about what is useful and what isn't must be made; therefore, Binah is also a bearer of limitation, decay. Therefore, in the highest sense, Chokmah is the provider of life and Binah the womb of death. But, in Chokmah we experience the thoroughfare of cosmic energy that is reflected from Kether. Chokmah takes that energy and shapes it into ideas before Binah builds them. Therefore, Chokmah is the progenitor of all creative energy.

---

180. Regardie, *Garden of Pomegranates*, 41–42.

Gimel: Path 13

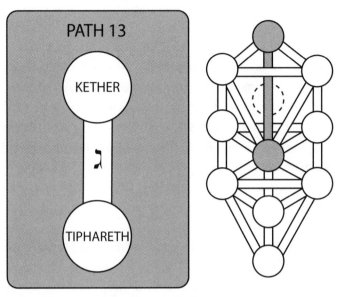

Figure 65: Path 13

Path: Path 13, Tiphareth to Kether

Hebrew Letter: Gimel

Hebrew Letter Meaning: Camel

Tarot Attribution: II, the High Priestess

Astrological Sign: The moon

Yetziratic Text: "The Thirteenth Path is named the Uniting Intelligence and is so-called because it is itself the Essence of Glory. It is the Consummation of the Truth of individual spiritual things." [181]

Path 13 is now the first contact to be made with Kether, the Fount of All Being and Manifestation. It would make sense that if you have gotten this far, it is now time—if you haven't already—to get your shit in order before continuing on to this direct connection to the Crown, the highest form of godhood. Because the Crown is the doorway into the Unmanifest, it is important to note the working of this path tends to be very abstract. Much

---

181. Westcott, *Sepher Yetzirah,* 2nd ed., 29.

time and patience need to be taken with Path 13, as results are likely to take months, even years, to manifest.

That being said, the 13th Path is rife with symbolism. After all, it is the final vertical path on the Tree of Life, uniting Kether to Tiphareth, the Divine with the individuality. More than any other path, this one is the direct route from soul to spirit, from creation to Creator (and vice versa). The *Sepher Yeztirah* calls it the "Uniting Intelligence" because the unity of the individuality with the Divine equals the essence of glory, and thus truth, which is the basis of the Great Work. It is on the Middle Pillar of the tree; along with Paths 32 and 25, the pathways along the Middle Pillar are collectively known as the Path of the Arrow, or the Way of the Mystic. Knowing this connection, we are reminded that one cannot traverse the higher realms of mysticism without first being rooted in this world, the here and now.

One of the primary symbols of this path is, of course, the High Priestess. A counterpart to the Magician card (Path 12), the High Priestess represents the spawning energies of creation templed, contained as principle rather than freeform. On either side of her stand the two pillars, Jachin and Boaz, making her the prime emblematic symbol of the initiate turned Divine Self. She is the first card in the tarot to represent the polarity of the universe, and she controls the influx of positive-negative, masculine-feminine from her throne. In her hand she holds the Torah, or book of knowledge. Through her, we can understand the true reality.

The Hebrew letter is *Gimel*, the "camel," and is indicative of two *Yods* connecting the top and bottom of a shaft. The top *Yod* represents life in heaven, whereas the bottom *Yod* represents life on earth. The camel is an animal with great stamina: it can hold water for extremely long periods while traversing the desert. Here is another desert we must cross, the Invisible Sephirah Daath, and thus we encounter another (though the final) dark night of the soul.

Understanding Daath is essential to understanding this path. For those who have encountered Daath, it is often portrayed as a desert landscape filled with androgynous forms. Being androgynous, a form loses its dualistic identity; in Daath there are no true forms. This is where the last remnants of the individual soul are stripped away to absolute nothingness so that true union with God can be achieved. It is where the Divine Wisdom comes to purify the soul so that the soul can continue its course to Kether, to God. In fact, it is the final purification.

Remember, Daath means knowledge, and as we discussed, the High Priestess is often shown holding a book or scroll of knowledge. There is another interpretation, according to Jungian psychoanalyst Dr. Irene Gad: "Some decks show the High Priestess with two keys—logic and intuition—in her left hand. Without their cooperation the book of secret knowledge, held in her right hand, could not become intelligible. They unlock the two doors to the white and black lights, whereby the white light can be found only after the black is known. Truth can be seen only by those to whom the High Priestess entrusts these keys, which in this context stand for equilibrium and equivalence of opposites."[182]

In some depictions there is a curtain stretched behind her between the two pillars. This, finally, is the veil, concealing the glory of Kether. Again, it is the High Priestess who holds the answer to lifting this veil. As we lift the veil, paradoxically, all of our previous knowledge is stripped from us. That's okay: that's part of the process. The only thing one can do is rely on that urge and need to keep moving onward to Kether.

Beth: Path 12

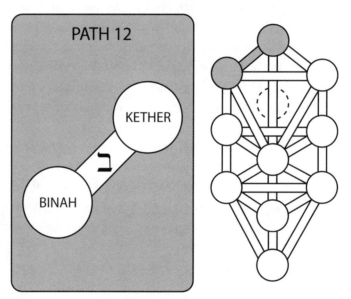

Figure 66: Path 12

Path: Path 12, Binah to Kether

Hebrew Letter: Beth

Hebrew Letter Meaning: House

182. Gad, *Tarot and Individuation*, 43.

Tarot Attribution: I, the Magician

Astrological Sign: Mercury

Yetziratic Text: "The Twelfth Path is the Intelligence of Transparency because it is that species of Magnificence called *Chazchazit*, which is named the place whence issues the vision of those seeing in apparitions. (That is the prophecies by seers in a vision.)" [183]

In the Yetziratic text, Path 12 is referred to as "the Intelligence of Transparency," which means this path brings about it a clarity of vision that goes beyond lower psychic powers; it implies that we will be able to see the true form of things. This is a higher spiritual vision, and that vision can sometimes reveal a reality most people do not, or are not able to, see. Bottom line, it is the Truth, with a capital *T*. Chic and Sandra Tabatha Cicero define this usage of vision concretely: "The student exploring this path should remember that the 'seership' alluded to on this path is spiritual knowledge in its highest form. Although there is nothing wrong with exploring visionary gifts (clairvoyance, etc.), it is important not to become an 'astral junky'—one who wanders aimlessly and carelessly on the astral planes. The key is to develop focused concentration, which allows the divine energy to be clearly seen." [184]

The tarot card is of course the Magician or Magus. The Magician brings the forces of the higher realms down to earth, fashioned and categorized on a table of manifestation: a mesa. The table of manifestation in the Magician card holds upon it the objects of magical working: a pentacle, a chalice, a sword, and in his hand a wand. These, of course, correspond to the elements of existence (respectively earth, water, air, and fire) on the altar of the Pachakuti mesa, holding the basic elemental properties of the Magician's table. The Magician is master over the elements, though the source of his power is indicated by his wand pointing upward, to Creator. Dolores Ashcroft-Nowicki again reminds us of our roots, no matter how adept a Magician we may become: "It looks glamourous, this idea of being a magician, in point of fact it is a tough, sometimes heart breaking discipline that lasts for the rest of your life. [...] The hardest thing for the aspiring magician to accept is the fact that the Path of the Hearth Fire is as important as the more glamourous studies. The earth side of yourself must be very stable and well realized before it is safe to go off on to other paths. The best magicians are those that give the Hearth Fire its just dues." [185]

---

183. Westcott, *Sepher Yetzirah*, 2nd ed., 29.

184. Regardie, *Garden of Pomegranates*, 461.

185. Ashcroft-Nowicki, *Shining Paths*, 163.

What is Dolores referring to by the "Path of the Hearth Fire"? This is not so much a reference to Path 31 but a walk of life as outlined by Dion Fortune. Dion describes the Path of the Hearth Fire as a way of life in which the duties of the real world come first and are often the very lessons one has to live through in order to achieve any amount of evolution.

The Hebrew letter for this path is *Beth,* which literally means "house." A house is a sanctuary, a place of dwelling, going within. This is representative of our bodies being the house, or temple, in which spirit can form itself. So, honoring our house, our bodies, is essential to becoming the Magician as depicted on Path 12. The Bible verse from Proverbs 24:3 directly references both Binah and Chokmah: "By wisdom is an house builded; and by understanding it is established."

Here we are reminded again of Dion Fortune's Path of the Hearth Fire. One's house must be built on a stable foundation, fit for God to dwell in. Because we are in physical incarnation, this must be accomplished first in the physical realms before the spiritual aims can be achieved.

This is true not only of our bodies as temples but also in the altars we use. The mesa especially is a reflection of the soul; therefore, the fitter it is as a container of spirit, the more direct connection a person has with the unseen realms. Caretaking one's body and altar or temple space is of utmost importance in the Great Work. This can be done with a strict regimen, but also there is a mindset the Magician teaches us in order to make the magic flow rather than be manufactured. The Magician is a master over his environment, the elements under his control. But, man cannot truly control nature. Man has to succumb to the natural forces and work with them, in a way in which there is little to no resistance while maintaining a mastery of focus. As expounded by an anonymous French monk on this particular major arcana card:

All practical esotericism is founded on the following rule: it is necessary to be *one* in oneself (concentration without effort) and *one* with the spiritual world (to have a zone of silence in the soul) in order for a revelatory or actual spiritual experience to be able to take place. In other words, if one wants to practise some form of authentic esotericism—be it mysticism, gnosis, or magic—it is necessary to be the *Magician,* i.e. concentrated without effort, operating with ease as if one were playing, and acting with perfect calm. This, then, is the *practical teaching* of the first Arcanum of the Tarot. It is the first counsel, commandment or warning concerning all spiritual practice; it is the aleph of the "alphabet" of practical rules of esotericism.[186]

The characteristic of being one with the world of spirit is revealed in the very posture of the Magician, whose right hand extends to the heavens, the above, and left reaches to the ground, the below. This stance is noted as being an ancient full-body mudra that has been displayed in many cultures throughout the world—shamanic or otherwise. From the several depictions of the Buddha and Christ with their right hands raised and left hands lowered, to Éliphas Lévi's rendition of Baphomet, and even more ancient examples such as the Mesopotamian *Pazuzu* figurine or the *Lanzón* monolith from the pre-Incan Chavín culture of Peru … all are embodiments of the role of the Magician, which we can ourselves personify: a pristine conduit of the axis mundi, where the above and the below interact and play in the universal game of life.

Aleph: Path 11

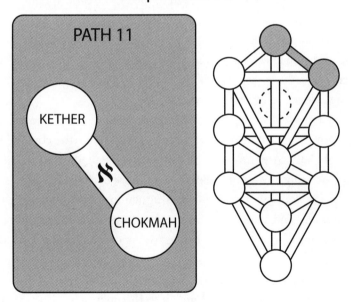

Figure 67: Path 11

---

186. Anonymous, *Meditations on the Tarot: A Journey into Christian Hermeticism*, trans. Robert Powell (New York: Jeremy P. Tarcher/Putnam, 1985), 11.

Path: Path 11, Chokmah to Kether

Hebrew Letter: Aleph

Hebrew Letter Meaning: Ox

Tarot Attribution: 0, the Fool

Elemental Sign: Air

Yetziratic Text: "The Eleventh Path is the Scintillating Intelligence, because it is the essence of that curtain which is placed close to the order of the disposition, and this is a special dignity given to it that it may be able to stand before the Face of the Cause of Causes." [187]

This is the final path in the pathworking as well as the first path on the Tree of Life. It extends from Kether (the Crown of Creation) to Chokmah (the King) and perhaps has more scholarship dedicated to its meaning and symbols than any other path in the Holy Qabalah. Crowley himself has almost an entire chapter dedicated to the Fool in *The Book of Thoth.* Other esoteric scholars have referred to the tarot trump as being one of the most profound symbols in the entire system of the tarot.

The *Sepher Yeztirah's* description of this path as the "Scintillating Intelligence" hints at the outpouring of divine energy from the Source of Creation. The "order of disposition" refers to Kether, which the curtain is veiling. The veil conceals and, because of that, is able to reveal the true essence of life in the universe.

The Hebrew letter is *Aleph,* the first letter of the alphabet, which means "ox." This is an animal that is a prime symbol of the earth in many traditions (the cow in Hindu mythology, the buffalo of Native American mythology, etc.) so being the first connection point to Kether—and the ox being a beast of the plow—we can see that spirit's aim is always rooted in the earth, in the material world, in Form. In agriculture, the plow is the tiller of earth, in which to plant seeds and bring forth fruit. Agriculture is the foundation of civilization, and it is our underlying task as incarnate beings to support civilization in its aim of survival and evolution.

As stated before, the tarot arcanum is the Fool. Traditionally, the Fool is shown to be stepping one foot off a cliff, ready to plunge into the unknown; this is representative of spirit's plunge from the beyond and into the process of creation. The Fool is a symbol of the potential of an experience. Within this resides an innocence one must always tap into

---

187. Westcott, *Sepher Yetzirah,* 2nd ed., 29.

no matter what level of attainment in the Great Work … in essence, the open mind of a beginner!

The fool in older times was always one to hold court with the king and to not only provide comic relief but also be a source of paradoxical wisdom as well. As such, often times the fool was the only one allowed to mock the king. As described by Ashcroft-Nowicki, "Fools down the ages have been honored and revered, the gift of laughter is theirs, and the ability to reduce great men to their common denominator. The Fool is as much the Great Leveller as the figure of Death." [188] Call to mind the *Heyokah* (sacred clown) or Coyote of Native American traditions, both acting as Tricksters to the people, yet at the same time they are some of the more sacred symbols or roles in the community.

This is where the wisdom of the Fool becomes paradoxical. The Fool abandons all expectation and cares little (if at all) for convention. The original French title of this card was *Le Mat*, the madman, and Crowley points out that all Native peoples saw the madman—the wandering lunatic—as one to bear great power and thus salvation for the people. This is why, he says, the number of the card is zero: "It represents therefore the Negative above the Tree of Life, the source of all things. It is the Qabalistic Zero. It is the equation of the Universe, the initial and final balance of the opposites; Air, in this card, therefore quintessentially means a vacuum." [189] The Fool is our reminder of the first implications of the Divine spilling into our world, which could make any personality mad. This is why all the previous work done thus far throughout the tree must be done in integrity: to prime one's individuality in relinquishing all understanding of the world as we see and experience it. For in zero, in the Unmanifest, we have no ability to understand.

Crowley also states that this card, this path, is a vacuum. This implies a void needing to be filled. So, what does this mean for us? Are we the vacuum, or are we that which is filling it? Again, paradox reigns supreme and the Fool turns a somersault in the court of the king. The essence of the mystic traditions will always throw us back into a Zen koan, the great riddle of the universe in which we ourselves become both the question and the answer in one. Or rather, zero.

---

188. Ashcroft-Nowicki, *Shining Paths*, 167.
189. Crowley, *Book of Thoth*, 53.

Kether: Path 1

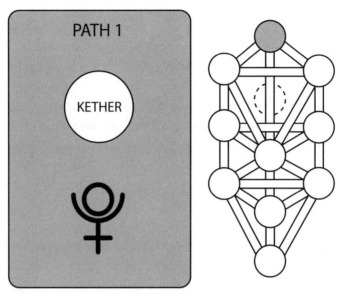

Figure 68: Path 1

God Name: Eheieh

Archangel: Metatron

Order of Angels: Chaioth He Qadesh

Animal Totem: Sponge

Color: White, sometimes gold

Virtue: Attainment, completion of the Great Work

Vice: N/A

Tarot Attributions: Ace of Pentacles, Ace of Cups, Ace of Swords, Ace of Wands

Spiritual Experience: Union with God

Titles: The Vast Countenance, the Most High, Existence of Existences, Concealed of the Concealed, Ancient of Ancients

Symbols: Point or point within a circle

Yetziratic Text: "The First Path is called the Admirable or the Hidden Intelligence (the Highest Crown): for it is the Light giving the power of comprehension of that First

Principle which has no beginning, and it is the Primal Glory, for no created being can attain to its essence." [190]

This may be the end of the pathworking, but it is the beginning of existence. No human can ever truly know God. In reality, God (the Source) resides in the Unmanifest, which is a whole other realm of esoterica that requires a whole other level of initiation. Kether is the first point of reality in which the Unmanifest begins the slightest notion of becoming Manifest. Here, there is not yet any division of pairs or opposites which beget the duality we experience in existence. In Kether, all is still one. All is light, and nothing more. Our minds, in actuality, cannot comprehend Kether in its purest form, for our minds operate within duality. We cannot comprehend it but merely infer its possibility.

Through Kether, all the other Sephiroth come into being. All are contained within the one. Pythagoras described the number one as the undividable monad. Through its own reflection, the monad can generate all of the other digits on the numerical scale proceeding it. This is exactly how the universe was conceived, by one digit adding itself to another of its reflection, thus creating two (Chokmah), and then adding another aspect of its reflection to that, creating three (Binah), and so on.

Another way to understand Kether and its relationship to the other Sephiroth is as a fount, spouting forth all the preceding Sephiroth, as described by Dion Fortune: "Let us conceive of Kether, then, as a fountain which fills its basin, and the overflow therefrom feeds another fountain, which in its turn fills its basin and overflows. The Unmanifest for ever flows under pressure into Kether, and there comes a time when evolution has gone as far as it can in the extreme simplicity of the form of existence of the First Manifest. All possible combinations have been formed, and they have undergone all possible permutations." [191]

Kether, meaning "crown," implies the Crown of Creation. A crown is above the head and not a part of it. Therefore, Kether (spilling over from the Unmanifest) is never fully a part of the knowable universe. In this, paradoxically (as all esoteric work is), we see the true colors of the pathworking process. Though we strive in esoteric work to repeat the process of Creation in reverse, to return to the very Source, we can never truly do just that. For fully returning to the monad of Kether means we in turn become uncreated. The attainment is the virtue of Kether; we see then that true attainment, the completion of the Great Work itself, is about returning to life and living within it.

---

190. Westcott, *Sepher Yetzirah*, 2nd ed., 28.
191. Fortune, *Mystical Qabalah*, 37.

This has been the ambition of this book all along: using shamanic practices, along with the Holy Qabalah of the Western Mystery Tradition, to achieve a state of connection with God. Pure and simple. There is no other motive. One should not be trying to "get" anything out of this—no money, no abundance, no happiness. One's sole desire, from the very beginning, should be a relationship with the Divine. In other words, attainment.

If there were one thing to take with you in the entire adventure in pathworking with the Tree of Life has to offer, it is one statement offered by Dion Fortune as the definitive mantra to understanding Kether, but also the entire makeup of the Great Work itself. It is the *one* statement, the ancients say, that is all that is ever needed to understand the Tree of Life. Meditation upon it is enough to last one lifetime, if not several. Remember always, as an initiate, forever reborn in the light of the first and only I AM: "Kether is the Malkuth of the Umanifest." [192]

Let us end with a final thought on this meditation of the Tree of Life: the animal totem for Kether is the sea sponge. The oldest living animal on the planet, the sea sponge is a member of Parazoa, which is a subkingdom of animals without tissues or organs. This makes the sponge vastly different from us in our current image, which is emblematic of Kether … we can scarcely imagine its countenance. So, what makes the sea sponge so special? Why does it represent the highest sphere of creation, the crown? The framework of the sea sponge's body is made up entirely of channels and pores. Its sole function is to allow water to flow through them. There is no nervous system or circulatory system. Its purpose is to flow, to permit the passage of water. This is the entire essence of Kether, the first inclination of existence. The crown Sephirah is a sponge for whatever it is that is on the other side of the veil, and it brings it into manifestation. This is a clear channel in its purest form. Surely, if we can replicate Kether's action here in Malkuth—much like the sea sponge—we may begin to learn what it is to create heaven here on earth.

---

192. Fortune, *Mystical Qabalah*, 29.

CONCLUSION

For millennia, humankind has searched for meaning. All the ancients had for their framework of understanding existence was the world around them, the stars glittering in the night sky, the fire in the hearth. Whether Judaic or not, Qabalah is about reception, opening up to the mystery beyond our senses in order to understand our origin, our sense of purpose. The archaic models of the shamanic paradigm are pure not just because they were the first expressions of religious experience, but because at their root they remain undistorted by centuries of dogma, reinterpretations, and misrepresentations.

Shamanism is the original religion, and its agenda lies primarily in seeking communion with the world. Like an open chalice waiting to be filled, a shamanic practitioner is naturally a Qabalist. There are those who dabble in ideas, but then there are those who are willing to roll up their sleeves and get dirty: physicists and explorers of the imagination.

Being a psychonaut requires work, perseverance, dedication, and devotion. It begs a natural balancing of the polarity inherent in every human. It is a call to service, for if the Great Work does not encourage the beneficial evolution of humanity, then it is no longer "great." Our job is to carry on the work of our ancestors, nurture the sacred knowledge, adapt to our understanding, and then sow the seeds for the next seven generations.

My hope and prayer is that this book provides an introductory understanding to Qabalah as understood in the Western Mystery Tradition via a shamanic perspective. This is only an introduction, though. There is so much more work to be done.

In the process of understanding and germinating the seeds of the Great Work, it is also my prayer that we see and honor the cross-cultural implications in the mystery traditions of all cultures and religious paths. Admittedly, I am a globalist. I want the world to be as one, to put an end to war, poverty, slavery, and disparity. However, I think there is a way to honor cultural differences and individuality as well as map the correlations among cultural memes in order to approach humanity as one race instead of many, with one common purpose: to explore and understand our place in the universe, in global peace and harmony.

It may be idealistic, but I think it is a noble cause. And it *is* achievable, if we would just allow our imaginations the bandwidth and flexibility needed for such an endeavor. Therefore, we are immediately caught in another balancing act: honoring the past as well as forging a new, daring future. But that is all we have, as time appears to move forward and not backward. Maybe if we can loosen the restrictions of fundamentalism, we will see a new fabric of connection threading its way through all ideologies that will unite rather than divide us.

Shamanic Qabalah is my contribution to this prayer. It is an unfinished work, as it is designed to be built upon, redesigned, and regrown into new gardens to feed children, grandchildren, and great-grandchildren. The great altar (mesa) of soul is waiting for us all to come and partake.

BIBLIOGRAPHY

Allen, Catherine J. *The Hold Life Has: Coca and Cultural Identity in an Andean Community.* 2nd ed. Washington, DC: Smithsonian Books, 2002.

Andrews, Ted. *Animal Speak: The Spiritual & Magical Powers of Creatures Great & Small.* St. Paul, MN: Llewellyn Publications, 1993.

———. *Pathworking: A Qabala Guide to Empowerment and Initiation.* Jackson, TN: Dragonhawk Publishing, 2009.

Anonymous. *Meditations on the Tarot: A Journey into Christian Hermeticism.* Translated by Robert Powell. New York: Jeremy P. Tarcher/Putnam, 1985.

Ashcroft-Nowicki, Dolores. *Highways of the Mind: The Art and History of Pathworking.* Sechelt, BC, Canada: Twin Eagles Publishing, 2010.

———. *The Shining Paths: An Experiential Journey through the Tree of Life.* Wellingborough: The Aquarian Press, 1983.

Barnstone, Willis, and Marvin Mayer, ed. *The Gnostic Bible: Gnostic Texts of Mystical Wisdom from the Ancient and Medieval Worlds.* Boston: Shambhala, 2003.

Berg, P. S. *The Energy of Hebrew Letters.* New York: The Kabbalah Centre, 2013.

———. *The Essential Zohar: The Source of Kabbalistic Wisdom.* New York: Three Rivers Press, 2002.

Bersin, Josh. "It's Not the CEO, It's the Leadership Strategy That Matters." *Forbes,* July 30, 2012. http://www.forbes.com/sites/joshbersin/2012/07/30/its-not-the-ceo-its-the-leadership-strategy-that-matters/#7e91d7235a3e.

Bible. King James Version. Bible Gateway. 1987. https://www.biblegateway.com/.

Blake, William. *The Poetical Works of William Blake.* Edited by John Sampson. London, New York: Oxford University Press, 1908. Electronic reproduction by Bartleby.com, 2011. http://www.bartleby.com/235/253.html.

Blom, Jan Dirk. *A Dictionary of Hallucinations.* New York: Springer Science+Business Media, 2010.

Bly, Robert. *A Little Book on the Human Shadow.* San Francisco: Harper & Row, 1988.

Campbell, Joseph. *The Hero with a Thousand Faces.* Princeton, NJ: Princeton University Press, 1973.

Chomsky, Noam. *On Anarchism.* New York: The New Press, 2013.

Crowley, Aleister. *The Book of Thoth: A Short Essay on the Tarot of the Egyptians.* Boston: Red Wheel/Weiser, 1969.

———. *The Confessions of Aleister Crowley: An Autohagiography.* New York: Penguin, 1989.

Crowley, Vivianne. *A Woman's Kabbalah: Kabbalah for the 21st Century.* London: Thorsons, 2000.

Davidson, Gustav. *A Dictionary of Angels: Including the Fallen Angels.* New York: The Free Press, 1967.

Delgado, Dante, and Orlando Salas. *Arquitectura Cósmica Inka: Arqueoastronomía.* Cusco, Peru: Biblioteca Nacional del Peru, 2016.

Descartes, René. *Descartes: Philosophical Writings.* Translated and edited by Elizabeth Anscombe and Peter Thomas Geach. New York: MacMillan Publishing, 1971.

Flammarion, Camille. *L'atmosphère: météorologie populaire.* Paris: Hachette, 1888.

Fortune, Dion. *The Cosmic Doctrine.* Boston: Weiser Books, 2000.

———. *The Mystical Qabalah.* Boston: Weiser Books, 2000.

———. *The Training & Work of an Initiate.* San Francisco: Weiser Books, 2000.

Gad, Irene. *Tarot and Individuation: Correspondences with Cabala and Alchemy.* York Beach, ME: Nicolas-Hays, 1994.

Gandhi, Mohandas. *The Collected Works of Mahatma Gandhi. Vol. III.* Ahmedabad, India: Navajivan Trust, 1960.

Gaus, Andy, trans. *The Unvarnished New Testament.* Grand Rapids, MI: Phanes Press, 1992.

Glass-Coffin, Bonnie. *The Gift of Life: Female Spirituality and Healing in Northern Peru.* Albuquerque: University of New Mexico Press, 1998.

Glass-Coffin, Bonnie, and don Oscar Miro-Quesada. *Lessons in Courage: Peruvian Shamanic Wisdom for Everyday Life*. Faber, VA: Rainbow Ridge Books, 2013.

Hall, Manly P. *The Mystical Christ: Religion as a Personal Spiritual Experience*. Los Angeles: The Philosophical Research Society, 1951.

———. *The Secret Teachings of All Ages: An Encyclopedic Outline of Masonic, Qabbalistic and Rosicrucian Symbolical Philosophy*. Reader's ed. New York: Penguin, 2003.

Harpur, Patrick. *Daimonic Reality: A Field Guide to the Otherworld*. London: Viking Arkana, 1994.

Iamblichus. *Iamblichus: The Platonic Commentaries*. Translated by John Dillon. Leiden, Netherlands: E.J. Brill, 1973.

Jodorowsky, Alejandro, dir. *The Holy Mountain*. Mexico City, Mexico: Producciones Zohar, 1975. DVD, 115 min.

John of the Cross. *Dark Night of the Soul*. Translated by E. Allison Peers. Dover Thrift Editions. Mineola, NY: Dover, 2003.

Joralemon, Donald, and Douglas Sharon. *Sorcery and Shamanism: Curanderos and Clients in Northern Peru*. Salt Lake City: University of Utah Press, 1993.

Jordan, June. *Directed by Desire: The Collected Poems of June Jordan*. Edited by Jan Heller Levi and Sara Miles. Port Townsend, WA: Copper Canyon Press, 2007.

Jung, Carl G. *Memories, Dreams, Reflections*. Edited by Aniela Jaffé. Translated by Richard Winston and Clara Winston. New York: Vintage Books, 1989.

———. *Mysterium Coniunctionis: An Inquiry into the Separation and Synthesis of Psychic Opposites in Alchemy*. Princeton, NJ: Princeton University Press, 1989.

Kalweit, Holger. *Dreamtime & Inner Space: The World of the Shaman*. Boston: Shambhala, 1988.

Knight, Gareth. *Dion Fortune & the Inner Light*. Loughborough: Thoth Publications, 2000.

———. *A Practical Guide to Qabalistic Symbolism*. One-volume edition. Boston, MA: Weiser Books, 2001.

Kraig, Donald Michael. *Modern Magick: Eleven Lessons in the High Magickal Arts*. 2nd ed. St. Paul, MN: Llewellyn Publications, 1988.

Krishnamurti, J. *On God*. New York: HarperCollins Publishers, 1992.

Lachman, Gary. *The Caretakers of the Cosmos: Living Responsibly in an Unfinished Universe*. Edinburgh, UK: Floris Books, 2013.

Larson, William M. "Those Mysterious Pillars." *Pietre-Stones: Review of Freemasonry*. Free-masons-freemasonry.com. http://www.freemasons-freemasonry.com/larsonwilliam.html.

Le Guin, Ursula K. *The Dispossessed*. New York: HarperCollins Publishers, 2015.

Lévi, Éliphas. *Transcendental Magic: Its Doctrine and Ritual*. Translated by Arthur Edward Waite. Mansfield Centre, CT: Martino Publishing, 2011.

Lewis, H. Spencer. *Mansions of the Soul: The Cosmic Conception*. San Jose, CA: Supreme Grand Lodge of AMORC, 1954.

Liungman, Carl G. *Dictionary of Symbols*. New York: W. W. Norton & Company, 1991.

Magee, Matthew. *Peruvian Shamanism: The Pachakúti Mesa*. Kearney, NE: Morris Publishing, 2005.

Malachi, Tau. *Gnosis of the Cosmic Christ: A Gnostic Christian Kabbalah*. St. Paul, MN: Llewellyn Publications, 2005.

McKenna, Jed. *Spiritual Enlightenment: The Damnedest Thing*. Wisefool Press, 2002.

McKenna, Terence. *The Archaic Revival: Speculations on Psychedelic Mushrooms, the Amazon, Virtual Reality, UFOs, Evolution, Shamanism, the Rebirth of the Goddess, and the End of History*. San Francisco: HarperCollins Publishers, 1991.

Moore, Alan, J. H. Williams III, Mick Gray, and Jeromy Cox. *Promethea*. Collected edition. Book 3. La Jolla, CA: Wildstorm, 2013.

———. *Promethea*. Collected edition. Book 4. La Jolla, CA: Wildstorm, 2013.

Nevi'im. *Tanakh: The Holy Scriptures*. Philadelphia: The Jewish Publication Society, 1985.

Odier, Daniel, trans. *Yoga Spandakarika: The Sacred Texts at the Origins of Tantra*. Rochester, VT: Inner Traditions, 2005.

Plato. *Republic*. Translated by G. M. A. Grube. Indianapolis, IN: Hackett Publishing, 1992.

Prabhavananda and Christopher Isherwood, trans. *Bhagavad-Gita: The Song of God*. New York: Mentor-Penguin Books, 1972.

Proudhon, Pierre-Joseph. *Property Is Theft!: A Pierre-Joseph Proudhon Anthology*. Edited by Iain McKay. Oakland, CA: AK Press, 2011.

Regardie, Israel. *A Garden of Pomegranates: Skrying on the Tree of Life*. Edited by Chic Cicero and Sandra Tabatha Cicero. St. Paul, MN: Llewellyn, 1999.

———. *The Golden Dawn*. 6th ed. St. Paul, MN: Llewellyn Publications, 1989.

———. *The Middle Pillar: The Balance Between Mind and Magic.* Edited by Chic Cicero and Sandra Tabatha Cicero. St. Paul, MN: Llewellyn Publications, 2000.

———. *The Philosopher's Stone: Spiritual Alchemy, Psychology, and Ritual Magic.* Edited by Chic Cicero and Sandra Tabatha Cicero. Woodbury, MN: Llewelyn Publications, 2013.

Rocker, Rudolf. *Anarcho-Syndicalism: Theory and Practice.* Edinburgh, Scotland: AK Press, 2004.

Ruiz, Miguel. *The Four Agreements: A Practical Guide to Personal Freedom.* San Rafael, CA: Amber-Allen Publishing, 1997.

Sharon, Douglas. *Wizard of the Four Winds: A Shaman's Story.* CreateSpace Independent Publishing Platform, 2015.

Shaw, Greogory. *Theurgy and the Soul: The Neoplatonism of Iamblichus.* Kettering, OH: Angelico Press, 2014.

The Emerald Tablet of Hermes & The Kybalion. Edited by Jane Ma'ati Smith. Lexington, KY: Enhanced Ebooks, 2008.

Seymour, Charles R. F. *The Forgotten Mage: The Magical Lectures of Colonel C. R. F. Seymour.* Edited by Dolores Ashcroft-Nowicki. Loughborough, Leicestershire, UK: Thoth Publications, 1999.

Soeng, Mu. "Worldly Happiness / Buddhist Happiness." *Parabola* 41, no. 2 (Summer 2016): 48.

Somé, Malidoma Patrice. *Ritual: Power, Healing and Community.* Portland: Swan / Raven & Company, 1993.

Stevens, José. *Transforming Your Dragons: How to Turn Fear Patterns into Personal Power.* Rochester, VT: Inner Traditions, 1994.

Tayler, Irene. "Blake's *Laocoön*." *Blake / An Illustrated Quarterly* 10, no. 3 (Winter 1976–77): 72–81. http://bq.blakearchive.org/10.3.tayler.

Tolle, Eckhart. "Eckhart on the Dark Night of the Soul." Eckhart Teachings. October 2011. https://www.eckharttolle.com/newsletter/october-2011.

Walsh, Roger. *The World of Shamanism: New Vision of an Ancient Tradition.* Woodbury, MN: Llewellyn Publications, 2007.

Westcott, William Wynn, trans. *Sepher Yetzirah: The Book of Formation and the Thirty Two Paths of Wisdom.* 2nd ed. London: Theosophical Publishing Society, 1893.

———. *Sepher Yetzirah*. 3rd ed. London: J. M. Watkins, 1911. Electronic reproduction by John B. Hare for the Internet Sacred Text Archive. http://www.sacred-texts.com/jud/sephir.htm.

Wilcox, Joan Parisi. *Masters of the Living Energy: The Mystical World of the Q'ero in Peru*. Rochester, VT: Inner Traditions, 2004.

Winkler, Gershon. *Magic of the Ordinary: Recovering the Shamanic in Judaism*. Berkeley, CA: North Atlantic Books, 2000.

Index

A

anarchism, 101–104, 117

animal totem, 127, 147, 151, 154, 157, 164, 166, 186, 194, 201, 222, 227, 229, 238, 240

ayni, 6, 105–107, 112

B

Binah, 51, 71, 73, 79–81, 84, 95, 128, 138, 140, 194, 207–213, 221–226, 228, 229, 232, 234, 239

C

Chesed, 51–53, 73, 80, 81, 121, 128, 194, 195, 199–206, 212, 213

Chokmah, 50, 51, 71, 73, 79–81, 84, 95, 128, 194, 212–215, 222, 223, 225–229, 234, 236, 239

curanderismo, 6, 58, 62, 89, 90, 92, 93, 195

D

Daat, 83

F

Fortune, Dion, 1, 2, 4, 5, 32–34, 47–49, 57, 68, 69, 76, 80, 91, 94, 99, 100, 119, 149, 184, 188, 189, 195, 199, 203, 223, 234, 239, 240

G

Geburah, 51–53, 73, 80, 81, 122, 125, 128, 191–197, 199, 201–207, 213

Great Work, xv, xvi, 3, 6, 7, 9, 12, 20, 21, 26–28, 31–34, 38, 39, 44, 52, 53, 61, 66–69, 71, 74, 80, 84, 85, 100, 108, 111, 116, 123, 131, 132, 139, 140, 143, 144, 146, 154, 160, 168, 171, 172, 179, 181, 182, 186, 188, 189, 195, 201, 209, 211, 216, 224, 231, 234, 236, 238–241

H

Hanaqpacha, 35, 36, 38, 39, 55, 86, 87, 111, 141, 200

Hebrew, 27, 34, 43, 47, 48, 50–52, 69–79, 83, 87, 107, 127, 139, 142–145, 148, 151, 153, 158, 159, 161, 162, 167, 168, 170, 171, 176, 179–181, 183, 185, 191, 196, 197, 199, 203–215, 220, 225, 226, 230–232, 234, 236

Hod, 52, 53, 73, 74, 80, 81, 87, 129, 148, 151–159, 162, 165, 166, 170, 176, 179, 181, 191–193, 200, 220

I

individuality, 22, 34, 35, 38, 52, 70, 71, 84, 87, 145, 153, 154, 167–169, 171, 173, 177–179, 182, 184, 185, 187, 189, 192, 197, 199, 203, 204, 206, 208, 211, 213, 229, 231, 237, 241

initiation, xvi, 1, 4–7, 12, 19, 20, 22, 27, 28, 30–36, 43–45, 52, 55, 60, 67, 77, 84, 96, 110, 122, 124, 125, 144, 146, 150, 152, 156, 168, 169, 171–173, 177, 181, 184, 185, 187, 202, 203, 206, 208, 219–221, 239

J

Jung, Carl, 31, 54, 62, 65–67, 83

K

Kamasqa, xvi, 6, 110–112, 117, 118, 130, 132

Kaypacha, 35–39, 55, 86, 87

Kether, 48–51, 53, 59, 73, 79, 81, 95, 97, 99, 116, 127, 140, 142, 149, 173, 187, 188, 204, 210, 226, 228–232, 236, 238–240

L

Lowerworld. See *Ukhupacha*

M

Malkuth, 53, 55, 57, 59–62, 64–68, 70, 74, 79–81, 87, 92, 97, 99, 121, 127, 129, 132, 138–153, 156, 159, 161, 162, 165, 172, 188, 200, 202, 220, 240

mesa, xvi, 6, 36, 60, 62–68, 78, 86, 89–92, 99, 120–124, 129, 131, 132, 140, 141, 165, 195, 233, 234, 242

Middleworld. *See* Kaypacha

Miro-Quesada, Oscar, xvi, 6, 60, 62, 68, 106, 107, 110, 111, 219

mitote, 25–27, 60, 67

mysticism, 2, 5, 15, 16, 21, 26, 27, 31, 32, 36, 43, 68, 100, 125, 146, 157, 166, 206, 213, 219, 231, 234

N

Neschamah, 34, 70, 153, 168, 187

Nephesch, 34, 70, 87, 209

Netzach, 52, 53, 73, 74, 80, 81, 129, 148, 151, 155, 156, 161, 162, 164–168, 170, 181, 183, 199, 200, 220

O

occult, 20, 21, 76, 77, 87, 109, 115, 126, 156, 164, 168, 181, 184, 206, 208, 221

P

Pacha, 36, 57, 68

Pachakuti Mesa Tradition, xvi, 6, 62, 86, 91, 120, 122–124, 131, 141

Paqokuna, 6, 59, 62

pathworking, 3, 5, 69, 107, 118–120, 125–127, 132, 140, 143, 144, 152, 159, 162, 171, 172, 176, 177, 189, 194–196, 205, 228, 236, 239, 240

personality, 16, 25, 31, 34–36, 38, 71, 84, 87, 167–169, 171, 172, 177, 178, 182, 184, 185, 195, 197, 203, 206, 208, 209, 213, 215, 218, 237

Plato, 23, 24, 26, 60, 115, 117

psychonaut, 1, 69, 108, 112, 118, 129, 176, 241

Q

Qabalah, xv, xvi, 2–5, 7, 12, 39, 41, 43, 44, 47–49, 53, 60, 68, 69, 71, 72, 74, 76, 77, 100, 108, 113, 116, 117, 119, 120, 132, 137, 149, 160, 181, 189, 190, 195, 196, 223, 228, 236, 239–242

Quechua, 6, 35, 59, 63, 85, 87, 104–107, 110, 111, 165, 173, 182

R

Ruach, 34, 71, 87, 168, 209

S

Sephiroth, xv, 45–50, 53, 54, 57, 69, 70, 72, 74, 77, 79, 81, 82, 85, 87, 95, 96, 98–100, 116, 118, 127, 128, 132, 137, 139, 140, 146, 148–150, 155, 165, 166, 168, 172, 175, 176, 178, 187, 190, 192, 200, 202, 206, 208, 210, 219, 222, 226, 228, 239

shadow, 26, 34–38, 47, 70, 71, 84, 87, 154, 196

shamanism, xvi, 7, 20, 36, 57–59, 62, 76, 90–92, 110, 132, 160, 241

T

tarot, xvi, 27, 76, 77, 79, 80, 127, 138, 144, 146, 147, 152–155, 158–164, 167–170, 172, 176, 178–180, 182–184, 186, 187, 191–194, 196, 197, 199, 201, 203–208, 210, 212, 214, 215, 218, 220, 222, 225–227, 230–236, 238

theurgy, xvi, 116–118, 120

Tiphareth, 52, 53, 70, 73, 79–81, 129, 149, 168, 169, 176, 178–180, 182–190, 194, 196, 197, 200, 202–204, 208–210, 214, 215, 230, 231

Tree of Life, xv, 2, 3, 5–7, 43–49, 52, 54, 57, 62, 67–70, 72, 73, 75–77, 79–85, 87, 91, 95–99, 118–120, 125–127, 129, 132, 139, 140, 142–144, 146, 148–150, 152, 155, 156, 159, 165, 169–172, 175–179, 181, 187, 190, 192, 194, 196, 201, 202, 205, 206, 208, 210, 213, 215, 219–226, 228, 229, 231, 236, 237, 240

U

Ukhupacha, 35, 36, 38, 39, 55, 86, 87, 146

Upperworld. *See* Hanaqpacha

W

Western Mystery Tradition, xv, 5, 32, 61, 69, 71, 76, 85, 115, 120, 121, 125, 141, 156, 163, 197, 206, 211, 219, 240, 241

Yesod, 53, 71, 73, 74, 80, 81, 129, 139, 143, 144, 146–151, 155, 156, 158, 159, 162, 165, 167, 168, 170, 175, 180, 182, 187, 200, 202, 220

To Write to the Author

If you wish to contact the author or would like more information about this book, please write to the author in care of Llewellyn Worldwide Ltd. and we will forward your request. Both the author and publisher appreciate hearing from you and learning of your enjoyment of this book and how it has helped you. Llewellyn Worldwide Ltd. cannot guarantee that every letter written to the author can be answered, but all will be forwarded. Please write to:

Daniel Moler
℅ Llewellyn Worldwide
2143 Wooddale Drive
Woodbury, MN 55125-2989

Please enclose a self-addressed stamped envelope for reply,
or $1.00 to cover costs. If outside the U.S.A., enclose
an international postal reply coupon.

Many of Llewellyn's authors have websites with additional information and resources. For more information, please visit our website at http://www.llewellyn.com.

GET MORE AT LLEWELLYN.COM

Visit us online to browse hundreds of our books and decks, plus sign up to receive our e-newsletters and exclusive online offers.

- Free tarot readings • Spell-a-Day • Moon phases
- Recipes, spells, and tips • Blogs • Encyclopedia
- Author interviews, articles, and upcoming events

GET SOCIAL WITH LLEWELLYN

Find us on  @LlewellynBooks

www.Facebook.com/LlewellynBooks

GET BOOKS AT LLEWELLYN

LLEWELLYN ORDERING INFORMATION

 Order online: Visit our website at www.llewellyn.com to select your books and place an order on our secure server.

 Order by phone:
- Call toll free within the US at 1-877-NEW-WRLD (1-877-639-9753)
- We accept VISA, MasterCard, American Express, and Discover.
- Canadian customers must use credit cards.

Order by mail:
Send the full price of your order (MN residents add 6.875% sales tax) in US funds plus postage and handling to: Llewellyn Worldwide, 2143 Wooddale Drive, Woodbury, MN 55125-2989

POSTAGE AND HANDLING

STANDARD (US):
(Please allow 12 business days)
$30.00 and under, add $6.00.
$30.01 and over, FREE SHIPPING.

INTERNATIONAL ORDERS, INCLUDING CANADA:
$16.00 for one book, plus $3.00 for each additional book.

Visit us online for more shipping options. Prices subject to change.

FREE CATALOG!

To order, call
1-877-
NEW-WRLD
ext. 8236
or visit our
website

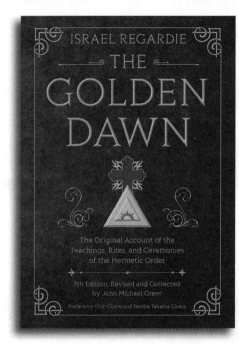

ISRAEL REGARDIE

THE GOLDEN DAWN

The Original Account of the
Teachings, Rites, and Ceremonies
of the Hermetic Order

7th Edition, Revised and Corrected
by John Michael Greer

Preface by Chic Cicero and Sandra Tabatha Cicero

The Golden Dawn
The Original Account of the Teachings, Rites, and Ceremonies of the Hermetic Order
Israel Regardie
John Michael Greer

First published in 1937, Israel Regardie's *The Golden Dawn* has become the most influential modern handbook of magical theory and practice. In this new, definitive edition, noted scholar John Michael Greer has taken this essential resource back to its original, authentic form. With added illustrations, a twenty-page color insert, additional original material, and refreshed design and typography, this powerful work returns to its true stature as a modern masterpiece.

An essential textbook for students of the occult, *The Golden Dawn* includes occult symbolism and Qabalistic philosophy, training methods for developing magical and clairvoyant powers, rituals that summon and banish spiritual potencies, secrets of making and consecrating magical tools, and much more.

978-0-7387-4399-8, 960 pp., 7 x 10   **$65.00**

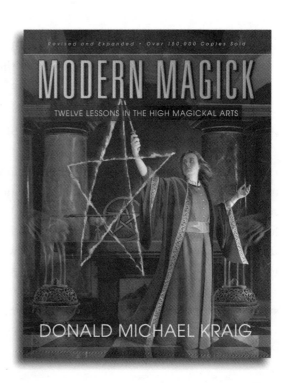

MODERN MAGICK

TWELVE LESSONS IN THE HIGH MAGICKAL ARTS

DONALD MICHAEL KRAIG

Modern Magick
Twelve Lessons in the High Magickal Arts
DONALD MICHAEL KRAIG

For more than two decades, *Modern Magick* has been the world's most popular instruction manual on how to work real magick. Now, author Donald Michael Kraig, with decades more experience, research, training, and study, has created the ultimate version of this contemporary classic. This expanded edition features an updated design, more personal stories, and a wealth of new information, including more than 175 original images and a completely new chapter on three emerging trends in magick and how readers can put them to use. What hasn't changed: the comprehensive scope and clear, step-by-step ritual instructions that have made this book an indispensable guide for more than 150,000 magicians.

978-0-7387-1578-0, 528 pp., 8½ x 11   **$34.99**

A

GARDEN
OF
POMEGRANATES

Skrying on the Tree of Life

ISRAEL
REGARDIE

Edited and Annotated with New Material by
Chic Cicero & Sandra Tabatha Cicero

A Garden of Pomegranates
Skrying on the Tree of Life
Israel Regardie
Chic Cicero and Sandra Tabatha Cicero

When Israel Regardie wrote *A Garden of Pomegranates* in 1932, he designed it to be a simple yet comprehensive guidebook outlining the complex system of the Qabalah and providing a key to its symbolism. Since then it has achieved the status of a classic among texts on the Hermetic Qabalah. It stands as the best single introductory guide for magicians on this complex system, with an emphasis on direct experience through meditation on the twenty-two paths.

978-1-56718-141-8, 552 pp., 6 x 9 $22.99

To order, call 1-877-NEW-WRLD or visit llewellyn.com
Prices subject to change without notice

THE
MIDDLE
PILLAR

The Balance Between Mind & Magic

ISRAEL
REGARDIE

Edited and Annotated with New Material by
Chic Cicero & Sandra Tabatha Cicero

The Middle Pillar: The Balance Between Mind and Magic
formerly The Middle Pillar
Israel Regardie
Chic Cicero and Sandra Tabatha Cicero

The classic book on working with the energy of the body for spiritual purposes, *The Middle Pillar* by Israel Regardie, is now more complete, more modern, more usable, and better than ever.

The exercise known as the Middle Pillar was devised by the Hermetic Order of the Golden Dawn. Regardie expanded upon it and made it public over sixty years ago in the first edition of this book. Since that time, the exercise has been altered and adapted for just about any spiritual use you could think of. It is a mainstay of many Western traditions of magic.

Now in its third edition, *The Middle Pillar* is better than ever. It has been edited by Chic Cicero and Sandra Tabatha Cicero, close friends of the late Regardie and senior Adepts of the Golden Dawn. They have also added new material in a separate section that more than doubles the size of the book with their valuable insights and knowledge.

Includes the complete original text, with nothing eliminated • Spelling has been standardized to Western traditions • Each chapter now has a title to identify its content • The Ciceros' notes to each chapter add insight and history to Regardie's work • Modern and clearer illustrations have been added • New, a further exploration of the relationship between magic and psychology • New, more than five techniques to enhance relaxation • New, the Middle Pillar and the Chakras • New, versions of the Middle Pillar exercise in Egyptian, Greek, and Gaelic • New, a shamanic version of the Middle Pillar • New, how to use the Middle Pillar to charge talismans and do healings

The Middle Pillar is now expanded to what it always should have been, a thorough, accessible examination and extension of the single ritual that has become the very embodiment of magic. Get *The Middle Pillar* and learn the real secrets of magic.

978-1-56718-140-1, 312 pp., 6 x 9   **$21.99**

NATURE
SPIRITUALITY
from the ground up

Connect with
Totems in Your
Ecosystem

LUPA

Nature Spirituality From the Ground Up
Connect with Totems in Your Ecosystem
Lupa

Nature Spirituality From the Ground Up invites you to go beyond simply exploring the symbols of nature and encourages you to bury your hands in the earth and work with the real thing. This is a book on green spirituality that makes a difference, empowering you to connect with totems as a part of your spiritual life.

Uniquely approaching totems as beings we can give to, rather than take from, Lupa shows how orienting yourself this way deepens your spiritual connection to the earth and helps you rejoin the community of nature. And while most books on totems focus on animals, *Nature Spirituality From the Ground Up* helps you work with interconnected ecosystems of totems: plants, fungi, minerals, waterways, landforms, and more.

978-0-7387-4704-0, 288 pp., 5¼ x 8 **$16.99**

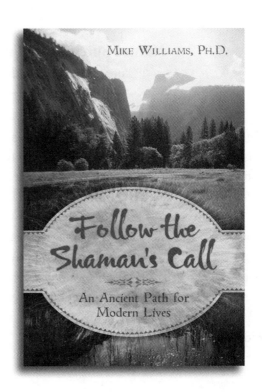

MIKE WILLIAMS, PH.D.

Follow the
Shaman's Call

An Ancient Path for
Modern Lives

Follow the Shaman's Call
An Ancient Path for Modern Lives
MIKE WILLIAMS, PH.D.

Drawing on 30,000 years of primeval wisdom, this engaging, hands-on guide teaches you how to transform your increasingly busy and stressful life by following the ancient shamanic path of your ancestors. You'll discover how to meet your spirit guides, journey to the otherworlds for healing and self-empowerment, and bring back lost souls.

As you begin to understand the powerful hidden forces of the unseen world, you'll also learn how to apply the knowledge in a variety of practical ways: predicting the future and understanding the past, using dreamwork to find answers to problems, and clearing your house of negativity and stale influences.

Written to appeal to both beginning and experienced practitioners, *Follow the Shaman's Call* shows how to use shamanic practices to take charge of your life, heal your friends and community, and live in harmony with the world.

978-0-7387-1984-9, 264 pp., 6 x 9   **$17.99**

Shamanism

For Beginners

Walking with the World's Healers
of Earth and Sky

JAMES ENDREDY

Shamanism for Beginners
Walking with the World's Healers of Earth and Sky
JAMES ENDREDY

Interest in shamanism is on the rise and people are eager to integrate this intriguing tradition into their own lives. *Shamanism for Beginners* introduces the spiritual beliefs and customs of the shaman—a spiritual leader, visionary, healer, diviner, walker between worlds, and so much more.

How is one called to be a shaman? How is a shaman initiated? Where does a shaman's power come from? Exploring the practices and beliefs of tribes around the world, James Endredy sheds light on the entire shamanic experience. The fascinating origins and evolution of shamanism are examined, along with power places, tools (costume, drum, sweat lodge, medicine wheel), sacred plants, and the relationship between the shaman and spirits. Enriched with the author's personal stories and quotes from actual shaman elders and scholars, Endredy concludes with incredible feats of shamans, healing techniques, and ruminations on the future of this remarkable tradition.

978-0-7387-1562-9, 288 pp., 5³⁄₁₆ x 8   **$14.95**

Elemental Shaman
One Man's Journey Into the Heart of Humanity, Spirituality & Ecology
Omar W. Rosales

This fascinating true story chronicles one man's journey into the mysteries of spiritual consciousness and indigenous healing practices. In his travels around the globe, Omar W. Rosales witnesses the powerful channeled spirit Niño Fidencio, receives messages and healing from a Toltec shaman, and experiences a dramatic soul retrieval from a Cherokee spirit walker. Rosales travels to Guatemala, where he meets a Mayan high priestess, or *Aj' k'ij*, and the secret brotherhoods called *Cofradias*, whose mission is to guard Maximon, the last living Mayan god. Rosales's last journey is to Bhutan, the Land of the Thunder Dragon, where he spends time with a holy lama. Along the way, Rosales encounters danger, sacred rites, secret rituals, and the guidance of a mysterious dream woman whom he finally meets on the physical plane.

978-0-7387-1501-8, 288 pp., 6 x 9   **$18.95**
